Speaking Up

Speaking Up

THE UNINTENDED COSTS OF FREE SPEECH
IN PUBLIC SCHOOLS

Anne Proffitt Dupre

HARVARD UNIVERSITY PRESS

Cambridge, Massachusetts

London, England

2009

Library of Congress Cataloging-in-Publication Data

Dupre, Anne Proffitt.
Speaking up : the unintended costs of free speech in public schools / Anne Proffitt Dupre.
p. cm.
Includes bibliographical references and index.
ISBN 978-0-674-03114-2 (alk. paper)
1. Educational law and legislation—United States.   2. Freedom of speech—United
States.   I. Title.
KF4124.5.D87 2008
342.7308'53—dc22
2008014218

*For Bill and Dad—and in memory of Mom,
my first and best teacher*

Contents

Acknowledgments *ix*

ONE   Outside the Schoolhouse Gate: A Free Speech Primer   *1*

TWO   The Vietnam War and "Hazardous Freedom"   *11*

THREE   The Second Wave and the Constraint of Civility   *39*

FOUR   Student Press Rights and Responsibilities   *74*

FIVE   Banning Books from School: The Right to Receive Speech, or Not   *107*

SIX   Religious Speech: On a Wing and a Prayer   *138*

SEVEN   Teacher Speech and the "Priests of Our Democracy"   *204*

EIGHT   A Long Way from Black Armbands   *230*

Notes   *259*

Case Index   *281*

Subject Index   *285*

Acknowledgments

Heartfelt thanks to my assistant, Cynthia Wentworth; to James M. Donovan, UGA Law Library Faculty and Access Services Librarian; to Jennifer Coalson and Charles McCrae, law student research assistants; and to Tonnya Norwood, project manager. Special thanks to Elizabeth Knoll, Senior Editor at Harvard University Press, for her sage advice from start to finish.

Speaking Up

CHAPTER ONE

✦

Outside the Schoolhouse Gate:
A Free Speech Primer

Must a government, by necessity, be too strong for
the liberties of its people, or too weak to maintain its
own existence?

—Abraham Lincoln

Too much, too little, just right.

—Goldilocks and the Three Bears

AT ITS ESSENCE, the school speech story in the United States is about
self-preservation. Any democratic nation will continue to exist as
such only if its citizens are ready, willing, and able to maintain its
core values. Thomas Jefferson observed, "Above all things I hope
the education of the common people will be attended to, convinced
that on their good sense we may rely with the most security for the
preservation of a due degree of liberty."[1] Of course, each nation has
a different set of core values. Some of these values may be shared
among nations, to some degree, and some values may change as society changes. But when citizens in a democracy care about protecting the ideal of self-government, their informed participation
in their country's democratic and economic institutions will help to
ensure that this ideal endures. And for citizens to understand which

ideals need to be protected, they must be taught. Otherwise, the ideals and practices of self-government cannot endure.

The story that unfolds in the next chapters is the tale of how one country has tried to come to terms with the question Abraham Lincoln posed: How does a nation "conceived in liberty" stay alive while giving its citizens the freedom to undermine its most sacred principles and institutions? That this particular national dialogue is focused on freedom of expression in the school raises an especially poignant aspect of the question. For the school, together with parents, has the important mission of educating each generation of new citizens so they will have the tools necessary to preserve and protect those tenets of democracy upon which the United States was founded. This process does not happen overnight, or by osmosis. To gain a serious understanding of the civic virtue that is necessary for self-government takes a concentrated discipline of mind. Teachers attempting to instruct their students about this subject (along with algebra and geography) need to maintain some form of order so that learning can occur. Thus, the paradox inherent in the issue of school speech surfaces: The state (in the form of the public school) takes away some liberty from the individual student in order to preserve the liberty of a nation.

Teachers, principals, legislatures, and judges have been wrangling for decades in their attempts to find the right doctrinal formula for school speech. This book chronicles that struggle, focusing on the U.S. Supreme Court and the cases it used to construct the school speech canon. As we view this controversy through the door at the schoolhouse gate, several themes emerge. Time and time again we see a clash between the principles of liberty and of order between local control and federal control over schools, and between the rights of individual students to speak in the face of the rights of other students to learn. Even the concept of "diversity," now a familiar term in the legal lexicon, made an appearance in some early school speech cases. Some judges have trusted teachers, principals, and elected school board members to make the decisions that generally are best for their constituents and the schools in their community. Others seem to have had a low opinion of local school officials and their ability to avoid oppressive conduct.

These themes have played out against the vibrant tapestry of some of the most riveting periods in recent American history that include the Nazi build-up in Europe, World War II, the McCarthy hearings, the Vietnam War, and the civil rights movement. The story of school speech is intertwined with the war on drugs and the Columbine shootings, and its story spans the fall of the Berlin wall and the rise of the Internet. In short, the school speech saga follows the path of the American adventure in the last half of the twentieth century. At times it was a bumpy ride while the nation lurched from traditionalism to modernism at the same time it grappled with becoming a world power.

The players in this rich drama are complex and fascinating characters. Trial court judges and Supreme Court justices alike were not afraid to reveal their passion about this issue. The complex interplay between the lower courts and the Supreme Court forms an important backdrop for the story. And the events that have transpired underscore the importance of the dissenting opinion. A dissenting judge may seem to be a voice crying in the wilderness, but that is not always so. The Supreme Court may adopt the view of a dissenting judge from the court of appeals, or the voice of a dissenting justice may appear years later in a majority opinion. Some justices who write majority opinions are vindicated in their views; others are humiliated when their colleagues publicly turn on them and later vote to overrule them. The litigants are no less colorful, as students (and sometimes teachers) push the envelope on school speech, and principals (and sometimes teachers) try to hold the line on school discipline.

Before considering the intriguing issues surrounding speech in school, I shall attempt to summarize some of the cardinal principles of the First Amendment as it applies generally to adults outside the schoolhouse. It is, of course, a daunting task to provide a summary of free speech in the United States in one introductory chapter. This chapter could not hope to address free speech issues to the same depth as scholars like Robert Post, Fred Schauer, Ed Baker, Larry Tribe or Marci Hamilton. It is not an exhaustive examination of the historical, philosophical or theoretical background of laws restricting speech. Instead, it sets the stage for the reader before we arrive at the schoolhouse gate by reviewing some of the basic principles of the federal Constitution's preservation of this fundamental liberty.

Throughout this book, I have tried to avoid getting tangled up in jargon that may make the reading more tedious for those not schooled in the intricacies of legal verbiage. I have also tried to explain terms that may not be obvious to a layperson attacking these difficult concepts. This has perhaps led to some oversimplification at times—a compromise I have accepted in the hope that the ideas presented here may become more widely understood.

> Give me the liberty to know, to utter, and to argue
> freely according to conscience, above all liberties.
>
> —John Milton

Justice Benjamin Cardozo described freedom of speech as "the matrix, the indispensable condition of nearly every form of freedom." When the framers of the Constitution drafted the Bill of Rights to articulate the areas where government could not interfere with individuals, the provision protecting freedom of speech appeared to speak in absolutist terms: "Congress shall make no law abridging the freedom of speech." Some U.S. Supreme Court justices have taken this language to mean that speech rights have a position elevated even above other rights set forth in the Constitution. Others have reasoned that the free speech right is subject to balancing—certain laws that do not intend to control the content of speech but have an incidental effect on speech are permissible if there is a valid governmental interest that justifies it.

Although the text restricts only Congress—the federal government—from making laws that abridge free speech, the U.S. Supreme Court determined that under the Due Process Clause of the Fourteenth Amendment, the First Amendment restrictions also applied to state government. This means that public school districts and public universities and colleges, which are considered arms of the state, are subject to the restrictions of the First Amendment.

It is important to realize at the outset that private schools, which are not considered "state actors" for purposes of the restrictions of the Bill of Rights, need not concern themselves with the Constitution, the Bill of Rights, or the First Amendment. Private schools nevertheless may opt to allow freedom of expression as a matter of choice or custom.

The text of the First Amendment mentions only "free speech," but a person's conduct may also communicate an idea. As the Supreme Court has stated, "The use of an emblem or flag to symbolize some system, idea, institution, or personality is a short cut from mind to mind."[2] The factual context in which the conduct occurs is important when determining when conduct will count as speech. There must be an intent to communicate a particularized message, and that message must be received and understood by others.[3]

Despite the protestations of Justices like Hugo Black and William Douglas, the U.S. Supreme Court has not treated the First Amendment guarantee of free speech as absolute. The Court has balanced the speech right against other important societal interests. In a famous example, Justice Oliver Wendell Holmes observed that the First Amendment would not protect a man who falsely shouted fire in a crowded theater and caused a panic. He pointed out that when words are used in circumstances where they would create a "clear and present danger," the government had the right to restrain them. The "clear and present danger" principle, like much that surrounds the First Amendment speech cases, is easy to state yet difficult to apply. Courts have struggled mightily to determine how much danger must be present and how clear the danger must be.

Other issues of speech restraint have proved no less complex. Although the Supreme Court has steadfastly held that obscenity does not receive First Amendment protection, determining whether an expression is obscene is not an easy task. Justice Potter Stewart's famous quip—"I know it when I see it"—illustrates the Court's frustration with this issue.

Despite the Supreme Court's willingness to balance some societal interests against the free speech right, its intrusions on individual freedom have been limited. The Court has narrowed the presumption of constitutionality when dealing with laws that impinge on free speech and has strictly construed laws to protect that freedom. The Court has been especially protective of political speech and especially wary of government attempts to restrict speech based on its message, its ideas, its subject matter, or its content.[4]

To be sure, the Supreme Court has allowed some kinds of speech only limited First Amendment protection or none at all. Commercial speech, libel, and child pornography are all areas that receive limited or no protection from the First Amendment. Words that are likely to provoke violence in the listeners or that seek to incite a riot—"fighting words"—may also be regulated. Distribution of a certain type of information that could damage national security is subject to prior restraint (though this is not true of opinions, arguments, or ideas that could have this effect). But with few (even though complicated) exceptions, adults "in the public square" have a broad and deep right of expression.

Courts use different levels of scrutiny to determine if laws pass constitutional muster. The lowest level of scrutiny merely requires the law in question to have a rational basis. Laws receiving inter-mediate scrutiny must further an important government interest. Under the "strict scrutiny" standard—the highest level—the gov-ernment must demonstrate that a restriction is narrowly tailored to meet a compelling government interest. Courts generally extend strict scrutiny analysis to speech legislation that is content-based. Although it is often difficult to decide whether regulation of speech is based on content or is content-neutral, content-neutral speech is viewed with less concern, as it is less likely to exclude ideas from the public discourse or what the Supreme Court has called "the mar-ketplace of ideas." Courts may use a more ad hoc balancing of the interest of the government and the speaker to determine if a content-neutral regulation is reasonable. For instance, a content-neutral regulation of the time, place, and manner of public protest that is narrowly drawn and reasonable may be upheld to promote the government interest in public safety and traffic flow.[5]

The Supreme Court's intermediate level of scrutiny—set forth in *United States v. O'Brien*—is perhaps the test that has been used most frequently in analyzing content-neutral laws that impose an incidental burden on free speech: a government regulation is suffi-ciently justified if "it furthers an important or substantial govern-ment interest; if the governmental interest is unrelated to the suppression of free expression; and if the incidental restriction of alleged First Amendment freedoms is no greater than is essential to the furtherance of that interest."[6]

The guarantee of free expression is deemed so important that a litigant is allowed to challenge restrictions on behalf of herself or on behalf of third parties who are not even before the court. Accord-ingly, First Amendment challenges may be based on the validity of the law "as applied" to a particular plaintiff, but another important method of attack is a "facial" challenge. A litigant may claim that the law is "facially" invalid because it is vague or overbroad and thus it may inhibit persons not before the court who may wish to engage in protected speech. If a facial challenge is upheld, the law is struck down. A law that is less than clear or that sweeps more broadly than necessary may inhibit protected speech. The courts have developed the "vagueness" and "overbreadth" doctrines to minimize a "chilling effect" on protected expression. To withstand a vagueness challenge, a law must be clear enough so the people who are subject to it will be able to know how to avoid its sanctions. Even if a law is written with sufficient clarity, it may be overbroad, that is, it may sweep too broadly so that it reaches both protected and unprotected speech.

One rationale for this substantial protection of free speech is its importance in the pursuit of political truth. Justice Oliver Wendell Holmes believed that "the best test of truth is the power of the thought to get itself accepted in the competition of the market."[7] Freedom of expression in the marketplace of ideas has become a powerful model that encourages a continuing dialogue even when the speech is pernicious. This model contains within it a presumption about the listener: it presumes that the listening citizens are educated decisionmakers who are able to understand not only the speech itself, but any corrupted motives that may underlie it.

This presumption has special significance in the school speech context. Students in school may range from five-year-old kindergarteners to twenty-two-year-old college students. This is a considerable time frame in the physical, cognitive, and psychological development of any child. Children are considered to be more vulnerable and need more protection during the earlier stages of development than later. As students move from elementary school through middle school, high school, and college, significant changes occur in their cognitive development, social skills, and impulse control. An eighteen-year-old college freshman may be better able to filter out corrupted speech and better able to control the impulse to respond to "fighting words" than a twelve-year-old in seventh grade.

These years of child development are significant for another reason. During this time—especially during the K–12 years—the state has a special interest in transmitting values of citizenship that will enable students to participate effectively in the nation's economic practices and democratic institutions when they become adults. Thus, the state, when acting as educator, has some interest in monitoring the marketplace in which ideas are developed, although this interest may change as a child ages and proceeds through the school system.

When the state acts as sovereign, its powers to limit speech are at its weakest, and the courts have been at their most vigilant in protecting free speech in this context. In the schoolhouse, however, the state is not acting only as sovereign but also as an educator for students and an employer for teachers. In this role, as explored below, the state's power to restrain speech changes in both character and substance.

Until fairly recently, the power to restrain school speech was mostly unfettered. Teachers were employed under at-will principles or under contracts that would be interpreted without reference to rights of expression. The principle of academic freedom, although first set forth by the American Association of University Professors in 1915, had no constitutional force, and the U.S. Supreme Court did not even mention it until 1952—in a dissenting opinion. Even today, teachers in lower (K–12) education have little protection based on academic freedom principles. Although the First Amendment provides some protection for teachers, the state has more power to constrain speech when it acts as an employer than when it acts as sovereign facing the general public (this is discussed in detail in Chapter 7).

The power of the state when it acts as an educator stems from a common-law doctrine that has deep roots. The scope of school authority over students was most often described by the Latin phrase *in loco parentis* (in the place of the parent). Blackstone's

Commentaries states that the father may "delegate part of his parental authority, during his life, to the tutor or schoolmaster of the child; who is then *in loco parentis,* and has such a portion of the power of the parent committed to his charge, viz. that of restraint and correction, as may be necessary to answer the purpose for which he is employed."

Historically, the authority of the schoolmaster over his students under the doctrine of in loco parentis was analogous to that of the master over his apprentice. When the basic educational model moved from apprenticeships and private tutors into the schoolhouse, the in loco parentis doctrine followed. Courts interpreting this doctrine allowed school officials the same power to make rules regarding student conduct at school as the parent would have at home—that is, virtually without limit—as long as the court considered the action reasonable and it pertained to the education of the student. During the cultural turbulence of the 1960s, a case reached the Supreme Court that would profoundly change this student-teacher dynamic: *Tinker v. Des Moines* is the cornerstone on which the student speech right was built.

Tinker is generally lauded as an opinion that was good for students, because it recognized their constitutional rights in school against adult school officials like teachers and principals. But lurking under all the rhetoric about student rights was a seed that could cause harm. The legal regime that followed this watershed opinion has more costs than are commonly recognized. It has dramatically changed the way public schools operate as they attempt to educate our children, and some of these changes have not benefited students. How that seed was planted and how it germinated and grew is the subject of this book. The *Tinker* opinion deserves its own chapter, and it is to that section that I now turn.

⋆

The Vietnam War and "Hazardous Freedom"

IF YOU WERE NOT THERE, it is hard to imagine the utter devastation most Americans felt when their president was assassinated in November 1963. It seemed as if the entire country stopped to mourn, with tearful eyes riveted to black-and-white television images. Less than a year later the nation was still reeling from this staggering blow when, during the summer of 1964, three young civil rights workers were murdered in Mississippi, and Congress passed the historic Civil Rights Act. Nineteen sixty-four also saw the start of the Organization for Afro-American Unity. Then its founder, Malcolm X, was shot dead early in 1965. The Watts riots followed this tragedy. They raged in Los Angeles for six days during the long, hot summer of 1965.

And, during that same summer, President Lyndon Johnson authorized the first deployment of U.S. ground combat forces in Vietnam. This action was not met with uniform approval across the nation. People who opposed the war held organized protests in several cities. In December 1965, some war protesters in Iowa took a stance that would result in a sea change for schools and students.

There was no hint when it all started that public schools in the

United States were about to undergo such a fundamental change. A small group of adults and their children in Des Moines decided to protest U.S. involvement in Vietnam by wearing black armbands and by fasting on two separate days. Although disagreement about the war had not yet reached the fever pitch that would occur later in the decade, debate had become intense in many localities. Principals in the Des Moines school system, concerned about the possibility of a disturbance at school, adopted a policy prohibiting the students from wearing the armbands to school. The students, aged fifteen, thirteen, eleven, and eight, nevertheless wore the armbands to mourn those who had died and to show support for Senator Robert Kennedy's proposal to extend the Christmas Day truce indefinitely. The students were sent home from school and told to return without the armbands (which they did after the Christmas holiday vacation).

Surely the Des Moines school principals thought that this was the end of the matter. In almost any school district across the country it certainly would have been. According to the standards of the day, the students would come back to school and studies would go on as before. This typical resolution did not occur in Des Moines in this instance, however, because the students, through their fathers, sued the school district in federal court. They requested both an injunction restraining the school system from disciplining the students and nominal damages. The next person making a decision about the schools in Des Moines would be a federal district court judge. (The trial court in the federal system is referred to as the "district court.")

The trial court's decision gave little hope to the student litigants when it ruled for the school district. Asked to determine whether the actions of the school officials had deprived the students of their right to free speech, the trial judge used a formula set forth by the well-respected Judge Learned Hand: "whether the gravity of the 'evil,' discounted by its improbability, justifies such invasion of free speech as is necessary to avoid the danger." The trial court took the view that school officials had not only a *right* but an *obligation* to prevent anything that might be disruptive to the scholarly, disciplined atmosphere of the classroom. Unless the conduct of school officials was unreasonable, courts should not interfere in the operation of the school.

Whether judges explicitly admit it or not, their decisions—especially in matters pitting the state against the individual—are often contextual. That is, opinions are often a product of the time in which they are issued. For instance, many judges in school cases after 1999 mention school shootings like the one that occurred in Columbine, Colorado. Chief Judge Stephenson, the trial judge in *Tinker,* did not hide the fact that he was well aware of the context in which the student speech took place in that case, and he recognized the effect that this context could have on public school officials.[1]

Judge Stephenson pointed out that the debate about the Vietnam War had become vehement in many localities. A protest march (a significant event in these times) had recently been held in Washington, D.C., and a wave of draft card burning (again, a significant event for the times) had swept the country. In fact, two highly publicized draft card burning cases were before the judge's own court, and individuals on both sides of the issue had been, in his words, "quite vocal in expressing their views."

For today's citizens, who have grown accustomed to (or who may have even participated in) ardent and widespread protest in the last forty years—over war, race, gender, sexual orientation, immigration—such commotion may seem like a minor squall, not worthy of institutional concern. But we have the advantage of knowing how it all turned out. Judges like Judge Stephenson were dealing with a new situation, and they had no idea what was coming next. Working without a safety net, they struggled in their efforts to reconcile this new brand of confrontation with a free speech clause that was written long before the first public school was established. Judge Stephenson expressly made this historical context a part of his opinion, stating that "it is against this background" that he reviewed the reasonableness of the school's regulation.

Noting that controversial subjects should not be excluded from the classroom, Judge Stephenson nevertheless would allow school officials to regulate the introduction and the discussion of these subjects. He observed that reactions and comments from other students to the armband protest demonstration would be likely to disturb the disciplined atmosphere required for any classroom. Most significantly, he said: "The actions of school officials should not be limited only to those instances where there is a *material or substantial interference with school discipline*" (emphasis added). Note well these words, as they will later become immensely important. But for now, if school officials reasonably anticipated that some type of a disturbance in school discipline would occur, they could permissibly regulate student speech. He pointed out that the students' free speech rights were infringed only to a limited extent, as they were free to wear the armbands off school premises and to express their views on the Vietnam War in any orderly discussion of the subject.

The Eighth Circuit Court of Appeals upheld the school's decision in a terse, one-paragraph opinion that merely stated that the district court's judgment was affirmed by an equally divided en banc court.[2] But the last word on the black armbands came from the highest court in the land. The U.S. Supreme Court reversed the two lower federal courts, sending shock waves down the corridors of public schools across the country.[3]

Although the overturning of a decision by school officials about student discipline was surprising enough, the *Tinker* opinion effected much more. It signaled that the Supreme Court was ready and willing to go further than merely allowing the Tinker children to wear their armbands. In a statement that has reverberated in court documents for decades since, the Court declared emphatically that students and teachers do not "shed their constitutional rights to free expression at the schoolhouse gate." Moreover, the Court explicitly upended the rule set forth by Judge Stephenson. The new Supreme Court standard set a high bar before schoolteachers and principals could regulate student speech. Unless the student expression caused "substantial disruption" or "material interference" with the education process, the school could not restrain it. This next section will examine this landmark decision in some detail, analyzing both the substance and the tone of the Court's opinion.

The Des Moines Public Schools and "Enclaves of Totalitarianism"

The *Tinker* case occurred during a time of great social and political upheaval, when authority at all levels was being challenged. By the time the Supreme Court handed down the *Tinker* opinion in 1969, Daniel Ellsberg had leaked the Pentagon Papers and both Martin Luther King and Robert Kennedy had been assassinated. One noted social critic observed that the turmoil during this period was as significant as the unrest surrounding the Protestant Reformation.[4] Whether that comparison was apt or not, there was little question that a tempest was brewing. College campuses were embroiled in frenzied demonstrations, and the K–12 milieu had not been left unscathed.

After the Supreme Court's decision in *Brown v. Board of Education,* the recalcitrance of some school boards faced with desegregation and the ensuing violence in many school districts had done little to shore up judicial trust in the decisions made by school officials. Viewing the opinion from this angle of historical context reveals how the Supreme Court's message, in contrast to that of the trial court, reflected a larger pattern of distrust of government institutions and authority in general. Of particular interest here, is the way the Court's language and tone conveyed that it accepted—and perhaps encouraged—challenges to school authority.

The *Tinker* opinion contains one of the most famous quotations in any case dealing with schools. Justice Abe Fortas, the author of the opinion, pronounced, "It can hardly be argued that either students or teachers shed their constitutional right to freedom of speech or expression at the schoolhouse gate." This right was not unfettered, however, as the Court acknowledged the "comprehensive authority" of school officials to "prescribe and control conduct in the schools." The problem, of course, occurs when a student fails to follow the official prescription. After all, the Des Moines school officials had prescribed a certain level of conduct (no war protest in school), and the protesting students simply refused to comply. Despite its nod to school administrators, the *Tinker* opinion narrowed that "comprehensive authority" considerably.

Although the district court had found the conduct of the school officials to be reasonable in anticipating a disturbance of some kind, the Supreme Court opinion dismissed any concerns about ensuing disorder. Justice Fortas bluntly stated that "undifferentiated fear or apprehension of disturbance is not enough to overcome the right to freedom of expression." The opinion did not explain how clear the fear of disturbance needed to be before school officials could act to control it.

In some places in the opinion, Justice Fortas's choice of words leaves the reader with the impression that public school students were in desperate need of outside help. Only the power of the Court and the Constitution could rescue them from oppression of the most serious nature. Justice Fortas sets up a scenario where only the most insensitive martinet could fail to conclude that someone (presumably the Court) must help rigid, provincial educators make the day-to-day discipline decisions in their school. His opinion leads us to believe that school officials left to their own devices would demand across-the-board subjugation from their students to avoid discipline problems, and that this suffocation would turn students into robotic simpletons. These educators were simply unable to discern for themselves when behavior in their schools needed to be restrained to keep order and when student conduct would not cause a problem. Because of their inability to make this distinction, teachers and principals overreact any time a student behaves in a way they fear might upset the learning process and, in so doing, crush their students' spirits.

Justice Fortas chided school officials for being overly concerned with keeping order. As he put it, *any* shift from "absolute regimentation" might cause trouble, and *any* variation from the opinion of the majority might "inspire fear." His use of the term "absolute regimentation" certainly painted an unpleasant picture, and he insinuated that school officials were so afraid of student agitation that they controlled student speech with an iron hand. In short, school officials were simply being too risk-averse. They should quit worrying so much about the risk of disorder among their students, because the Constitution does not allow it. Far from allowing school officials to avoid the risk of trouble, Justice Fortas proclaimed, "Our Constitution says that we must take this risk." The opinion acknowledged that this view of the world in school is not without danger. This freedom for students has its hazards. Despite potential problems that may occur while guarding the safety of hundreds of students, Justice Fortas insisted that it is "this sort of *hazardous freedom*" that is "the basis of our national strength."

Of course, the school principals—if they are to be believed—were not attempting to constrain all speech that varied from the majority opinion. They were merely concerned about an organized protest at school that they believed might cause a disturbance and distraction from the learning process. These educators, entrusted with the well-being of hundreds of children, may not have been comfortable with a freedom that presents hazards for the children in their custody.

The willingness (or lack thereof) of a court to defer to the judgment of educators is a recurring theme throughout the school speech cases. If you look hard enough as you read these cases, you might also discern a hint of classism surrounding this issue. Judges and justices—though better educated than most teachers and principals—are not trained to run schools, and they are far removed from the day-to-day problems in the classroom. Yet time and time again, their opinions reveal their lack of understanding of—and perhaps lack of respect for—those who work in school systems as teachers, principals, superintendents, and board members.

Justice Fortas simply did not trust the judgment of the Iowa educators. He refused to countenance the idea that a disturbance was a possibility and never addressed to what extent distraction from a task could affect the learning process. Unlike Judge Stephenson, who deferred to the judgment of the school administrators about the day-to-day operations of their schools, the Supreme Court recast the concern about a disturbance as a "mere desire to avoid the discomfort and unpleasantness that always accompanies an unpopular viewpoint." The Court did not even attempt to consider the extent to which discomfort or unpleasantness can affect disciplined study and the learning process.

In addition, the school officials were in more hot water because, as it turned out, they got it wrong. As the Court saw it, there had been no major disturbance in the Des Moines schools. The Court stated that although a few students made hostile remarks to the protesters, there were no threats or acts of violence on school grounds. Because the student expression did not result in disorder or disturbance, the Court concluded that it did not intrude on the work of the schools or on the rights of other students.

Vietnam War protests were not the only protests that were occurring throughout the country. Protests about civil rights for African Americans were also a part of the landscape, and sympathetic courts had developed some guidelines that would make it hard for those who would obstruct the implementation of the Civil Rights Act to interfere with peaceful demonstrations. It was to this milieu that the Supreme Court turned for its standard for student speech. The Fifth Circuit Court of Appeals had decided a case dealing with a civil rights protest at school a few years before, and Justice Fortas used the rule from that case in *Tinker.* The Court required that school officials show that wearing the armbands would "*materially* and *substantially* interfere with the requirements of appropriate discipline and the operation of the school." At the time, the Fifth Circuit consisted of Florida, Georgia, Alabama, Mississippi, Louisiana, and Texas. The case the Supreme Court borrowed from is *Burnside v. Byers* (discussed in greater detail later in this chapter).[5] The Supreme Court determined there was no showing in Des Moines that the school authorities had anticipated such a degree of disruption. In fact, school officials had been quoted in the newspaper as simply stating that the public schools were not the place for anti-war demonstrations. They had also made the mistake of allowing other symbols of political or controversial significance in school. These included political buttons and the Iron Cross, although there was nothing in the record that showed that they believed these symbols would have the same kind of effect on students as the Vietnam protest, and there was nothing in the record that showed that there was any viewpoint discrimination. That is, if students had wanted to wear armbands to support the war in Vietnam, they would have been banned also.

As noted, Justice Fortas was not averse to using rhetoric to reinforce his conclusions. This rhetoric reached its apex when he proclaimed, "In our system, state-operated schools may not be enclaves of totalitarianism." Of course, no one could disagree with that statement, but Justice Fortas put forth no evidence that this was occurring in Des Moines or anywhere else. It was a clever device, though. This solemn declaration that schools "may *not* be enclaves of totalitarianism" insinuated that this was exactly what was going on in Des Moines. These would be biting words at any time, but they were especially caustic when the country was in the midst of the Cold War against these oppressive regimes.

The opinion continued with this kind of polemic, implying that students would become overly programmed by a rigid school experience: "In our system, students may not be regarded as closed-circuit recipients of only that which the State chooses to communicate."

The Court then conjured an image that had been used in a 1923 Supreme Court opinion—the specter of the abstemious rules of ancient Sparta. "In order to submerge the individual and develop ideal citizens, Sparta assembled the males at seven into barracks and intrusted their subsequent education and training to official guardians." After repudiating this kind of restriction (and implying that the school officials in Des Moines were headed down this path), the Court stated that "the principal use to which the schools are dedicated is *to accommodate students* during prescribed hours for the purpose of certain types of activities" (emphasis added). Because one of these activities is "personal intercommunication among students," a student's rights embrace more than the hours in the classroom. The student may express his or her opinion, as long as it does not lead to substantial disruption or material interference with school activities.

That Justice Fortas authored an opinion that was fervid in its support of a student's right to protest is not surprising. Like Chief Judge Stephenson, Fortas, too, was coming at the case from his own perspective. In May 1968, one year before the *Tinker* decision, he had published a book entitled *Concerning Dissent and Civil Disobedience*.[6] Thus, Justice Fortas had been thinking about protest and its ability to change social constructions for a long time. His book explained what he called the "weapons of protest, dissent, criticism and peaceful assembly." The main focus was on demonstrations for racial civil rights and protests where men burned draft cards because they were opposed to the war in Vietnam.

In parts of the book, written in the first person, Justice Fortas said he hoped that he would have had the courage to disobey state Jim Crow laws that segregated white from black or to refuse to "Heil Hitler" or submit to genocide. The theme of the book is that as long as this power of dissent—what he called freedom's instrument—is used "forcefully, but prudently, we shall continue as a vital, free society." Although none of the examples in the book relate to elementary and high school students protesting in public schools, some of the text presages the text of the *Tinker* opinion. For example, Justice Fortas noted that the Constitution protects dissent and protest within broad limits, but he cautioned that the state should act when the protester's actions involve "substantial interference" with the rights of others.[7] The term "substantial interference" reemerged in *Tinker* as the new standard for student speech.

At the end of the book Justice Fortas makes an interesting point: civil disobedience—the deliberate violation of a law—is never justified when the law being violated is not the target of the protest. For example, entering a public waiting room reserved for "Whites only" was directed at the law that separated white from black. But *the violation of the law as a technique of demonstration* "constitutes an act of rebellion, not merely of dissent." Disobeying an unrelated law to dramatize dissent "may be morally, as well as politically unacceptable." To be sure, *Tinker* was not categorized as a civil disobedience case, but the thesis of the Fortas book concerns more than civil disobedience narrowly defined. It is about the need to promote dissent. Because he determined that the Tinkers had a constitutional right to engage in their protest, Justice Fortas did not make any attempt to explain how the Tinker protest comported with the principles he so forcefully expounded in his book. After all, the Tinkers were not protesting anything the school had done. The very purpose of the armbands was a demonstration—to dramatize their disagreement with the war. Although the protesters were not violating a state criminal law, they did violate a school rule that school officials, as arms of the state, had put in place to avoid a violent disturbance in school. Justice Fortas claimed that the state must ensure that individuals are granted the facilities (including the schoolhouse) to express their dissent. This duty of the state was also something he had emphasized in his book.

Justice Fortas and the *Tinker* majority did not hand down the Court's pronouncement without protest. Traditionally, the justices convene in the Supreme Court courtroom to issue their opinions to the public. The justice who wrote the majority opinion reads a brief summary of the case and the decision. On rare occasions, when a justice in dissent is especially disturbed by the majority opinion, he or she may also read his or her dissent.

Justice Hugo Black, considered a First Amendment purist in other contexts, was outraged at the *Tinker* decision, and he gave an impassioned reading of his dissent. As a counterpoint to Justice Fortas's affirmation of student autonomy and liberty (and highlighting the theme that will occur frequently throughout this book), Justice Black argued for the importance of discipline and order. He noted that uncontrolled liberty is an enemy to domestic peace and insisted that school discipline, like parental discipline, is an integral and important part of training our children to be good citizens.

Justice Black took issue with the majority opinion's disregard of the effect of this particular student protest. He pointed out that testimony in the record showed that the armbands caused comments, warnings by other students, the poking of fun at the protesters, and an incident in which a football player intervened and told other students to leave the protesters alone. One math teacher had testified that his class had been "wrecked" by a dispute with Mary Beth Tinker.

The armbands thus diverted the students from their regular work and focused thought on the subject of the Vietnam War. Indeed, this was the likely purpose of the protesters, and it was exactly what the school officials foresaw. Justice Black was adamant that allowing students to flout the orders of school officials to keep their minds on their schoolwork was "the beginning of a new revolutionary era of permissiveness in this country fostered by the judiciary."

Justice Black argued that it was a myth to say that any person has a constitutional right to say what he pleases, where he pleases, and when he pleases. For him, schools were different. He believed that students had not reached the level of experience and wisdom that enabled them to teach their elders. They were not sent to schools to broadcast political views; at their age, they needed to learn, not to teach. Disputes over the Vietnam War divided the country as few other issues ever had. Students could not help but fail to concentrate on their schoolwork when black armbands called their attention to the wounded and dead of the war, some of whom were their friends and neighbors. "One does not have to be a prophet," he warned, "to know that after the Court's holding today students turned loose with lawsuits, will be ready willing and able to defy their teachers on practically all orders."

Justice Harlan, nearly blind at the time, also wrote a dissent in *Tinker*. This short opinion, not joined by any other Justice, is significant because a different panel of Justices—without attribution—reconstituted the essence of this dissent in a *majority* opinion nearly twenty years later.[8] Justice Harlan acknowledged that school officials are not exempt from respecting freedom of expression. But he would have required the challenging student to show that the school official's decision was motivated by something other than "legitimate school concerns" (for example, prohibiting the expression of an unpopular view while permitting the expression of the dominant opinion).

The *Tinker* opinion continues to fascinate us because it reaches into so many layers of our social fabric. And, like a kaleidoscope, it changes color and meaning depending on how one looks at it. Certainly it had a decided impact on day-to-day life in our public schools, but it also affected our view of how the world works. The effects of this multi-faceted opinion were both immediate and far-reaching.

The New Reformation

Tinker was indeed a watershed for student speech rights. As the *New York Times* reported, "The Court had never before said that students of public schools—or colleges, for that matter—have free speech rights that the courts will enforce against their elders."[9] A new age had arrived for teachers and students, resulting in more cases challenging school decision making. The *Tinker* opinion made it clear that students had every right to challenge teachers and principals as long as they believed their right of free speech was being infringed. Not surprisingly, after *Tinker,* "public schools and state-supported colleges and universities [became] involved as never before in constitutional litigation with respect to student expression."[10]

The fulcrum on the school speech scale was now decidedly on the side of student liberty, and many school officials had a difficult time adjusting to what Professor Perry Zirkel has called a "stunning blow" to their authority, a turnabout that left many ill-prepared for its consequences. Even some lower courts seemed uncomfortable with this stark change in the character of the relationship between student and teacher. A standard like "substantial disruption" and "material interference" invites countless challenges and endless litigation regarding precisely what these terms mean in a school context: How much disruption may occur before it is deemed to be "substantial"? What kind of interference with the learning process is "material"? It was left to the lower courts throughout the country to determine on a case-by-case basis what kinds of student conduct in school constituted speech and whether that speech would be protected.

Records from the time show only those cases that went far enough through the legal pipeline for a lawsuit to be filed and an opinion written and reported by a federal judge. They do not show the instances where a court did not report its opinion, where a case was settled early in the process, where a lawsuit was not filed, where a principal chose to forgo discipline to avoid a lawsuit, or where a teacher refrained from reprimanding a student to avoid controversy.

One issue that came to the fore as the *Tinker* opinion began to find its sea legs concerned school rules on hair length for boys. The issue was litigated extensively, and there was substantial disagreement in the federal courts of appeal regarding whether hair length was speech and, if so, whether rules about its length passed constitutional muster under the *Tinker* standard. The U.S. Supreme Court was asked on more than one occasion to resolve the conflict in the circuits. It never did so, despite a written dissent by Justice Douglas when the Court refused to grant a hearing: "The question tendered is of great personal concern to many and of unusual constitutional importance which we should resolve. I would grant this petition and set the case for argument."[11]

Other issues that arose included the removal of books from school libraries, banning a school play because of sexual content, distribution of underground newspapers on school grounds, and school discipline measures after a student "walkout." As the *Wall Street Journal* reported, a "striking new development in student dissent"—using the courts to air grievances—in both colleges and high schools resulted in "an explosion of student-rights litigation." Litigation "has grown overnight."[12] Students were less accepting of the authority of school officials (a development encouraged by the rhetoric in the *Tinker* opinion), and there was a tremendous increase in the availability of free or inexpensive legal counsel (who now had the *Tinker* opinion to use as a potent weapon against school officials). Lawyers at the time were not concerned that students lost most of these initial cases, stating that "winning isn't as important right now as educating the courts to the problem."[13] Student advocates predicted: "By next year no one will be able to keep track of all the cases."[14]

Indeed, *Tinker* had set a tone that allowed the law surrounding student rights to develop along an upward trajectory for almost two decades. But let us turn the kaleidoscope away from its most famous setting—the view of the *Tinker* opinion as a trailblazer for student speech rights—and to a different setting that highlights some interesting questions about the role of the *parents* whose children were involved in the protest.

The father of the Tinker children was a Methodist minister without a church, who had been appointed "peace education secretary" for the American Friends Service Committee (though he had no connection with the Friends church). The mother of Christopher Eckhardt, the other named plaintiff, was an officer in an organization called Women's International League for Peace and Freedom. These adults had been active in protesting the war, and the respondent's brief in the case discusses a connection to the Students for a Democratic Society (SDS). (SDS began as a student organization to promote the civil rights movement and was widely considered to be the most radical of militant student organizations.)

The children named as plaintiffs in the case were age thirteen, fifteen, and sixteen, but children as young as eleven and eight had also participated in the protest by wearing the black armband to school. Leaving the younger children out of the case was undoubtedly good litigation strategy. It would have called attention to the question whether the *Tinker* opinion upheld the speech rights of children or whether the children were merely acting as a conduit for the political views of their parents.

A case decided three years after *Tinker* raised some questions about parents and children that the *Tinker* court had ignored. In *Wisconsin v. Yoder,* the Supreme Court addressed whether parents in the Old Order Amish religious community could circumvent compulsory school law and remove their children from school after the eighth grade (about thirteen or fourteen years old). Although a majority of the Court upheld the right of the parents to make this decision on religious grounds, questions arose both in separate written opinions by the Justices and in commentary on the case as to whether the children's views had been properly taken into account.[15] There was nothing in the *Yoder* record to indicate that the Amish children's own views differed from that of their parents, and the same was true in *Tinker.* Yet Justice Douglas in dissent argued that the claims of both parent and child were inextricably linked, and he would have canvassed the Amish children to see if they wished to continue in school in opposition to their parent's wishes.

Even Justice Douglas, however, missed the larger question. To what extent do children (especially in 1965 and later in 1972), who are dependent on their parents for the necessities of life and infused by religious and political ideas that their parents impose on them, have a viewpoint that is different from their parents? Research shows that even in today's society, parents have a significant influence on the religious or political beliefs of their children. A Gallup Poll Youth Survey showed that 71 percent of teens aged 13–17 said that their views about social and political issues were "about the same" as their parents'.[16]

To the extent that the *Tinker* opinion was actually allowing the children's *parents* to use the school as an outlet to promote their own agenda, it has important repercussions for the schoolhouse today. The next group of parents may have an agenda that is not as appealing as a protest against an unpopular war. School districts today spend enormous amounts of time and resources as they continue to deal with the legal issues spawned by this facet of *Tinker*. For example, students have used *Tinker* to bolster the claim that they have the right to proselytize and distribute religious messages at school and to denounce homosexuality as a sin against God. These ideas are likely generated from their parents' political or religious beliefs and their parents' desire to use their children to spread this message to others at school.

Another facet of the *Tinker* decision that has eluded searching examination is the extent to which it was influenced by America's Original Sin—a Constitution that first allowed slavery and then state-mandated segregation. *Tinker* was argued in November 1968. The Civil Rights Act had been in effect only four years and the Supreme Court had dealt with such issues as civil rights in public accommodations and interracial marriage in the years leading up to

Tinker.[17] The year 1968 saw the assassination of both Martin Luther King and Robert Kennedy. Moreover, it had been over fourteen years since the Court had handed down *Brown v. Board of Education,* and many school boards across the country still continued to ignore the Court's 1954 call for desegregation. This defiance in the area of race gave courts little reason to believe that school officials were to be trusted with other important issues of social policy.

Justice Fortas saw a strong connection between the actions of the Tinkers and the student protesters in another case called *Burnside v. Byars.* In that case high school students in an all-black school in Philadelphia, Mississippi, decided to wear what they called "freedom buttons."[18] They had obtained the buttons from the headquarters of the local Council of Federated Organizations, an umbrella organization for various civil rights groups working in Mississippi. The buttons had the words "One Man One Vote" around the perimeter with "SNCC" in the center, the acronym of the Student Nonviolent Coordinating Committee, a political organization of black college students dedicated to overturning segregation. The school principal, concerned that the buttons would cause a disturbance, gave the students the option of taking the buttons off or being suspended from school. Unsurprisingly the students brought a civil rights action. (In a segregated school in Mississippi in 1964, the principal was also black). The Fifth Circuit handed down its decision in *Burnside* the same day it handed down its decision in *Blackwell v. Issaquena County Board of Education,* a case regarding a situation where the issue of freedom buttons had caused disruption and a breakdown in discipline.[19] The Court of Appeals made a clear distinction between the two cases, allowing the buttons in *Burnside* but not in *Blackwell,* because the students in *Blackwell* had violated the privacy and physical security of others and had interfered with the operation of the school.

Justice Fortas seized on these cases and this distinction. In fact, he used the words for his new constitutional standard—whether the exercise of speech rights materially and substantially interferes with the requirements of appropriate discipline in the school—from the Fifth Circuit's opinion in *Burnside*. And he cited *Blackwell* for the proposition that conduct that materially disrupts classwork, causes substantial disorder, or invades the rights of others gets no constitutional protection. Thus, the new student right the Court promulgated in *Tinker* has deep roots in the judiciary's response to and protection of student protest during the civil rights movement.

Justice Fortas must have thought a great deal about this issue when he was writing his book, which places heavy emphasis on the significance of African American dissent. He observed that "the fundamental justice of their demands" made certain steps necessary "in the long, difficult, and enormously costly and disruptive task of reparation and reform."[20] He also pointed out that these changes came about only because protesters went outside the boundaries of polite conduct. Although their behavior was not confined "to the polite procedures that other segments of our society would wish," it was necessary to make their point. "We can hardly claim that their deserving demands would be satisfied if they did not vigorously assert them."[21] Less than one year after his book was published, he must have seen the *Tinker* protest in the same light. Even though that protest had occurred in a school—a place others thought was inappropriate for this kind of activity—the civil rights protesters had shown that pushing the envelope in the school setting was necessary to inspire change.

Turning the kaleidoscope to yet another setting shows another interesting issue buried within *Tinker*. Even under the best of circumstances, it can be difficult to maintain a learning environment where students receive a serious education. Consider the scenario in a school that makes every effort to follow *Tinker*. How much learning is lost before the standard set by the Supreme Court—substantial interference and material disruption to education—is reached? Was the only danger that mattered in *Tinker* the possibility of physical violence? Or is there a danger that students exercising their free speech rights will change the classroom in a way that harms the learning process?

Students are easily distracted from the learning task at hand, and they often have a hard time returning to that task when other diversions are available. Any teacher knows that the learning process can be disrupted by something as small as a fly buzzing in the room, and teachers try to keep distractions—even small ones—to a minimum. Even a minor distraction can undermine a class for a whole period.[22] Research bears out what teachers have observed throughout the ages: "Quantitative analysis suggests that a distracting comment or action does have a statistically significant effect on the probability an individual becomes inattentive at a later point in the lesson, even when controlling for a number of individual and group characteristics."[23]

The Tinkers and Eckhardts wore the armbands to attract attention to their cause. They were successful. The armbands diverted their classmates' minds away from their studies and toward the "highly emotional subject of the Vietnam War."[24] By setting a standard of *substantial* interference and *material* disruption, the *Tinker* decision invited a significant change in the classroom dynamic. It expanded the role of the courts in the day-to-day decisions about classwork. It allowed judges to second-guess teachers when determining how student speech at school can influence a student's emotional state and cognitive focus, while subverting the learning process.

Because of its profound effect on student speech rights (and perhaps even on student learning), the dust that the *Tinker* opinion raised reached far beyond the schoolhouse in Des Moines, Iowa. The thesis that underlay the opinion dug deep into the columns that had upheld the structure of local governance since the time public schools were first established. *Tinker* fundamentally changed the matrix that had determined how and by whom our schools, the institution that socializes our young, are run. *Tinker* is often touted as a rights-expanding decision because it challenged students to question school authority. But when rights expand on one side, they contract on another. Viewed from a different perspective, the *Tinker* decision might be criticized as antidemocratic. For in some ways, as it expanded student rights in school, *Tinker* contracted the rights of other voting citizens. After *Tinker,* the last word regarding student speech within this singularly local endeavor—the schoolhouse—resides in unelected federal judges, rather than elected school board members or their agents (school principals).

Once student speech rights were deemed protected by the Constitution, students began to ask what other rights could be imported from the street to the schoolhouse.

In the Wake of *Tinker:* The Bill of Rights and the Schoolhouse Gate

Given the invitation in *Tinker,* it was not particularly surprising when other students' rights issues began appear on court dockets. After all, the *Tinker* Court stated that students do not shed their constitutional rights at the schoolhouse gate, and the right of free expression is only one of many constitutional rights that may be relevant to students in school. In *Goss v. Lopez,* the Supreme Court allowed another constitutional right to pass through the schoolhouse gate. The Court determined that a student's entitlement to a public education was a property interest that was protected by the Due Process Clause of the Fourteenth Amendment.[25] The Due Process Clause states that no State shall "deprive any person of life, liberty, or property without due process of law."[26] Once the Court decided that students have a property right in their education, it followed that schools could not deprive students of the right to attend school for misconduct without complying with the procedures the Constitution requires. The upshot of *Goss* was that students have the right to the "notice and hearing" protections of the Due Process Clause before they can be suspended for ten or more days.

Once again, the Court's tone is interesting. When explaining why courts need to intervene in disciplinary decisions, the opinion suggests that without courts to ensure fairness, teachers and principals would likely make "secret, one-sided," "self-righteous" determinations of fact regarding student discipline. A flood of lawsuits filed after *Goss* attempted to define just what kind of notice was sufficient and under what circumstances and to what extent counsel, cross-examination, evidence rules, and other accessories were necessary to a suspension hearing. The claims for due process reached far beyond the facts addressed in the *Goss* opinion—student suspension. Cases arose in which students challenged placement in a time-out area and removal from a varsity cheering squad, a high school band, and a softball team.

New Jersey v. T.L.O. was the Court's first foray into the application in the school setting of the Fourth Amendment, which states that "the rights of the people to be secure in their persons, houses, papers and effects, against unreasonable searches and seizures shall not be violated."[27] The Court rejected the argument that teachers and principals act in loco parentis (in the place of the parent) in their dealings with students, although some lower courts had accepted this argument.[28] Instead, the Court determined that the Fourth Amendment's proscription against unreasonable searches applies to searches conducted by school officials. While teachers do not need the same "probable cause" that is required of the police to search students, they must have a "reasonable suspicion" that the search will turn up evidence that the student has violated the law or a school rule.

Like *Tinker*, the *T.L.O.* opinion had a long reach. Although the Court undoubtedly thought it was issuing an opinion that was favorable to schools when it gave school officials more leeway than the police, the ambiguity of its legal standard—like that of *Tinker*— had a much bigger effect on the running of schools than the justices imagined it would. Fear of running afoul of its edicts is one reason why public school principals could not keep guns, knives, and drugs out of their schools. When litigation ensued after a school search, lower courts were left with the task of determining whether a teacher's suspicion had been reasonable enough to make the search constitutional. The diverging opinions there only led to more confusion and uncertainty. The *T.L.O.* opinion was not the last word on the Fourth Amendment in school. The Supreme Court has found it necessary to grant certiorari in school search cases on two subsequent occasions. Both of these cases addressed the quantity and the character of the suspicion that would pass muster to perform drug tests on students.

In a 5–4 decision, the Court shut the schoolhouse gate on one constitutional provision, determining that the Eighth Amendment prohibition against cruel and unusual punishment applied only to those convicted of crimes, not to the paddling of schoolchildren.[29] Nevertheless, despite this setback, the *Tinker* opinion had opened a Pandora's box regarding constitutional rights for students who wished to challenge punishment for misconduct.

In *Judging School Discipline,* Richard Arum points out that the Supreme Court's sanction of free speech rights altered the mindset of all the actors in the school setting.[30] After courts supported student challenges in the context of freedom of expression and the right to protest, students, parents, and schools began to operate under the assumption that courts could be used effectively to overturn school discipline in other contexts, including carrying a weapon to school, as well as drug and alcohol use.[31] Arum observes that the institutional environment around schools changed the boundaries within which disciplinary practices emerged. He argues that court decisions overturning school discipline had "a significant role in contributing to the decline in moral authority and the erosion of effective disciplinary practices" in public schools in the United States. Most interesting is his assertion that the change in the public schools was not an inevitable result of broader changes in the political and popular culture. Similar cultural changes in Europe and other developed countries—without the same level of interference in matters concerning school discipline—did not lead to the same kind of institutional changes that have occurred in the United States.

Arum is certainly correct that a spectacular increase in education litigation occurred during the late 1960s and early 1970s, a period he calls the student rights contestation period. This litigation, if not directly spawned by the *Tinker* opinion, was at least encouraged by its language and holding. It left in its wake a sense of entitlement on the part of both students and parents regarding the student's ability to circumvent school discipline. Beginning with *Tinker*, and later through *Goss* and *T.L.O.*, students learned from none other than the Justices of the U.S. Supreme Court that school rules could be broken. Many students and their parents developed a level of scorn—even contempt—for school discipline and those who attempt to enforce it, and an increased willingness to use the power of the courts to undermine those who would enforce school rules to maintain discipline.

As a result, schools changed their disciplinary practices. They set up processes that would comport with *Tinker* and *Goss* and *T.L.O.* and avoided any restraint that might become the subject of litigation. Teachers and principals refrained from reining in behavior for fear of parent outrage or a lawsuit. There was little upside and a big downside here for teachers and principals who attempted to maintain a high level of student discipline. The huge cost of this change, as Arum points out, is that the legitimacy and the moral authority of the public school as the institution that had the trust and the capacity to socialize the young for a constructive role in society was seriously undermined.

Tinker was decided at a time when the idea of discipline in many contexts was disfavored and there was much skepticism about authority and tradition. This worldview may have influenced the Supreme Court as much as the Court influenced its world. And other changes in society at large within families and other institutions affecting children certainly played into the hand that *Tinker* had dealt the schools. But not all schools were similarly affected by the *Tinker* regime, and here the school speech story brings to light a disconcerting incongruity.

Private schools were not exempt from litigation demanding constitutional rights. In a decision that had important repercussions for public schools, especially after *Goss* and *T.L.O.* expanded constitutional rights for students in the schoolhouse, the Supreme Court was asked to decide whether private schools, as well as public schools, were constrained by the First Amendment. The First Amendment is, of course, a proscription against *government* infringement of free speech. Unless the private school is viewed as being a "state actor," the protections in the Bill of Rights simply do not apply. In 1982 the Court determined, in *Rendell-Baker v. Kohn*, that a private school did not carry out its functions as a state actor, despite the fact that it performed a public function, received federal funds, and was subject to state regulation.[32]

This case has had a huge effect on how K–12 education has developed in the United States. It meant that private schools are not bound by *Tinker, Goss,* or *T.L.O.* Private schools can make disciplinary rules as they see fit without fear of a lawsuit for violating the constitutional rights of their students (although they may be liable for violating contractual promises if they make them in a school handbook or admissions document).

Has the lack of constitutional rights in private schools caused their downfall? Far from it. Despite the fact that constitutional rights do not pass the schoolhouse gate into the private school, parents are clamoring to get their children through that portal. Parents from all across the political spectrum are delighted when their child is admitted to a tony private academy. Those who do not have the financial ability to pay private school tuition are also eager to have their children enter the private school classroom. This demand, in turn, has led to the political hot-button issue of school vouchers.

As the school voucher movement has gained considerable strength in recent years, many parents seem unconcerned that their children will be without these constitutional rights during the time that they are learning in the private school environment. And there is no evidence that students emerging from a private school education are singularly lacking in their ability to understand the nature of constitutional liberty. As W. Stuart Stuller wryly observed, "Big Brother never had to deal with the likes of John Lennon and Tupac Shakur. So long as the First Amendment remains vital after students exit the schoolhouse gate, parents, friends and the uproar of popular culture all combine to remind students that there are other voices."[33]

K–12 students were not alone in the quest for constitutional rights. Challenges to rules about school speech also proliferated in the college and university setting. The *Tinker* melody continued to play in this context, beginning with two cases decided in the early 1970s. The first, *Healy v. James,* like *Tinker,* was rooted in protest about Vietnam. It was based on facts that occurred in 1969, the same year *Tinker* was handed down. Some students at Central Connecticut State College attempted to organize a local chapter of Students for a Democratic Society (SDS). Because the national chapter of SDS had been involved in campus protests that had resulted in disruption and violence, the committee in charge of recognizing new student organizations asked the students several questions about how the chapter would respond if these issues arose. Although the committee approved the request for campus recognition, the president of the college denied it, and the students sued.[34]

The Supreme Court opinion wasted no time before invoking *Tinker,* starting its analysis with the now-famous quotation that students do not shed their constitutional rights at the schoolhouse gate. Remanding the case to the lower court, Justice Lewis Powell's opinion stated that if the college president's rejection was based on a disagreement with the philosophy of SDS, the decision was unsupportable on First Amendment grounds. If, however, the president had rejected the request because he feared disruption, this might be an acceptable reason—provided that the actions would materially and substantially disrupt work and discipline, as required by *Tinker*. Yet despite its nod to *Tinker*, the *Healy* opinion added two additional phrases to the *Tinker* test. The college need not tolerate expressive activities that would "infringe reasonable campus rules," "interrupt classes," or (now explicitly using the *Tinker* standard) "substantially interfere with the opportunity of others to obtain an education."

The decision is interesting because the *Healy* opinion, unlike *Tinker*, set forth the historical context in detail. The Court explained at the outset that a climate of unrest prevailed on many college campuses at the time, together with the seizure of buildings, vandalism, arson, looting, and destruction of manuscripts—even the shutting down of some colleges completely. An opinion dealing with free expression during these trying times had to perform a difficult balancing act between the interests of students and faculty in having a learning environment that is free from disruptive interference and the significant interest in giving wide latitude to free expression. The Court attempted to balance these interests by placing on the college administration the burden of justifying its decision on the basis of something other than a disagreement with the ideas underlying SDS.

Both *Healy* and *Papish v. Board of Curators of the University of Missouri*, decided the next year in a per curiam opinion, forced the courts to think about how and why the fulcrum on the school speech scale might change in higher education. *Papish* involved a graduate student who had been expelled for distributing an under-

ground newspaper on campus that contained a cartoon of a policeman raping the Statue of Liberty and an article entitled "Mother
f—Acquitted" (about a youth who was a member of a gang by that
name). The Supreme Court opinion did not spell out the word
Motherfucker but left dashes for the omitted letters as shown in the
text. The student had been expelled for violating the university's
Standard of Student Conduct, which prohibited "indecent conduct
or speech."[35]

Again, the Court cited *Tinker* at the outset of its analysis. Then
the Court stated that the dissemination of ideas—no matter how offensive to good taste—on a state university campus cannot be constrained because of "conventions of decency." The Court did not
explain if a university had a particular mission that made it special,
but merely cited *Healy* for the notion that this student could not be
expelled because administrators disapproved of the content in the
newspapers.

This lack of concern with "conventions of decency" on a college
campus did not transfer to the K–12 setting. After the Tinkers set
the stage for litigation, federal courts were asked to decide many issues about student speech. In 1986, the Supreme Court once again
reviewed a case from a high school that was very different from the
silent war protest of the Tinkers. The next chapter explores how the
Court added a new element—"the habits and manners of civility"—
to the school speech analysis.

✦

The Second Wave and the Constraint of Civility

ALTHOUGH THE SUPREME COURT made it clear in *Papish* that disciplining a student for language that was offensive to good taste would not pass constitutional muster at the University of Missouri, younger students presented a different problem and a new consideration when setting the school speech fulcrum. The facts in *Bethel School District v. Fraser* did not concern war protest and armbands.[1] This 1986 case is, in part, an example of just how different the world had become for teachers and principals dealing with student speech during the years after the *Tinker* decision.

> First Amendment problems in the school area are
> not easy of solution and much depends upon the
> specific facts before us.
>
> —Thomas v. Board of Education, 607 F.2d
> 1043, 1049 (2d Cir. 1979) (Chief
> Judge Irving R. Kaufman)

At an official school assembly addressing a high school student council election in Spanaway, Washington, Matthew Fraser gave a

nominating speech for his friend. His speech compared his friend
to a penis during erection, intercourse, and orgasm. He stated that
candidate Jeff was "firm in his pants," "takes his point and pounds it
in," "does not attack things in spurts," "drives hard, pushing and
pushing until finally—he succeeds." He "will go to the very end—
even the climax, for each and every one of you."

Six hundred students, many of them fourteen-year-olds, attended the assembly. Their reactions varied: some hooted, others
simulated masturbation and sexual intercourse with their hips, and
others appeared embarrassed or bewildered. One teacher reported
that she needed to use class time to discuss the speech with her students. The next day the principal suspended Fraser for violating the
school rule that prohibited speech that materially and substantially
interferes with the educational process (a rule obviously based on
the standard set forth in *Tinker*), including obscene or profane language or gestures. Fraser received his school district hearing (as required by the *Goss* opinion), which affirmed the discipline meted
out, and after serving two days of suspension, he returned to school.

The journalist Jonathan Yardley once observed that it is almost
impossible for a contemporary American to imagine the respect
that was granted the authority of teachers in the first half of the
twentieth century.[2] In the same vein, it would have been nearly impossible for a school principal in the in loco parentis era, before
Tinker, to imagine being the subject of a lawsuit in federal court for
disciplining a student after a speech like Fraser's. It would have
been even more difficult to imagine that Fraser would *prevail* both.
at the trial court and at the court of appeals. Indeed, these victories
for Fraser—as well as the language and tone used in the lower
courts—exemplify some of the changes that were wrought by
Tinker.

Fraser's name had been on a list of graduation speakers to be
elected by students, but his name was removed from the ballot after his speech at the assembly. His classmates nonetheless voted

him to be speaker by a write-in vote, but school officials refused to permit him to speak. If Fraser had been a student in a private school, he could have been disciplined and even expelled (and then sent to a public school, which has no choice in the students it must accept). He would not have had any claim that the school had deprived him of a constitutional right. But Fraser was in a public school. He grieved his case to the superintendent and then, joined by his father as guardian ad litem, filed an action for declarative relief, for an injunction permitting him to speak at graduation, and for $12,750 in attorney's fees.

Filing this lawsuit was probably easier for the Frasers than it had been for the Tinkers. In the time since the Supreme Court issued the *Tinker* opinion, Congress had passed a statute that made it easier for plaintiffs like Fraser to turn to the courts. Civil litigation in the United States generally follows the "American Rule," which assumes that plaintiffs and defendants choose and pay their own lawyers. In 1976, Congress passed a statute called, The Civil Rights Attorney's Fee Awards Act of 1976. It allows plaintiffs making constitutional claims against state officials or local governments to make the governmental defendants pay their legal fees when the plaintiffs are the prevailing party.[3] Before this fee-shifting arrangement, plaintiffs who were "seeking purely equitable relief or expecting small monetary awards had great difficulty locating competent counsel. Contingent fee arrangements offered little incentive to lawyers in either context."[4] The fee-shifting statute gave lawyers more economic incentive to pursue constitutional cases like that of Matt Fraser. At the same time—perhaps because of the ease of obtaining counsel, or perhaps due to other changes in societal norms—parents were becoming more confrontational about school discipline. Where students in years past did not want their parents to learn of trouble at school (fearing they would be punished worse at home), students increasingly saw parents as their allies against school discipline. So Matt Fraser and his father went to court. After an evidentiary hearing at which Fraser, the school principal, two assistant principals, and several teachers testified, the district court ruled for Fraser on all counts. The school district appealed the decision to the Ninth Circuit Court of Appeals.[5]

The Ninth Circuit started its opinion by quoting Fraser's speech in its entirety and then described the actions school officials took in response (calling Fraser to the principal's office the next day, giving him notice that he had violated the school's misconduct rule, giving him the opportunity to explain himself, and suspending him for three days). The court of appeals pointed out that Fraser was a member of the Honor Society and the debate team and had received the "Top Speaker" award in statewide debates. (It is not clear from the opinion whether the court was hinting that school officials should treat honor students who break school rules differently from other students who commit infractions, but there is some suggestion in this case and in others that school officials should treat students with this background with special care.)

After describing the facts surrounding the speech, the appeals court first determined that the student response had not met the *Tinker* disruption standard. The speech "evoked a lively and noisy response from the students, including applause and . . . a few of the students reacted with sexually suggestive movements." The court pointed out that teachers had been able to maintain order and that the assembly had been dismissed on schedule. This reading of the case means that student speech does not meet the *Tinker* "material disruption" standard as long as teachers are ultimately able to control the situation. The court dismissed out of hand evidence that even the next day, one teacher found that students were more interested in discussing the speech than in attending to classwork.

The two judges in the majority (Judge Norris, who wrote the opinion, and Judge Goodwin, who joined him) viewed the situation as indistinguishable from that in *Tinker* and saw no evidence that the speech had materially interfered with activities at the high school. "The mere fact that some members of the school commu-

nity considered Fraser's speech to be inappropriate does not necessarily mean that it was disruptive of the educational process."
Although the behavior could be characterized as "boisterous," testimony by the school counselor indicated that it was not atypical of a
high school assembly.

This opinion by the court of appeals revealed at least two interesting facets of the *Tinker* rule, which lower courts were applying in
school districts across the country. First, some courts would allow
considerable disruption to occur before agreeing that the *Tinker*
standard had been met. A significant factor in this case was that the
teachers at Bethel High School had been able to maintain order after the speech. This could mean that only a physical disruption that
careened out of control would pass the test. And the focus on the
actions of the listening students lets these students dictate the rules
for expression in school. As long as the *listeners* do not react in a
way that results in teachers losing control of the group, there is no
constraint on the speech. Conversely, if the listeners react in a violent manner that reaches the level of "material" disruption, they can
exercise their "heckler's veto," and the speech can be constrained.

In addition to its (losing) argument that Fraser's speech met the
Tinker standard for disruption, the school district set forth a new
theory. This argument ended up at the heart of the ultimate ruling
in the case, and it had repercussions that are still being heard in
school speech codes today. To what extent do school officials have a
legitimate interest in protecting teachers and students from speech
that is offensive, and when does that interest outweigh a student's
right to free expression?

The school district asserted that Fraser's speech could be restrained because it was offensive, and teachers had a duty to protect
students in their charge from offensive speech. The court of appeals viewed the school district's position as tantamount to a request to expand the doctrine of a 1985 Supreme Court case about
radio broadcasts—*FCC v. Pacifica Foundation*—to the school setting.[6] The *Pacifica* case addressed the power of the Federal Com-

munications Commission (FCC) to regulate a radio broadcast that included profanity but was not considered obscene. The broadcast in question was George Carlin's *Filthy Words,* a twelve-minute monologue containing words that, according to Carlin, you could not say on the public airwaves.[7] A New York radio station played the monologue at two o'clock in the afternoon, and a man who heard the broadcast with his young son complained to the FCC.

The Supreme Court noted in that case that the broadcast media have a pervasive presence in the lives of Americans. Patently offensive material can confront children in public and in the privacy of their homes, where the right to be let alone outweighs the First Amendment rights of an intruder. The *Pacifica* Court deemed that the government's interest in the "well-being of its youth" and in supporting the "parents' claim to authority in their own household" justified FCC regulation and special treatment of "indecent broadcasting." The Court also pointed out that adults who wanted to hear this kind of speech could purchase tapes or records or go to theaters or nightclubs, and that the FCC had not closed off the broadcasting of this kind of speech late in the evening. Of course, children today need only turn on satellite radio, cable television, or their computers to receive almost any kind of language. (The issue of a student's right to receive speech at school will be more fully addressed in Chapter 5.)

The court of appeals refused to import the *Pacifica* rationale to the school setting. It determined that high school students voluntarily attending an assembly do not expect the same measure of protection from unwelcome language as at home (as with the *Pacifica* radio broadcast) since the assembly is a public place, not a sanctuary for privacy. Moreover, the court found the second *Pacifica* rationale—the fact that broadcasting routinely reaches impressionable young children—equally inapposite. The court stated that Matthew Fraser was talking to young adults who were "beyond the point of being sheltered from the potpourri of sights and sounds we encounter at every turn in our daily lives." Being offended by some of what we see and hear, the court said, is the price we pay for living in a free and open pluralistic society. To allow school officials unbridled discretion to apply a subjective and amorphous "indecency" standard "would increase the risk of cementing white, middle-class standards for determining what is acceptable and proper speech and behavior in our public schools." In the appeals court's view, whether Fraser's speech went over the line of good taste and became offensive was not a matter to be decided by the school principal or another adult. Instead, this was a matter for Fraser's fellow students to judge when they cast their ballot for the election in question (Fraser's candidate had gone on to win the election).

To the extent that the court is suggesting that a concern about offensive language in school is a "white" and "middle-class" value, the court seems to be making a distinction based on race and class that some might argue is itself racist and classist. And the assertion that middle and high school students are the best judges of what crosses the line of good taste in the school environment surely strikes many who know youngsters of that age as downright silly.

The school district argued that school officials may control the language used at school-sponsored events. The court acknowledged that schools have broad discretion to control the content of the school curriculum. But it determined that this school assembly—where attendance was not compulsory, was run by a student, and where students gave speeches that were not prescribed by school officials—was not part of the curriculum. According to the court, Matthew Fraser was as free to express himself in the assembly as he would be if the students had organized a campaign rally in the cafeteria or outside on the school steps. (The themes presented here were not picked up in the Supreme Court opinion in the *Fraser* case, but they reappeared later in *Hazelwood School District v. Kuhlmeier,* discussed in Chapter 4.)

The opinion's final paragraph left little doubt about the inability of educators to restrain student speech merely because they deem it inappropriate. "Just as in the political world outside the school, the First Amendment requires that the principal restraint on the choice of words and ideas in political dialogue is the risk of disapproval by the audience the speaker hopes to influence." Thus, this court went even further than *Tinker* by making the "political world outside the school" the measure of restraint, equating the constitutional rights of adults with those of schoolchildren. As long as the speech was not disruptive (based on the court's view of disruption) or obscene, the decision Matthew Fraser made to use sexual innuendo in his speech was his and his alone to make.

Judge Wright in dissent took the two judges in the majority to task for failing to make the "delicate accommodations" necessary to ensure that "First Amendment freedoms coexist with institutional needs." Courts should begin with the presumption against judicial involvement in the schools. Quoting an article in the *Georgetown Law Journal,* he observed that "the school environment is unique, due to its physically confining nature, the immaturity of its population, and the special demands and needs of the educational purpose."[8]

The dissent described in detail one of the most important functions of the public school. Noting first that schools have the "difficult task of educating children and preparing them for full participation in adult society," Judge Wright also explained that the function of schools was more than merely "transmitting necessary information and techniques of learning." Schools also have the mission to "instill citizenship, discipline and acceptable morals. In short, we expect schools to inculcate society's values and help children become fully adjusted adults." Given this function of transmitting our culture's values, school authorities have both the right and the duty to "condemn language that falls below the minimum standards of decency expected in the local community." Moreover, the local school board is in the best position to determine what these values are in its own particular community. (As I will discuss later, the Supreme Court picked up on this theme and wove it through its own opinion.)

According to Judge Wright, *Tinker* was distinguishable because it concerned a political matter, toward which schools should remain neutral. But even if *Tinker* applied here, the dissent argued, the majority's notion of what constituted substantial disruption was overly constrained and failed to take into account the "delicate environment necessary to sustain learning." Speech that may appear harmless to the outside observer may nevertheless disrupt the education environment. "A speech which causes great distraction, excitement or embarrassment among the students may disrupt the educational process as greatly as one which results in fist fights." The dissent believed that teachers and principals were in a better position than judges to understand the sensitive nature of the learning process and were thus owed great deference by the courts.

The decision from the court of appeals was only a temporary victory for Matthew Fraser. When the Supreme Court heard the case, a new chapter was added to the school speech story.

> Tradition wears a snowy beard, romance is always young.
>
> —John Greenleaf Whittier

Both the Supreme Court and the country it serves had changed in the seventeen years since *Tinker* was handed down in 1969. The Vietnam War that had spawned the armband protest in Iowa had ended "officially" in 1973 and finally in April 1975, when the last American soldier was killed and the last American was evacuated by helicopter from the rooftop of the U.S. embassy in Saigon. The scars from that war have never healed.

The country had also seen hearings on the Watergate break-in, learned about secret White House tapes, and witnessed the resignation of a president. American hostages had been paraded in front of cameras in Iran, and the United States had boycotted an Olympics held in Moscow. In the two years before the oral argument, the AIDS virus was discovered, crack cocaine started to appear on the streets, and Mikhail Gorbachev had become the general secretary of the Communist Party in the Soviet Union. By the time the *Fraser* case came before the Court, Ronald Reagan was in his second term as president.

There had been major changes on the Supreme Court in the intervening years. Only three of the Justices who had been on the Court for the *Tinker* case remained. Justices Black, Douglas, Harlan, Stewart and Fortas were gone, replaced by Justices Powell, Rehnquist, Blackmun, Stevens, and O'Connor. Chief Justice Warren Burger had replaced Chief Justice Earl Warren. Court employees called the new Chief the "judge from Central Casting" because of his shock of white hair and his regal manner. He grew up in St. Paul, Minnesota and was a close boyhood friend of Harry Blackmun, who joined him at the high court. (The friendship later withered in the rarified atmosphere at the Court.)[9] Burger had played a key role in the nomination of Dwight Eisenhower for president, and Eisenhower later appointed him to the Court of Appeals for the District of Columbia Circuit, where he served for thirteen years, until President Nixon appointed him to succeed Earl Warren as chief justice.

Thirteen years before the *Fraser* decision, Chief Justice Burger had written a dissent in *Papish* that foreshadowed his opinion in *Fraser.* He stated that a university was not merely an arena for the discussion of ideas, but an institution where students learn to express themselves in acceptable, civil terms with the self-restraint necessary to the functioning of a civilized society.[10] When he expanded on this theme in *Fraser,* this time he found four justices who would join him.

If *Tinker* can be viewed as setting the benchmark for the student autonomy/liberty side of the speech conundrum, *Fraser*, decided seventeen years later, serves as the crowning point for those supporting socialization and order. The *Tinker* majority believed that the preservation of speech values would continue only if students could practice free speech in school. The *Fraser* majority believed that high school students could only learn about democratic values in a more disciplined atmosphere. If they are able to learn these values while they are in school, they will be better able to understand their importance to the self-preservation of the nation when they become adults. Students should gain a substantive knowledge base and a broader perspective before being turned loose with their freedoms. In fact, the *Fraser* majority quotes Justice Black's *dissent* in *Tinker* with enthusiastic approval. The *Fraser* opinion, without overruling *Tinker*, fashioned a new overlay to the school speech analysis.

The Court first took the court of appeals to task for equating *Fraser*'s speech with *Tinker*'s armbands, observing that there was a "marked distinction" between the "nondisruptive, passive" expression in *Tinker* and the sexual content of Fraser's speech. The Chief Justice pointed out that the *Tinker* opinion itself stated that "the case did not concern speech or action that intrudes on the *work of the schools* or the *rights of other students*" (emphasis added). The opinion then proceeded to explain the "work of the schools"—that is, the mission of the American public school system. In doing so, the Court was taking on a significant task. The institution that is our nation's public school system touches close to 50 million students each year.[11] The *Fraser* Court's conception about the mission of this institution would become part of court opinions, legal briefs, and motion documents in the decades that followed.

Fraser was not the first Supreme Court decision that attempted to set forth a view regarding the purpose of the public school. Justice Jackson declared in *West Virginia v. Barnette* that schools are "educating our young for citizenship," and the *Brown v. Board of Education* opinion maintained that the public schools help to awaken students to cultural values.[12] But the *Fraser* majority did not focus on the language from these cases. Instead, Chief Justice Burger used another case as the guidepost for his opinion.

Decided in 1979, *Ambach v. Norwick* addressed a New York law that prohibited teacher certification for persons who were not citizens of the United States.[13] In upholding the statute, the majority opinion, written by Justice Lewis Powell, explained the role of education in the United States and the responsibility teachers have in fulfilling that role. Citing philosopher John Dewey, the *Ambach* Court stressed the "assimilative force of the public schools in bringing together diverse and conflicting elements in society on a broad but common ground." Teachers can influence "the attitudes of students towards government, the political process and a citizen's social responsibilities," an influence the Court stressed was "crucial to the continued good health of a democracy."

The *Fraser* Court built on this self-preservation model, but it is significant that the Court did not start its analysis with either the *Ambach* case or with quotes from any other of its own opinions. Rather, the first sentence of the analysis in the *Fraser* opinion is a quotation from a 1968 history book, *The Beards' New Basic History of the United States,* by Charles Austin Beard and Mary Ritter Beard. The Court used the Beards' conception of the public school as the foundation of its opinion: "The role and purpose of the American public school system were well described by two historians, who stated: '[Public] education must prepare pupils for citizenship in the Republic. . . . It must inculcate the habits and manners of civility as values in themselves conducive to happiness and as indispensable to the practice of self-government in the community and the nation.'"

We do not know for sure how Chief Justice Burger found this phrase and why he decided to make it the cornerstone of this opinion, but reading the amicus briefs submitted for the case yields some clues. The United States wrote an amicus brief under the direction of Solicitor General Charles Fried. That brief included the exact quote from the Beards' book that was to form the basis of the *Fraser* opinion, and it is likely where the Chief Justice found this quotation to describe the role of the public school for lower courts and policy makers for generations to come.[14]

Who were Charles and Mary Beard, the historians who came to have such influence on General Fried, Chief Justice Burger, and consequently, American public education? Charles (1874–1948), the more renowned of the two, gained his reputation as a scholar interested in the relationship of politics and economics. His fame (or notoriety) began when he wrote *An Economic Interpretation of the Constitution of the United States* in 1913, which focused on the motivations behind the Constitutional Convention. His suggestion that the Constitution had been a triumph for property and business caused a furor; he was castigated for invoking "dangerous thoughts" that tarnished that document's image.[15] In a 1938 *New Republic* survey entitled "Books That Changed Our Minds," this work was one of two titles mentioned most frequently by American intellectuals.[16] (The other book was Thorstein Veblen's *The Theory of the Leisure Class*.) Mary Beard (1876–1958), had a reputation in her own right as a scholar of the labor movement and feminism; and she published *Women's Work in Municipalities* in 1915.

The couple was recognized by the reading public of the day for their four-volume history of the United States (published from 1927 to 1943). But it was their brief survey, *The Beards' Basic History of the United States* (1944, revised in 1960) that caught the eye of the amicus brief writer and then the fancy of Chief Justice Burger. While he was influential during his lifetime, Charles Beard's posthumous standing has been debated among historians. In 1968, one noted commentator, Richard Hofstadter, called Beard's reputation "an imposing ruin."[17] If Hofstader was correct about Beard in 1968, that message apparently had not reached all of the legal world in 1986.

The quote from the Beards became the lodestar for the theme the Court developed in the *Fraser* opinion and the new standard the Court tacked on to its *Tinker* ruling.

The chief justice pointed out that the theme he used from the Beard quotation had its genesis in earlier Court opinions, including *Ambach,* which he said "echoed the essence" of the quotation. *Ambach* had indeed stated that "perceptions of the public schools as inculcating fundamental values necessary to the maintenance of a democratic political system have been confirmed by the observations of social scientists."[18] *Ambach* cited three sources: Richard E. Dawson and Kenneth Prewitt, *Political Socialization* (1969); Robert D. Hess and Judith V. Torney, *The Development of Political Attitudes in Children* (1967); and Validmer O. Key, *Public Opinion and American Democracy* (1961). Thus, aside from the quotation from the Beards' 1945 book, the core of this concept was plucked from the views of historians and social scientists of the 1960s.

The next step was to determine how Fraser's speech fared under this new standard. The Court acknowledged that these fundamental values of "habits and manners of civility" included tolerance for divergent, even unpopular, viewpoints. Indeed, the Court has suspended the enforcement of civility norms in other contexts. It allowed Paul Cohen to wear his jacket bearing the words "Fuck the Draft" in the Los Angeles County Courthouse. And the Court would later say that burning the U.S. flag was protected conduct.[19] But when it came to the public schools, it balanced the freedom to advocate controversial views against the countervailing interest of society in teaching students the boundaries of socially appropriate behavior and in protecting the sensibilities of other students. "The process of educating our youth for citizenship in public schools is not confined to books, the curriculum, and the civics class; schools must teach by example the shared values of a civilized social order."

What nature of speech, then, will fail to pass muster? The Court stated emphatically: "Surely it is a highly appropriate function of public school education to prohibit the use of vulgar and offensive terms in public discourse." The school may determine that "the essential lessons of civil, mature conduct cannot be conveyed in a school that tolerates lewd, indecent, or offensive speech."

Chief Justice Burger must have realized that he needed more than quotations from historians, citations from social scientists, and a broad theme from the *Ambach* opinion to bolster the legitimacy of this new standard for student speech. After pointing out that the sexual innuendo in Fraser's speech was offensive to both teachers and students (particularly teenage girls), the Court turned to its own past opinions to demonstrate how First Amendment protections for adults could change when children were exposed to speech with sexual content.

Using *Ginsberg v. New York* (1968), *Board of Education v. Pico* (1982), and *Pacifica*, the *Fraser* Court explained how these previous First Amendment opinions had recognized a state interest in protecting children from sexually explicit, vulgar, or offensive speech.[20] *Ginsberg* had upheld a New York statute that prohibited the sale of sexually explicit material to minors, even though the material would be protected by the First Amendment if sold to adults. *Pico* (discussed in Chapter 5) was a divided and fragmented opinion dealing with the removal of books from a school library because the school board believed they were "anti-American, anti-Christian, anti-Semitic, and just plain filthy." The *Fraser* Court read *Pico* as acknowledging that school boards have the authority to remove books that are vulgar. More significant, the Court used these two cases to equate the power of school authorities with that of parents—a power that cases from the time of *Tinker* had taken pains to dissolve.[21] *Ginsberg* and *Pico,* the Court said, "recognize the obvious concern on the part of the parents, and *school authorities acting in loco parentis* to protect children—especially in a captive audience—from exposure to sexually explicit, indecent, or lewd speech" (emphasis added).

The Court then used *Pacifica* as the basis of its claim that the state has an interest in protecting minors from exposure to "vulgar and offensive spoken language." As discussed above, *Pacifica* addressed a 1973 broadcast of a radio monologue by George Carlin wherein Carlin's performance, presaging today's shock jocks, focused on stating words forbidden on the airwaves.[22] A splintered Court, in an opinion by Justice Stevens, held that the action of the Federal Communications Commission (FCC) in response to the broadcast was constitutionally permissible under a federal statute that allowed the FCC to regulate "indecent broadcasts."[23]

The *Fraser* Court saw Carlin's broadcast as similar to the speech in *Chaplinsky v. New Hampshire* (often called the "fighting words" case), that is, it was speech of the lowest value and deserved little or no protection. "Such utterances are no essential part of any exposition of ideas, and are of such slight social value as a step to truth that any benefit that may be derived from them is clearly outweighed by the social interest in order and morality" (quoting *Chaplinsky*).

All that remained was to put the Beard formulation of the school mission with the *Ginsberg-Pico-Pacifica-Chaplinsky* hierarchy of First Amendment values: "The First Amendment does not prevent the school officials from determining that to permit a vulgar and lewd speech such as [Fraser's] would undermine the school's basic educational mission. . . . [I]t was perfectly appropriate for the school . . . to make the point to the pupils that vulgar speech and lewd conduct is wholly inconsistent with the 'fundamental values' of public school education."

The Court ended its First Amendment analysis with a quotation from Justice Black's dissent in *Tinker*, a point the Court said was especially relevant to the *Fraser* case: "I wish therefore . . . to disclaim any purpose . . . to hold that the Federal Constitution compels the teachers, parents, and elected school officials to surrender control of the American public school system to public school students."

Justice William Brennan concurred in the Court's judgment but wrote a separate opinion to show his disagreement with the reasoning in the majority opinion. In his view, Fraser's speech was not in the same basket with the speech that was regulated in *Ginsberg* and banned in *Pacifica*. Nevertheless, Brennan acknowledged that the speech contained "disruptive language," and he allowed that school officials have the discretion to teach high school students civil and effective public discourse. In the circumstances of the case, he believed that it was not unconstitutional for school officials exercising that discretion to conclude that Fraser's speech at the assembly had exceeded permissible limits.

Both Justice Marshall and Justice Stevens dissented. Justice Marshall would have applied the *Tinker* disruption standard. Since the lower courts were not convinced that education at the school had been disrupted, Fraser's speech could not be restrained. Justice Stevens began his dissent with a quotation from the end of the film *Gone with the Wind:* "Frankly, my dear, I don't give a damn." He pointed out that when he was in high school, the use of those words by Clark Gable in the film had shocked the nation.[24] Despite the fact that the word "damn" was now "less offensive" than it had been at that time, Justice Stevens asserted that school officials may ban that word in classroom discussions and at other activities on school premises because "a school faculty must regulate the content as well as the style of student speech in carrying out its educational mission." He did not believe that Fraser's speech rights had been violated. Instead, his dissent anchored in the Due Process Clause of the First Amendment, as he believed that Fraser had not had the proper notice either that his speech was prohibited or the likely punishment.

The *Fraser* case was not over yet . . . at least for Fraser's attorney. Apparently well versed in the Civil Rights Attorney's Fees Award

Act, he filed a motion with the Ninth Circuit requesting "partial attorney fees," contending that Fraser had prevailed on one claim of relief he had sought, since he had been allowed to speak at graduation. By the time the Ninth Circuit reviewed the district court opinion, the issue was moot. Judge Norris, who had written the original Ninth Circuit opinion that had been reversed by the Supreme Court, agreed with Fraser (and his lawyer, who was the one who stood to benefit from the motion) that Fraser was a prevailing party since he benefitted from the injunction. He wrote a dissent when the other members of the panel denied the motion.

Matt Fraser attended the University of California at Berkeley and majored in political science. He says that the term "graduated" is a "strong word for the culmination of my studies."[25] For nearly twenty years he has served as the director of The Stanford Debate Society at Stanford University and at the Head-Royce School, a private school in Oakland, California.[26] He occasionally speaks publicly about his experience, and he still believes that students in a school assembly should be able to give speeches that are not disruptive, lewd, or obscene.

One interesting aspect of the case was not part of the opinion. According to Fraser, Jeff Kulman's parents were deeply religious and were very upset about Fraser's speech about their son. Jeff told his parents he knew nothing about the speech before Fraser gave it. Fraser says that Jeff knew about the speech beforehand: "He was in the room when I wrote it." As of 2006, Fraser reported that he had not spoken with Jeff—the focus of the most famous student council election in history—since high school.[27]

The *Fraser* opinion changed the mission of the public school from that set forth in *Tinker*—accommodation of students—to the inculcation of the habits and manners of civility. At its marrow, the inculcation mission is a call for self-preservation—what the Supreme

Court has termed "the subtle process of securing effective loyalty to the traditional ideals of democracy."[28] In *Government and the Mind,* Professor Joseph Tussman observed that the state's "teaching power" is even more fundamental to the state than its war power. This "teaching power" is the "inherent constitutional power" of the state to establish and direct the institutions, like the schools, that are necessary to ensure its continuity.[29] The heart of both the *Tinker* and the *Fraser* opinions was aimed at preserving our nation's core values, but the opinions differed on exactly what was needed to do so. For the *Tinker* majority, allowing students the freedom to express themselves with little constraint would give them the opportunity to "practice" their freedoms so that they will be better able to understand and cherish these freedoms when they become adults. In the view of the *Fraser* majority, teaching the habits and manners of civility while setting the boundaries for public discourse would allow all students the freedom to learn in an environment that encourages the self-discipline that is necessary for sustained and reflective study.

Despite its spirited attempt to cabin *Tinker,* the *Fraser* opinion could not come close to restoring the student-teacher relationship of the pre-*Tinker* days. The constitutional right of free expression in the schoolhouse is here to stay, along with the right of due process and the right to be free from unreasonable searches. The strains of the *Tinker* melody continued to be heard in court opinions throughout the following decades.

But the civility limitation on school speech has taken on a new twist. This time, the impetus lies outside of the ambit of the courts and history professors. It has gained momentum with the help of some new federal and state statutes. Even the education institutions themselves have gotten into the act by passing school speech codes. Although the *Fraser* opinion is never mentioned in the legislative history, these statutory constraints on speech certainly resonate with *Fraser*'s notion that education institutions must infuse "the habits and manners of civility."

> When once the forms of civility are violated, there
> remains little hope of return to kindness or decency.
> —Samuel Johnson

Two federal statutes—Title VI of the Civil Rights Act of 1964 and Title IX of the Education Amendments of 1972—address discrimination because of race or sex in educational institutions. Courts have determined that students can sue school districts and collect money damages for failure to address speech by teachers or students that meets the standard for racial or sexual harassment. Title VI prohibits discrimination on the basis of race, color, and national origin in programs and activities that receive federal funding. Title VI states: "No person in the United States shall, on the ground of race, color, or national origin, be excluded from participation in, be denied the benefits of, or be subjected to discrimination under any program or activity receiving Federal financial assistance."[30] A recipient of federal funds (like a school or university) may be responsible for "hostile environment" harassment (physical, verbal, or written harassing conduct) that is sufficiently "severe or pervasive and objectively offensive that it deprived the student of access to educational benefits or opportunities."[31] The educational institution may be liable for money damages if, once it has notice of the problem, it is "deliberately indifferent." Deliberate indifference is a term of art used by courts that requires the educational institution to take "reasonable steps" to eliminate the harassment.

Similarly, the Supreme Court has determined that educational institutions may be liable for money damages when sexual harassment occurs in school. Congress modeled Title IX on Title VI of the Civil Rights Act of 1964 (though Title VI protections are not limited to education programs, as Title IX is). Title IX provides that "no person . . . shall, on the basis of sex, be excluded from participation in, be denied the benefits of, or be subjected to discrimination under any education program or activity receiving Federal financial assistance."[32] Indeed, the Supreme Court has stated that Title VI provides important guidance in applying Title IX.[33] The standards are similar to those of Title VI: after a school receives notice of harassment based on sex that is sufficiently severe, pervasive, and persistent, the school must not act in a way that is "deliberately indifferent."[34] The Court has determined that schools may be liable for both teacher-on-student and student-on-student harassment.[35] Although the Supreme Court cases that have focused on sexual harassment in school have all involved male-on-female harassment, some lower courts have addressed same-sex harassment scenarios—where the victims are harassed because of their actual or perceived sexual orientation—and found that Title IX offers these students protection when the harassment is based on the failure to meet masculine stereotypes.[36]

During the 1980s and early 1990s, many colleges and universities—and even school districts—passed speech codes to curb discrimination and harassment. At the time, there was a perceived "epidemic" of racial harassment on college and university campuses.[37] Professor Jon Gould discusses three distinct motives for the speech codes: (1) universities needed a symbolic response to racial incidents on campus to assure campus constituencies the university was acting against intolerance; (2) the codes served as the higher education version of "keeping up with the Joneses," universities instituted speech codes to stay in what looked like the mainstream of higher education; and (3) administrators legitimately believed in the merits of the codes (Gould asserts that the third is true for a much smaller group of schools than the first two).[38]

An incident at the University of Massachusetts, Amherst, may have provided the spark that set off a "grand firestorm that enveloped American society and its opinion leaders for the better part of a decade."[39] After the Red Sox lost the sixth game of the 1986 World Series, a racial brawl took place in Amherst between white Red Sox fans and black Mets fans that became "symptomatic for a souring racial climate among college students."[40] Other schools, including the University of Michigan, began to see evidence of a deteriorating racial climate in the late 1980s, when reported incidents of racial harassment seemed to be increasing.[41] Unknown persons in Ann Arbor distributed a flier declaring "open season" on blacks and referring to "saucer lips, porch monkeys and jigaboos." A student disc jockey at a campus radio station allowed the broadcast of racist jokes. A Ku Klux Klan uniform was displayed outside a dormitory window.

The University of Michigan expressed outrage and reaffirmed its commitment to a diverse campus, but it was highly criticized at a public hearing for its response to these racial incidents. The United Coalition Against Racism, a campus antidiscrimination group, announced that it would file a class action civil rights lawsuit against the university "for not maintaining or creating a non-racist, nonviolent atmosphere" on campus. After discussions and hearings, the university's acting president presented what was called the Policy on Discrimination and Discriminatory Harassment to the Board of Regents. The board adopted it unanimously in April 1988, even though some of its members expressed concern that the policy would unduly restrict the free speech rights of students.

The policy prohibited behavior that "stigmatizes or victimizes an individual on the basis of race, ethnicity, religion, sex, sexual orientation, creed, national origin, ancestry, age, marital status, handicap, or Vietnam-era veteran status, and that . . . creates an intimidating, hostile, or demeaning environment for educational pursuits, employment of participation in University sponsored extra-curricular activities." The university's *Interpretive Guide* to the policy stated that one example of sanctionable conduct occurs if "a male student makes remarks in class like 'Women just aren't as good in this field as men,' thus creating a hostile learning atmosphere for female classmates." The guide further stated:

"YOU are a harasser when . . ." (among other examples):

You exclude someone from a study group because that person is of a different race, sex or ethnic origin than you are

You tell jokes about gay men and lesbians

You display a Confederate flag on the door of your room in the residence hall

You comment in a derogatory way about a particular person's physical appearance or sexual orientation, or their cultural origins, or religious beliefs.

A graduate student in biopsychology challenged the policy in a lawsuit, using the pseudonym John Doe to preserve his privacy and protect himself from adverse publicity arising from the case. He claimed that his right to discuss certain controversial theories about biologically based differences between sexes and races was impermissibly chilled by the policy.

Avern Cohn, the federal judge who heard the case, agreed. He recognized that he was faced with the difficult task of mediating an appropriate balance between two important values: freedom and equality. In this instance, freedom prevailed. The court cited both *Fraser* and *Pacifica* (among other opinions) for the proposition that speech that is vulgar, offensive, and shocking is not entitled to absolute constitutional protection in all circumstances. But the university was not permitted to establish a policy that prohibited speech because the university disagreed with the idea the speech conveyed. Nor could the university proscribe speech merely because it was offensive to a large number of people.

Two important and closely related doctrines that come into play when dealing with speech issues are the prohibitions against "overbreadth" and "vagueness." A prohibition is overbroad when it sweeps in too much speech—not only the speech that government can legitimately regulate, but speech that is protected by the First Amendment. Although the university argued that its policy did not apply to protected speech, the court reviewed the way the university had applied the policy to complaints filed regarding classroom discussion and determined that the policy "was consistently applied to reach protected speech."

The policy also failed to withstand the court's review for vagueness, that is, whether the policy was clear enough about what speech it was prohibiting. The court explained that "it was simply impossible to discern any limitation . . . or any conceptual distinction between protected and unprotected conduct." The terms "victimize" and "stigmatize," as used in the policy, are general and have no precise definition. The court went even further and stated that speech that may victimize or stigmatize another may not be stripped of its First Amendment protection entirely. Based on these infirmities, the court permanently enjoined the University of Michigan from enforcing the policy.

Although the University of Michigan case was arguably the most famous campus speech code opinion, other cases followed from challenges to codes at the University of Wisconsin, Stanford University, and Central Michigan University, each meeting the same fate.[42]

The Supreme Court has also weighed in on hate speech, although not in the specific context of schools and universities. In *R.A.V. v. City of St. Paul*, a juvenile was charged with violating the city's hate crime ordinance when he burned a cross on the lawn of a neighboring African American family.[43] The hate crime ordinance was an attempt to follow the "fighting words" rule of *Chaplinsky* (no First Amendment protection for words that "tend to incite an immediate breach of the peace").[44] It was a misdemeanor to place an object like a Nazi swastika or burning cross on private property when the perpetrator knew or had reason to know that it would arouse anger, alarm, or resentment in others on the basis of race, color, creed, or gender. All nine justices agreed that the ordinance was unconstitutional, though they did not agree on the same rationale. There were four opinions written in *R.A.V.*, and Justice Scalia garnered the necessary five votes for his view that the ordinance did not pass First Amendment scrutiny because it singled out certain "fighting words" based on their content or viewpoint. In other words, government could prohibit all fighting words, but it could not prohibit only fighting words about race: "Government may not regulate use based on hostility—or favoritism—towards the underlying message expressed."

Despite the fact that the case had nothing to do with school speech codes, the opinion bristled with language that could easily be applied to codes on the campus. Justice Blackmun recognized this possibility and wrote in his concurring opinion: "I fear that the Court has been distracted from its proper mission by the temptation to decide the issue over 'politically correct' speech and 'cultural diversity,' none of which is presented here." Legal commentators across the political spectrum saw the case as the Court's attempt to derail campus speech codes. Most commentators saw *R.A.V.*, together with the decisions from the lower courts striking down code after code, as the end of the road for this phenomenon. In fact, after *R.A.V.*, the lead counsel for the plaintiffs in both the University of Michigan and Central Michigan University cases (who is also a law professor at Wayne State University) wrote: "Under the law of the First Amendment, virtually any campus ban on racist speech in a public university will be found to be unconstitutional."[45]

Despite this apparent victory of "freedom" over "equality" in the world of campus speech codes, Professor Jon Gould argues that hate speech regulation has sustained a significant "afterlife."[46] In his book *Speak No Evil: The Triumph of Hate Speech Regulation*, he points out that five years *after R.A.V.*, "almost half of American colleges and universities had hate speech policies on the books, a rise of nearly 30 percent from the time of the Court's opinion. The rate was even higher for those schools that adopted more constitutionally suspect policies—codes that banned offensive speech—where numbers had tripled."[47]

Instead of putting an end to college hate speech regulation, Professor Gould asserts, "the court decisions were ignored, evaded, and resisted."[48] Gould's critics counter that since universities are not actively enforcing these policies, the codes will not create a chilling effect on the discussion of unpopular ideas.[49] Gould does not disagree that these institutions seldom enforce their speech policies, but he argues that the policies still "continue to wield great power." "Their symbolic power has flourished as student services staff and other college officials continue to advance the underlying message of the speech policies. [Moreover] the conceptual kernel has taken root in American society, bringing with it greater acceptance of hate speech regulation."[50]

Although some observers suggested that unenforced restrictions on speech would be immune from challenge in the courts, colleges and universities with dormant speech codes may nonetheless be brought to heel. Even after acknowledging that the student code at Shippensburg University was enacted "with the noble purpose of making that institution a better place to live and learn" and had not been used to punish students (and was unlikely to be used) during the term of the current university president, a federal court in Pennsylvania issued a preliminary injunction prohibiting the university from enforcing certain provisions of the code.[51] The court declared that other provisions of the code, local ordinances, the state criminal code, and federal antidiscrimination laws would provide adequate safeguards against improper behavior.

The contradiction between the acceptance of antidiscrimination statutes by courts and the (so far) universal rejection of speech codes presents a legal and social conundrum that deserves a more penetrating analysis than is possible here.[52] There is no question that speech that constitutes harassment is regulated under Title VI (racial) and Title IX (sexual). As noted, educational institutions at both the K–12 and the higher levels can be penalized by a loss of federal funds or by paying money damages to the victim if they fail to act after they receive notice of harassment. Many school districts and colleges and universities have policies that prohibit harassment based on sex or race (certainly a reasonable response to the threat of a lawsuit under Title VI or Title IX).[53] The problem is that these policies forbidding harassment, at some level, look suspiciously like the University of Michigan Policy on Discrimination and Discriminatory Harassment. When challenged, these K–12 and university nonharassment policies could meet the same fate.

For example, in 2001, then-Judge Samuel Alito wrote an opinion for the Third Circuit Court of Appeals that addressed a school district policy that prohibited harassment. "Harassment" included "any unwelcome verbal, written or physical conduct which offends, denigrates or belittles another" because of actual or perceived race, religion, color, national origin, gender, sexual orientation, disability, or "other personal characteristics." These characteristics could include "clothing, physical appearance, social skills, peer group, intellect, educational program, hobbies or values, etc."

The district court had dismissed the plaintiff's free speech claims because it believed that harassment received no protection from the First Amendment. Judge Alito and the Third Circuit panel determined that there is "no categorical 'harassment exception'" to the First Amendment and that the school district policy was overbroad—it prohibited a substantial amount of speech that would not be actionable harassment under either federal or state law.[54] A year later the Third Circuit allowed a school district's racial harassment policy to stand, with the exception of a section that prohibited clothing or material that is racially divisive or "creates ill will." The court reasoned that the "creates ill will" language focused on the reaction of the listener. The court then focused on Justice White's concurrence in *R.A.V.*, which stated that expressive activity that causes offense or resentment does not render the expression unprotected.

Although the court determined that this clothing section of the harassment policy did not pass constitutional muster, the part of the policy limited to racially provocative speech was an acceptable nondiscriminatory response by school officials to past racial disturbances. The school district had simply gone too far in disciplining a student for wearing a tee shirt that was inscribed with "redneck" jokes. The school district had not established that the shirt violated any particular provision of the harassment policy, except perhaps the problematic "ill will" provision.[55]

Professor Gould agrees that restrictions on harassment can have the same effect as restrictions on hate speech. He claims that the words courts use to determine whether harassment has occurred under Title VI or Title IX (whether it is "severe" or "pervasive") are just as vague as the words "stigmatize" and "victimize" in the University of Michigan speech code.[56] Some courts even include "offensive" speech in the harassment analysis, requiring the harassment to be severe, pervasive, *and* objectively offensive, while other courts require the harassment to be severe *or* pervasive. (Compare *Bryant v. Independent School Dist.*, 334 F.3d 928 (10th Cir. 2003), harassment standard for Title VI and Title IX violation is "severe, pervasive, and objectively offensive," with *Qualls v. Cunningham*, 1006 WL 1476123 (7th Cir. 2006), for Title VI hostile environment violation, need to show harassment was "severe or pervasive enough to deprive [the student] of access to educational benefits.") Gould's assertion about harassment statutes rings true: "The hostile environment prong of sexual harassment law rests on the same basis as does hate speech regulation: Words not only wound, but severe and pervasive messages may also discriminate."[57]

So what is the explanation for the willingness of the courts to approve of sanctions under harassment statutes while tearing apart speech codes? Professor Gould argues that judges addressing this issue are influenced by three forces, which are all political rather than legal. First, the history and strength of interest groups behind sexual harassment litigation helped to convince the courts over time of the seriousness of sexual harassment.[58] According to Gould, speech codes lacked this kind of passionate and committed support, since for the most part they were merely measures put in place by administrators as a sop to certain constituencies.[59]

Second, opponents of speech codes were successful in framing the issue as a free speech issue and an extension of "political correctness." Professor Gould also points out that most of the judges deciding the speech code cases had graduated from college during a different era, one where few minorities attended college and no one made harassment claims. Finally, Professor Gould posits that judges may be more comfortable regulating sexualized speech because of this nation's cultural history of "collective prudishness" that "leads to the repression of sexual expression."[60]

It is impossible to determine to what extent Professor Gould's theories are correct, but his first two reasons seem to make intuitive sense. Without question, dedicated interest groups that understand the power of patience can help to change public perception of an issue over time. We have seen time and time again in social and legal controversies throughout the last decades—whether about abortion rights or immigration—that framing an issue can influence policy makers and the public. And Professor Gould is surely correct that judges are not completely immune from societal influences.[61] His assertion about the influence of cultural history may also have merit, but on its face the connection seems a bit more attenuated, and it fails to explain the courts' embrace of harassment regulation based on race under Title VI. Nonetheless, Professor Gould's observations highlight this inconsistency in how speech is regulated in educational institutions and points to an area for further scholarly exploration. One such endeavor is Timothy Shiell's book *Campus*

Hate Speech on Trial.[62] Shiell suggests that sanctions should be confined only to "hate speech that targets a specific individual or individuals in a captive-audience context . . . is intended to cause harm to that individual or individuals, is clearly unrelated to any legitimate academic purpose, and is repeated (or in an individual instance, sufficiently egregious) or done in conjunction with illegal conduct."

Not to be outdone by Congress and university councils, some state legislatures have passed statutes regarding uncivil speech in school. "School bullying" has been increasingly viewed as a community problem that needs a societal response, and state legislatures have responded by passing "antibullying" legislation. According to the National Institutes of Health, bullying may be physical (hitting or another kind of attack), verbal (name calling or threats), or psychological (spreading rumors or excluding).[63] It is distinguished from other kinds of aggression because (1) it is intended to inflict suffering; (2) this infliction is repeated and persistent; and (3) there is a power imbalance between victim and perpetrator.[64] One study reported that about 28 percent of the students questioned said they had been bullied at school within the last six months.[65] Indeed, bullying behavior seems to be a part of human nature. "Bullying is a problem in every school in the world, which may seem like a simplistic answer, but it's true."[66]

Bullying is not confined to students. Teachers, who should be part of the solution, can be part of the problem—not just with students, but with each other. "Mobbing" is a term that stems from the behavior of songbirds. When birds perceive danger (say, a cat) a group of birds will fly at the threat, make a racket, swoop down on it, and draw other birds to the assault until the intruder leaves. Researchers have coined a term for situations where employees gang up on someone at work: "workplace mobbing"; and university faculties are notorious for using this kind of behavior to target weaker colleagues. The pattern begins with social isolation—for example, the rolling of eyes when the target speaks at meetings—and then escalates to petty harassment and a request for action by an administrator.[67]

Although concerns about bullying predated the Columbine school shootings, that tragedy undoubtedly contributed to renewed attempts to curtail school bullying. In the aftermath of the Columbine shootings, facts emerged that suggested the shooters were lashing out at classmates who had ridiculed and taunted them.[68] Indeed, a 2002 U.S. Secret Service and Department of Education study found that two-thirds of school shootings in the previous 30 years were committed by victims of bullying.[69]

Stopping shooting rampages like that in Columbine may be only one of the benefits of curtailing bullying. Bullying disrupts learning, and it can result in increased absenteeism, physical and emotional illness, and even substance abuse. Bullying can even foreshadow criminal adult behavior. One report claims that nearly 60 percent of the male bullies in sixth through ninth grade were convicted of at least one crime by age 24 (40 percent had three or more convictions).[70] Some policy makers have tried to find a legislative solution to the problem, and by 2007 at least 18 states had passed antibullying legislation.[71]

It is not yet clear whether these state initiatives will meet the same fate as campus speech codes, but not all of these attempts to promote civility have fared well. For example, legislation in the state of Washington was derailed because of claims that antibullying statutes could violate the free speech rights of students who wished to express their opposition to homosexuality.[72] Another student code of conduct that addressed bullying-type behavior was struck because it infringed on free speech. The code of conduct was authorized by a Michigan state statute that required school discipline for "verbal assault." Despite the paradoxical nature of the term (at common law, words alone do not constitute an assault) the school district policy was to punish students who "verbally threaten the well-being . . . or dignity of persons on school property." Although the statute does not mention bullying, it addresses conduct that would easily be part of any bully's repertoire. If a student above grade 6 commits a verbal assault, as defined by school board policy, at school, the school board "shall suspend or expel the pupil from the school district" for a time to be determined by the school board.[73] The district court in Michigan acknowledged that the legislation was enacted with a "laudable purpose" in response to tragic assaults in schools in other states, and that it attempted to address confrontational bullying and disruptive speech. Nonetheless, the court found that the statute and the corresponding policy were overbroad and vague, and it enjoined the school district from enforcing them.

As schools and courts continue to grapple with the contours of free speech and civility in face-to-face confrontations, the Internet adds a new dimension to the problem. "Bullies who once cornered their victims on the playground are now tormenting them in cyberspace."[74] Text messages, email messages, and websites are the tools of the "cyberbully," who can distribute (often irretrievable) postings worldwide. Schools report violent school incidents and even suicides that are connected to cyberbullying, but "legal remedies for the victims of bullying continue to be woefully inadequate."[75] Even if school officials learn about it, much of the activity may occur off-campus. Although some state legislatures have attempted to address cyberbullying, the courts that have addressed school authority to punish students for speech on the student's own website have not been in agreement about the appropriate analysis. For example, the Pennsylvania Supreme Court affirmed a lower court decision that addresses student-on-*teacher* harassment. It determined that a student website entitled "Teacher Sux" hindered the educational process, noting the effect the site had on a teacher who viewed a picture of her severed head dripping with blood, a picture of her face morphing into Adolf Hitler, and a solicitation for funds to hire a hit man.[76] But in a case where a student posted mock obituaries and allowed visitors to the website to vote on who would "die" next, the court enjoined the school from enforcing a short-term suspension because the website was out of the school's control and the school had not shown that the student intended to or had actually threatened anyone.[77] The U.S. Supreme Court has not yet weighed in on cyberbullies, and its guidance would be useful to lower courts and school districts dealing with this issue.

Hate speech and cyberbullying may be offensive, but "offensive" speech—is not the only kind of speech that undercuts the habits and manners of civility. The *Fraser* opinion also gave school officials the right to discipline K–12 students for "vulgar" speech. Students and administrators continue to wrangle about what speech is vulgar. Yearbooks designating students "most likely to be a pimp" and a student literary magazine containing stories and poems using the words "fuck," "pussy," and "homo" have resulted in complaints by parents and have been confiscated by school officials. Although the speech is a far cry from Matthew Fraser's allusions at the assembly, students defend this kind of speech as an accepted part of today's culture.

It is not hard to see why students may have trouble ascertaining the dimensions of speech that is vulgar. The *American Heritage Dictionary* defines "vulgar" as "deficient in taste, delicacy or refinement," "marked by a lack of good breeding, boorish," and "crudely indecent," but, like obscenity (remember Justice Potter Stewart), vulgarity is difficult to define with anything approaching clarity.

To add to the problem, students are bombarded with crude speech daily in almost every avenue of popular culture—in music lyrics, television, and films. And all this occurs at a time when they are most vulnerable to peer pressure that entices them to be a part of the picture that popular culture paints for them. This media blitz has given rise to what author Tom Wolfe calls the "fuck patois" that occurs in the language of many young people.[78] When this language erupts in the school setting, the clash can be bitter.

The essence of this issue stems once again from the conception of the school's mission. Should the school be a reflection of society so that language that is accepted in music lyrics and films becomes acceptable at schools? Should the minds and appetites of screenwriters and songwriters be the benchmark for students? Or should the school be a special place that sets a different tone from that seen in popular culture?

These questions are at the core of the debate between the majority and the dissents in both *Tinker* and *Fraser*, and they go to the heart of our conception of the public school. One side believes schools should be a place where students are free to make choices about how they see fit to express themselves. The other side believes schools should teach students how to make those choices in an atmosphere free from the vagaries of generational popular culture.

Even though the *Fraser* Court was much friendlier to schools than *Tinker*, school officials did not really benefit much from the changes *Fraser* attempted to make. Throughout the school speech story, regardless of the ideological makeup of the Supreme Court, the one constant has been uncertainty about what schools can do about student expression. The *Fraser* opinion added yet another uncertain legal line for school officials to figure out. It is not legal lines in and of themselves that impose high costs on regulated actors like teachers and principals; but when these lines are vague and fuzzy, it makes it hard for these actors to know how to order things to avoid litigation. Ascertaining whether speech is "vulgar" or "offensive" or the extent to which it undermines the inculcation of the "habits and manners of civility" under *Fraser* is not much easier for school officials than determining whether school speech would cause a "substantial" disruption under *Tinker*. This uncertainty, combined with the asymmetry brought about by the attorney's fees statute, leaves school officials in a vulnerable position that surely has consequences for the day-to-day learning environment in schools.

Students have many ways of expressing themselves at school. They often use school newspapers as a forum for stating their viewpoint on current issues, and their speech may at times present issues that bring the *Fraser* analysis into play. But even if the speech in a school newspaper does not meet the broadest definition of vulgarity, it may be harmful to others in a different way. When the Supreme Court chose to hear its next case in the student speech line, it set its sights on a school newspaper this time. The Court once again attempted to explain how the school's mission affects student expression in this arena. The following chapter focuses on issues surrounding the student press and other student publications.

.✦.

Student Press Rights and Responsibilities

> What one knows is, in youth, of little moment; they
> know enough who know how to learn.
>
> —Henry Adams, *The Education of Henry Adams*

> When I think back on all the crap I learned in high
> school, it's a wonder I can think at all.
>
> —Paul Simon, "Kodachrome" (1973)

ONLY SIX MONTHS AFTER the Supreme Court imprinted the "habits
and manners of civility" into the legal lexicon—a millisecond in
Supreme Court time—the Court agreed to review another school
speech issue. Instead of oral expression, this case centered on the
written word. Although the Court granted certiorari on January 20,
1987, the opinion was not handed down until a full year later, on
January 13, 1988. The Court used this opinion, *Hazelwood School
District v. Kuhlmeier,* to carve out a special niche for school newspapers.[1]

The lawsuit that was to ripen into what one commentator called
"probably the most significant free speech case involving public
school students since . . . *Tinker*" was filed after a high school principal deleted two articles (one about teen pregnancy and one about
students with divorced parents) from an issue of the school news-

paper, the *Spectrum*.[2] The *Spectrum* was written and edited as part of the high school's Journalism II class. A faculty member taught the class, and students received academic credit and a grade. The class met every day, and the students and instructor worked on the production of the paper during this period. Some of the stated goals for the course were to give students an experience in journalistic techniques "by publishing the school newspaper under pressures of pre-established deadlines" and learning "the legal, moral, and ethical restrictions imposed upon journalists within the community." The duties of the teacher included selecting the editors, scheduling publication dates, assigning and editing stories, and counseling students on story development.

The *Spectrum* was published every three weeks, funded in part by money allocated by the local school board, and it had a distribution of over 4,500 copies. The publication procedure was for the journalism teacher to submit page proofs to the school principal, Mr. Reynolds, for review before publication. When the teacher delivered the proofs for the edition in question, the principal objected to two articles that were slated to appear. Because there was not enough time to change the articles (in an era long before computers and desktop publishing, he got the page proofs for the May 13 edition on May 10), he simply deleted the two pages on which these articles were to appear; the newspaper was printed with four pages instead of the planned six.

Three staff members of the *Spectrum* filed a complaint in federal court against the school district and various school officials, including principal Reynolds, and the journalism teacher. Interestingly, the students who filed the complaint were *not* the students who had written the deleted articles. Cathy Kuhlmeier, whose name was soon to become part of a significant episode in the school speech story, was layout editor; Leslie Smart was newswriter and movie reviewer; Leanne Tippett was news feature writer, cartoonist, and photographer. The students' complaint sought an injunction, money damages, and a declaration that their First Amendment rights had been violated. District Judge John F. Nangle of the Eastern District of Missouri dismissed the request for an injunction as moot, because the plaintiffs had graduated. He then conducted a bench trial on the First Amendment issue.

Since he sat without a jury, Judge Nangle made his own determination of which view of the facts was most credible. His written opinion starts with a lengthy section in which he sets forth his factual findings in the case. Because the factual findings of the trial judge are given great deference by courts of appeal, his findings proved significant as the case worked its way up the ladder. Judge Nangle found that the journalism teacher was the final authority with respect to "almost every aspect of the production and publication of *Spectrum,* including its content." The testimony of the student plaintiffs that "they believed that they could publish 'practically anything' in *Spectrum* was not credible." Judge Nangle also quoted at length from the ethical rules of journalism that appeared in the class textbook. These included ethical rules adopted by the American Society of Newspaper editors about respecting the rights of people involved in the news and a section entitled "Fair Play" about giving those who are publicly accused the right to respond.

The first deleted page contained three articles. One article surveyed statistics on teen pregnancy and included some discussion of birth control and abortion. The second, entitled "Squeal Law," discussed a law that would require federally funded clinics to notify parents when teenagers sought birth control. The third—the article the principal saw as problematic—contained "personal accounts of three Hazelwood East students who became pregnant." The article stated that "all names have been changed to keep the identity of these girls a secret." In each account, the student discussed her reaction and her parents' reaction to the pregnancy, her future plans, her relationship with the father, details of her sex life, and use or nonuse of birth control. The author of the article had told the students that their names would not be used. No parental consent was obtained.

Three other articles appeared on pages 4 and 5. The first addressed the divorce rate of teen marriages, and the second discussed runaways and juvenile delinquents. The third article—the one that had concerned the school principal—was entitled "Divorce's Impact on Kids May Have Life Long Affect [*sic*]." One student, identified as Junior, was quoted as saying that his dad did not make any money and was an alcoholic who always came home drunk. Another student, identified in the article as freshman Diane Herbert, was quoted as saying, "My dad wasn't spending enough time with my mom, my sister and I [*sic*]. He was always out of town on business or out late playing cards with the guys. My parents always argued about everything." Similar statements were provided by two other named students. No parental consent was obtained, and no parents were contacted to explain or rebut the statements of their children.

Reynolds testified that only two of the articles raised concerns, and he explained why. First, he believed that the privacy rights of the three girls who spoke anonymously about their pregnancies were compromised, as readers might be able to identify the particular three students, despite attempts to keep their identity secret by using false names. Testimony at trial convinced Judge Nangle that this concern was legitimate. Reynolds also believed that the references to sexual activity and birth control were not appropriate for younger children at the school.

Reynolds also had a concern about the other article that was rooted in journalistic "fair play." Because the second article had statements by one student criticizing her father for his behavior before the divorce, Reynolds believed that fairness required that her parents should have been notified and given an opportunity to respond to the remarks or to consent to their publication.

Reynolds thought there was no time to make the necessary changes before the scheduled publication, and he was concerned that delaying printing too long would mean there would be no newspaper issue before the end of the school year. Thus, he believed his options were to publish a truncated issue with the two articles excised or to publish no issue at all. He decided to publish a four-page issue, instead of the six usual pages. It was this decision that landed him in court. Reynolds testified that he had no objection to the other articles that appeared on the two pages; they merely happened to be on the pages he deleted.

Trial lawyers often say a case can be won or lost by the testimony of the expert witnesses, and this case certainly was no exception. Both sides presented an expert witness, but Judge Nangle clearly viewed one as more credible than the other. The student plaintiffs' expert witness, a professor of journalism, testified during direct examination that the articles at issue complied with professional journalism standards. But skillful questioning elicited testimony on cross-examination that suggested that this witness had a personal interest in the outcome of the case. He admitted that he attended a national convention of investigative reporters where he had distributed materials about the case and tried to get others to come to the aid of the student plaintiffs. The court was concerned that this witness might have been biased by his personal views supporting the expansion of student press rights.

On the other side, the school district's expert witness, a former college instructor and editorial page editor of the *St. Louis Globe Democrat,* had no particular axe to grind and had not even been paid by the defendant. Judge Nangle thought he was "an objective and independent witness." This witness testified that the divorce story did not meet the standard required for journalism "fairness and balance," because the student's father was not given an opportunity to respond. He explained that the pregnancy stories involved invasions of privacy, and he pointed out the difference between censorship and editing. Censorship originates from an outside source, but editing is the prerogative of someone in authority within the publishing entity.

Perhaps Judge Nangle's most important finding appeared in a

short paragraph near the end of his finding of the facts. He noted that the school officials involved—from the teacher to the school district superintendent—were all professional educators with many years of experience. Their judgment that certain articles were not appropriate for high-school-age readers or for publication in a school-sponsored newspaper was reasonable and *entitled to great deference*. This statement pretty much says it all. Although the court went on to set forth conclusions of law and analyze whether the school was a public forum, a court that indicates that it trusts and will defer to the professional judgment of educators is not likely to rule against the school. (Recall how Justice Fortas showed no deference to educator judgment regarding the distraction presented by the *Tinker* armbands, and how the lower courts in *Fraser* paid little heed to the idea that Matthew Fraser's speech was inappropriate for a school assembly.)

Despite this early hint of the final outcome, the court nonetheless set forth its conclusions of law in an analysis that later became the basis of the U.S. Supreme Court's opinion. Two lines of cases had developed in the aftermath of *Tinker*. The first line addressed situations where student speech was privately initiated and was independent of any school program or activity. The focus in these cases is on whether the speech would materially disrupt the educational process.

In the second line of cases—those where student speech is in the context of school-sponsored publications, activities, or curricular matters—the focus moved away from the effect of the student's speech on others to an analysis of the nature of the school-sponsored program. That is, courts decided whether the program is an open forum for free expression or an integral part of the curriculum. If a program is an integral part of the educational function, a standard less than substantial disruption is applicable.

According to Judge Nangle, the *Spectrum* was an integral part of the curriculum and not a public forum. The *Spectrum* was produced by members of the Journalism II class, who were taught by a faculty member. A grade and academic credit were awarded for completion of the class and for work on the newspaper. Significantly, the teacher had control over virtually every aspect of the newspaper's production, including prepublication review. Given this degree of involvement with the high school curriculum, the school district had not created a public forum.

Judge Nangle used a 1979 case from a district court in New York, *Frasca v. Andrews,* to articulate the standard to use when analyzing an educator's decisions about an integral part of the educational function.[3] In essence, the decisions of school officials will be sustained in this line of cases if there was a "substantial and reasonable basis for the action taken." The Supreme Court opinion would later borrow heavily from this formulation.

All that was left was for Judge Nangle to apply the standard it had obtained from *Frasca* and analyze whether the school officials could demonstrate that there was a reasonable basis for their actions. First, the court determined that the principal's concern about the students' anonymity in the pregnancy story was legitimate and reasonable. The court reached back to *Tinker* to justify its analysis, noting that *Tinker* had listed "invasion of the rights of others" as one situation where school officials would be justified in restraining student speech. Second, the court pointed out that the school could properly prevent the publication of material in a school-sponsored newspaper to avoid giving the impression that it endorsed the sexual norms of the students in the articles. Finally, and "most importantly," the court credited the principal's judgment that this material, in the context of a school-sponsored newspaper, was not appropriate for some of the readers of the *Spectrum,* given their age and maturity.

With respect to the divorce article, because the father of the student quoted in the article had not been given a chance to respond to the allegations she made about his conduct, there was "serious doubt" that the article complied with the standard rules of journalistic fairness that were covered by the textbook used for the class. Because the principal's objections were legitimate with respect to both articles, the court decided the student's First Amendment rights had not been not violated. Much of this analysis found its way into the Supreme Court's opinion as well, but the Eighth Circuit Court of Appeals weighed in first; in a 2–1 split, it rejected Judge Nangle's analysis.

Contrary to the district court, the Eighth Circuit decided that the *Spectrum* was a public forum for the free expression of student opinion. The two judges in the majority believed that the *Spectrum* was operated as a conduit for student viewpoints.[4] Since students chose the staff members and determined the content of the articles, the newspaper was a "student publication in every sense." Moreover, as part of the Journalism II class, the school encouraged students to express their opinions freely. Interestingly, this court bolstered its analysis with the Ninth Circuit opinion in *Fraser* (on which the Supreme Court had not yet filed its opinion). The court pointed out that this Ninth Circuit opinion had even held that a school-sponsored *assembly* where Matt Fraser made his famous speech was not a part of the curriculum but was instead a student activity where students were "free to exercise their individual judgments about the content of their speeches." Ironically, the Supreme Court's *Fraser* opinion was filed the very same day that the Eighth Circuit filed its opinion in *Hazelwood*—July 7, 1986. Unfortunately for these two Eighth Circuit judges, the Ninth Circuit *Fraser* opinion was struck down by the U.S. Supreme Court, and their own analysis would soon meet a similar fate.

But that day was yet to come. The Eighth Circuit determined that since the *Spectrum* was a public forum, the educators had to meet the standard set forth in *Tinker*. They had to show that they could reasonably forecast that the speech would materially disrupt classwork, cause substantial disruption, or invade the rights of others. The court determined that they had failed to do so. The school had not claimed on appeal that the articles would disrupt classwork or cause substantial disorder, and unlike the district court, the court of appeals gave short shrift to the justifications given by the school administrators. The court found no evidence that the pregnancy article would create the impression that the school endorsed the sexual norms of the students involved. And unlike the district court, the court of appeals was unimpressed with the professional educators' years of experience dealing with high school students and their opinion that the article was inappropriate and unsuitable for younger students. Rather than according their views "great deference" like Judge Nangle, the appellate judges simply set forth their own view that students in the high school were aware of teenage pregnancy and said "it is most unlikely that anything in the article would offend their sensibilities."

Like that of the Ninth Circuit in *Fraser,* this analysis focused on "the students" and whether *they* would think the speech was a problem. It did not take into account an adult judgment whether a particular speech is appropriate for children or teens or whether it is appropriate in the school setting. This analysis presents several problems. Given the diversity of student cultural and religious viewpoints in many schools, it may be difficult to ascertain how some kinds of speech might affect the sensibilities of all of—or even a majority of—the students. Moreover, the sensibilities of students may not be the best way to sort out school speech issues. If part of the mission of schools is to socialize students, adult guidance regarding appropriate speech may help facilitate that socialization. For example, many high school students today might say that the word "fuck" does not—to use the words of the Eighth Circuit— "offend their sensibilities." Under the socialization model, students would still need to learn that this word is not considered appropriate speech in many contexts, and school officials would be well within their rights to say that its use was unsuitable in school, whether the students were bothered by it or not.

For the Eighth Circuit, the crux of the case was whether the articles invaded the rights of others under *Tinker.* As discussed in Chapter 2, the Supreme Court in *Tinker* had drawn its language about rights invasion from another source, *Blackwell v. Issaquena.*[5] In that case, the court allowed the school to prohibit students from wearing certain protest buttons when the students initiating a protest, accosted their peers on school grounds and pinned buttons to them. This caused an unusual degree of commotion and "a collision with the rights of others."

Although few cases since *Tinker* had delineated the boundaries of this type of collision, the court of appeals in *Hazelwood* was persuaded by an article written by a law student in the *Michigan Law Review* that argued that this invasion-of-rights justification refers only to a tortious act.[6] Thus, school officials could limit student speech only when allowing it could result in tort liability for the school (e.g., assault, battery, or defamation).

The court of appeals found that neither the divorce article or the pregnancy article met this requirement. With respect to the divorce article, the court completely ignored the school district's concern with the "fairness and balance" journalism standard. Instead, the court asserted that the real reason for the deletion was the school district's view that divorce was an inappropriate subject for high school newspapers. The court decreed not only that this topic was appropriate, but that "responsible treatment of this subject" would provide a helpful perspective on it.

The court's failure to address the school's main argument is curious. But its statement about the principal's true motive for deleting the article is even more curious, considering the content of other articles that had been published in the *Spectrum* in the past and the content of articles that passed without objection in the very issue in question. Topics discussed in the *Spectrum* in the seven years preceding the case included student use of drugs and alcohol, race relations, teenage marriage, the death penalty, the St. Louis desegregation case, runaways, teenage pregnancy, religious cults, the draft, school busing, and student's rights against search and seizure. In the very issue in question, the principal had no problem with another article on teenage pregnancy that covered such issues as birth control and abortion, an article entitled "Squeal Law" discussing a proposed rule that would require federally funded clinics to notify parents when teenagers sought birth control assistance, an article on runaways and juvenile delinquents, and an article entitled "Teen Marriages Face 75% Divorce Rate." In light of the subject matter of these articles—published without any objection to content—it seems a bit far-fetched to claim that the underlying reason for deleting the divorce article had absolutely nothing to do with journalism standards but was based on the view that the subject of divorce was an inappropriate subject for an article in the *Spectrum*.

The pregnancy article fared no better under the Eighth Circuit analysis. School officials stated that they believed that the girls in the articles could be identified, and they were concerned because neither their boyfriends or parents had consented to being subjects of a newspaper story. Again using the standard set forth by the law student in the *Michigan Law Review* article, the court noted that the only tort action that could have been maintained against the school district after publication was that of invasion of privacy. The court defined this tort as violating another's "right of privacy by publicity exposing details of such person's life, the exposure of which would be offensive and objectionable to a reasonable person of ordinary sensibilities" (taken from the American Bar Association Standards Relating to Schools and Education). Under this definition, there was no possible tort action: the female students had consented to the article, and neither the parents nor the fathers could sue, since the article did not expose any detail of the parents' lives or disclose who the fathers were.

This approach is yet another instance of a court setting a difficult course for those who make decisions in schools. It is not always easy to tell whether published words will be a tort. The torts of invasion of privacy and defamation are slippery legal concepts, even for legal scholars and judges, let alone teachers and school principals. Newspapers and other publishers in the commercial press have their own lawyers and often hire law firms with attorneys who specialize in this area to help to unravel these complex issues. Most major media companies in the United States (who own the dominant media outlets in almost all the major markets) use both in-house and outside counsel. Their lawyers perform a variety of day-to-day tasks, including prepublication broadcast review. This review is conducted at a number of levels by different departments, including both Editorial and Legal Standards and Practices. Of course, this is a costly endeavor. Typical outside counsel rates can easily run $500 an hour in the large media markets and somewhat less in the smaller markets. In addition, these media companies also pay large insurance premiums to cover their expenses when mistakes do occur.[7]

As Judge Wollman observed in dissent, although the commercial press may be able to afford to retain counsel to advise them daily on complicated liability questions, school districts—limited in funding to what the taxpayer can or will bear—are unlikely to have these resources. Making the allusion to mythology that many judges seem to find so irresistible, he observed that the court's opinion forced school officials to chart a course between the Scylla of student-led First Amendment suits and the Charybdis of tort actions by those claiming injury from student-published articles. For those unfamiliar with Greek mythology, the Scylla and Charybis were two sea monsters that inhabited either side of a narrow strait between which Odysseus had to sail. The sailor who chose to sail away from one monster had to sail closer to the other and face certain doom.

It is odd that the Eighth Circuit never mentioned the fact that the students interviewed about their pregnancies had been told that their names would not be used and may have believed that this would be enough to keep their identity secret. If the students believed that they would remain anonymous, the scope of their consent might not have been as broad as the court assumed. Moreover, the article discussed each pregnant student's statements about both her relationship with the baby's father and the reaction of her parents, and both of these might have exposed details that either the parents or the father wanted to keep private. Although the article itself did not disclose the names of the fathers, even the appeals court admitted that they could be identified by persons who had knowledge of the facts revealed in the article. The court also failed to address the extent to which educators could restrain students when their journalism failed to meet ethical standards. Nor did the court discuss whether the state as educator has an interest in its students that exceeds or differs from the dollar amount a school district is willing or able to pay during tort litigation.

The court's reliance on a law student's note in the *Michigan Law Review* also deserves mention. Student "Notes" are generally written by second-year law students who are on their school's law review editorial board. Law Reviews are student-run journals, and the student articles seldom, if ever, receive any review for content except by the third-year law students who make the selections for publication. The court in this case was putting some heavy weight on a notion proposed by a second-year law student in a journal edited only by other students.

The Scylla and Charybdis picture painted by Judge Wollman is an entertaining one, and it is not far off the mark. Even though the Supreme Court would later reverse the Eighth Circuit opinion regarding school-sponsored newspapers, school districts are often in a First Amendment Scylla/Charybdis (or rock/hard place or devil/deep blue sea—pick your metaphor) quandary. The principal who suspends a student who writes a poem about murdering his teacher and classmates is open to a lawsuit for violating the student's First Amendment rights. In the recriminations that occurred after the Virginia Tech massacre, it became clear that the school official who fails to recognize that a student is about to commit a violent act may also be open to a lawsuit for failure to act in time. For example, the school officials in the Columbine case have been roundly criticized for their failure to identify the killers' severe breakdown before the shootings.

These two opinions in the *Hazelwood* lineage, together with *Tinker* and *Fraser*, exposed some significant issues that underlie the school speech cases. Economic resources, although seldom mentioned, certainly play a part in the educator's decision-making process, and they may have even deeper implications for policy debates about the future of public schools. After *Tinker* ushered the federal constitution through the schoolhouse gate, school districts needed to change their policies about student expression. To avoid personal or institutional liability, school officials in the wake of *Tinker* and its progeny must keep informed of new cases to make sure their policies adequately address current issues and changes in the law regarding student expression (or due process and search and seizure). Every case after *Tinker*, not just those decided by the Supreme Court but also those in the lower courts, could require another policy change. And every time a situation arises where an educator feels the need to restrain student speech means that they must carefully assess whether they are allowed to do so. No superintendent or principal or teacher wants his or her name on the next test case, so they call in legal counsel to assess whether they should sail closer to Scylla or Charybdis. Of course, all this discussion of what principals and teachers are allowed to do requires a huge amount of time, money, and energy, and the upshot often is that there is no clear answer.

Public schools are at a distinct disadvantage with regard to private schools in this area of resource expenditure. Any instance where public schools compare less favorably to private schools puts one more arrow in the quiver for those hoping to influence public opinion in the school choice wars. Given the dismal state of some public schools, some might argue that the limited funds that *are* available could be better spent on students. Others might counter that defending student speech in the public schools is worth every penny. Perhaps the first question to ask those folks is where they send their own children to school. At the very least, the school choice debate highlights the fact that many parents are clamoring to get their children *out* of schools where the First Amendment is in play and *into* schools where it is not.

Perhaps the explanation lies in parental trust that private school educators are principled enough to maintain an environment that will keep their children safe and enable them to learn in a disciplined atmosphere. Court mistrust of public school officials erupted in *Tinker,* and the perception judges have about how much to trust educators was still the hidden linchpin in the *Hazelwood* opinions filed years later. The district court trusted the experience of the professional educators; two judges in the court of appeals were dismissive of their experience and their judgment. The dissent in the court of appeals summed up the argument on one side of the line. Judge Wollman wrote, "We judges are not journalists . . . and even less school administrators. Granting the defendant school administrators the deference due them, I would hold that they committed no constitutional violation."

When the Supreme Court took up the case, Justice Byron White agreed with Judge Wollman's ultimate conclusion. His opinion borrowed many of the ideas set forth by Judge Nangle. Justice White noted that the *Hazelwood* case must be considered in light of both *Tinker* and *Fraser.* Like the two lower courts, his opinion focused on First Amendment forum analysis, but it also revived a dissent from years past.[8]

Justice Harlan Redux

Justice White explained that public schools are not like streets and parks and other traditional public forums that "time out of mind" have been used by citizens for assembly and discussion. Thus, a nontraditional forum like a school will be deemed a public forum only if—by policy or practice—the school facilities have been opened for indiscriminate use by the public (or some segment of the public, such as student organizations). No public forum is created if the facilities are reserved for other intended purposes, and school officials in that circumstance may impose reasonable restrictions on the speech of those in the school community.

Under the school district's policy, the writing for the *Spectrum* was a regular classroom activity that was part of the educational curriculum. The journalism teacher was the final authority on virtually every aspect of the newspaper, including its content, and the newspaper was subject to final review by the school principal before publication. The evidence relied on by the court of appeals failed to demonstrate a clear intent to open the pages of the *Spectrum* to indiscriminate use by the students or to otherwise create a public forum by policy or practice.

Justice White then spent a portion of his opinion explaining how *Hazelwood* differed from *Tinker*. He pointed out that in *Tinker* the Court addressed whether a school was required to *tolerate* student speech—a matter of the student's personal expression. In *Hazelwood,* the question was whether the school was required affirmatively to *promote* particular student speech that occurred in activities the school sponsored, like newspaper publications, theater productions, and other expressive activities. Because these activities are supervised by faculty and designed to impart particular knowledge or skills, they are part of the school curriculum. The school may exercise greater control over this form of student expression to ensure that the students learn what the activity is designed to teach, that they are not exposed to material that is inappropriate for their maturity level, and that the views of a speaker are not erroneously attributed to the school. As in *Fraser,* the majority opinion in *Hazelwood* quoted Justice Black's *dissent* in *Tinker* "disclaim[ing] any purpose . . . to hold that the Federal Constitution compels the teachers, parents and elected school officials to surrender control of the American public school system to public school students."

Moreover, the *Tinker* standard—substantial disruption and material interference—"need not be the standard for determining when a school may refuse to lend its name and resources to the dissemination of student expression." Instead, the Court, without attribution to Justice Harlan, resurrected the standard offered by Justice Harlan in his long-dormant dissent in *Tinker* (requiring the student to show that the school's restraint was "motivated by other than legitimate school concerns"). When exercising editorial control over the style and content of student speech in school-sponsored activities, school officials are not constrained by the First Amendment, "so long as their actions are reasonably related to legitimate pedagogical concerns."[9]

After setting forth this new standard, the majority then applied it to the actions of the school principal. According to the Court, Reynolds had acted reasonably in the circumstances, given his concern that students had not mastered the portions of the journalism curriculum relating to anonymity, journalistic fairness, sensitivity to privacy interests, and inappropriate content for some students.

Justice Brennan wrote a dissent that was joined by Justices Marshall and Blackmun. The dissenters would have applied the *Tinker* standard to the student speech in *Hazelwood:* The principal's actions "cannot by any stretch of the imagination have been designed to prevent material disruption of classwork." The dissenters also agreed with the court of appeals that the newspaper stories failed the invade-the-rights-of-others prong of *Tinker,* since that term must be limited only to rights that are protected by law.

Justice Stevens, who had dissented in *Fraser,* joined the majority this time. His vote was crucial for Justice White's 5–3 majority, as the Court had only eight members at the time the case was argued on October 13, 1987. Justice Powell had resigned on June 26. One of President Reagan's nominees for Powell's spot was not confirmed by the Senate; a second withdrew. Justice Anthony Kennedy was not sworn in until February 18, 1988. If Justice Stevens had voted with the dissenters to make a 4–4 tie, the Eighth Circuit decision upholding the rights of the students would have remained valid.

The writer of the majority opinion in *Hazelwood* has always been a bit of an enigma. Justice White was President John Kennedy's only appointment to the Supreme Court, and he joined the Court after serving as deputy attorney general under Robert Kennedy. White was a Rhodes Scholar, but many outside the legal world knew him as the All-American football halfback from the University of Colorado nicknamed "Whizzer" (a name he supposedly disliked). He is certainly the only Justice ever to have played professional football (for the Pittsburgh Pirates, now the Steelers), and he was a "big money" player for his day—making $15,000 in 1938, the year he led the NFL in rushing (reportedly the highest paid athlete in history at the time). He was gruff-voiced and he had a handshake that could bring you to your knees. (I know this first-hand—sorry for the pun.)

Law professor Dennis Hutchinson, a former clerk for Justice White, recalled that White "went after arguments aggressively, wrestling them to the ground."[10] His clerks claimed that he would often start typing away, drafting opinions immediately after the justices conferred on the day a case was argued. Although he may be most famous to legal cognoscenti for his majority opinion in *Bowers v. Hardwick* (upholding a state's criminal statute on sodomy) and for his dissent in *Roe v. Wade*, he wrote two important opinions concerning student rights—*Hazelwood* and *T.L.O.*, discussed in Chapter 2. His opinion in *T.L.O.* held that the Fourth Amendment restraint on unreasonable searches by government officials applied to a school principal (although the principal needed only "reasonable suspicion," rather than probable cause, to conduct a legal search). His opinion in *Hazelwood* certainly made its mark in the student press world.

After the decision was announced, the front page of the *Washington Post* declared, "The Supreme Court gave public school officials sweeping power to censor school-sponsored student publications yesterday, rejecting the complaints of three dissenting justices that it was approving "brutal censorship."[11] The *New York Times* described the "broad power to censor school newspapers, plays and other 'school-sponsored expressive activities.'"[12] Many school officials and their advocates supported the decision. Ivan Gluckman, counsel for the National Association of Secondary School Principals, maintained that although most high school principals do not want to act as censors, they nonetheless need to have the final word on what is printed. "They are responsible for what comes out in the newspaper," Gluckman said, as is the chief editor of a regular newspaper. "No reporter has an unfettered right to publish whatever he wants in the paper."[13] Editorial comment was generally critical of the *Hazelwood* opinion, but some writers hailed it as "a lesson in reality" for students that "with freedom goes responsibility, and that goes for the First Amendment."[14]

Most commentators view *Hazelwood* as a watershed opinion: "The Court's sweeping language . . . moved far beyond the narrow issue of school censorship. It even moved beyond the question of appropriate or acceptable speech in public secondary schools. It was clear that *Hazelwood* could have far-reaching consequences for student rights, school governance, and the scope of official authority to make curricular decisions that reflect the values of the local community."[15]

Just how much did *Hazelwood* change the legal matrix? *Tinker* had advised courts to use what looks like a form of strict scrutiny in reviewing student First Amendment claims by requiring "*material disruption*" and "*substantial* interference." *Hazelwood* adjusted that scrutiny by defining it down: whether the educator's decision was "*reasonably* related to a *legitimate* pedagogical concern." At least where school-sponsored expression was concerned, courts could overturn a decision by a school official only if the official did not have a "legitimate" reason for the decision. The decision does not have to be the best alternative under either educational or legal theory, as long as the educator can show that there was a "legitimate" concern with respect to education.

Although Justice Harlan used "legitimate school concerns" years earlier in his *Tinker* dissent, the Court had also used the term "legitimate concerns" only six months before *Hazelwood* was decided, in *Turner v. Safly*.[16] In this case, Justice O'Connor, writing for the majority, ruled that prison officials could impinge on prisoner's constitutional rights if the action was reasonably related to legitimate penological interests—giving commentators ample ammunition to claim that the Court was treating students like prisoners.[17]

With this new *Hazelwood* overlay, school officials and their attorneys need not worry about showing material disruption of the educational mission. Instead, they must be prepared to convince a court that their actions were based on a legitimate pedagogical concern. Unless an educator was disciplining a student out of sheer spite, it would not be too difficult now to set forth a reason that would pass muster. For example, in one opinion from the Sixth Circuit, regarding a student being declared ineligible for an election after he made rude remarks about the high school assistant principal at a campaign speech at a school assembly, the court stated: "Local school officials, better attuned than we to the concerns of the parents/taxpayers who employ them, must obviously be accorded wide latitude in choosing which pedagogical values to emphasize, and in choosing the means through which those values are to be promoted. We may disagree with the choices, but unless they are beyond the constitutional pale, we have no warrant to interfere with them."[18] In light of how Matt Fraser won both his lower court cases for his speech at a school assembly when the courts applied the *Tinker* standard, and how the lower courts in *Hazelwood* differed in their willingness to defer to the judgment of educators, it becomes clear how the Supreme Court's *Hazelwood* opinion changed things, at least in the context of school-sponsored speech.

Hazelwood's ambit is not limited to newspapers. Other forms of expression—for example, yearbooks, even the school mascot—may also bear the stamp of school approval. When a high school principal in Virginia ended the use of a school mascot called "Johnny Reb," the court of appeals stated that it was sufficient that the principal's decision was "based on legitimate concerns." The court expressly affirmed that the most important question in the analysis was whether the decision had an educational basis. Once that decision was made, the court backed off: "[The principal] received complaints that Johnny Reb offended blacks and limited their participation in school activities, so he eliminated the symbol based on legitimate concerns. *Except to make the rough threshold judgment that this decision has an educational component, we will not interfere,* and it is clear that educational concerns prompted [this] decision."[19]

Sometimes even teachers may fall into the *Hazelwood* net. When parents complained about a teacher who made a remark in the classroom about some students' lack of moral values, the teacher was disciplined. The school district set forth three concerns to justify sanctioning the teacher: (1) the school has an interest in preventing a teacher from using his or her position of authority to confirm an unsubstantiated rumor; (2) the school has an interest in ensuring that its teachers exhibit professionalism and sound judgment; and (3) the school has an interest in providing an educational atmosphere in which teachers do not make statements about students that embarrass them before their peers. The court had no trouble deciding whether the asserted concerns were legitimate, simply stating, "The interests asserted by the school in this case clearly are legitimate pedagogical interests."[20]

When a teacher was terminated for allowing students to use profanity in her creative writing class, in violation of school policy, the teacher claimed that the school district had violated her First

Amendment rights. She argued that as a teacher she was facilitating the speech of her students, and that the school's prohibition on profanity in creative activity did not serve a legitimate academic interest. The court cited both *Fraser* and *Hazelwood* and stated that "[a] flat prohibition on profanity in the classroom is reasonably related to the legitimate pedagogical concern of promoting generally acceptable social standards."[21] Thus, the *Hazelwood* doctrine has wandered a long way from its original moorings—where it merely allowed a school principal to remove student-written articles from a school-sponsored newspaper.

So is there any set of circumstances where a court applying the *Hazelwood* standard will find against the school? *Desilets v. Clearview Regional Board of Education* is often used to show how courts occasionally will buck the tide. In this case, school officials refused to allow middle school students to review R-rated movies in the school newspaper. The asserted pedagogical concern was that the educators did not want the school to be perceived as promoting R-rated movies to middle-school-aged children. The trial court determined that the decision was reasonably related to a legitimate pedagogical concern, but the court of appeals disagreed. "Substantial deference to educational decisions does not require a wholesale abandonment of First Amendment principles simply because the medium for the student's expression is funded by a school board." The court thought that *Hazelwood* should apply only to decisions based on content or journalistic style. According to the court, the school's decision was not based on content, which it defined as "what is written," but on subject matter, which it defined as "what is written about." The articles were not lewd, ungrammatical, or likely to cause disruption. The only reason school officials wanted to restrict them was because the movies in the reviews were R-rated. The court ruled that the decision whether to allow a middle school child to view an R-rated movie was a parental, not an educational, decision, and the pedagogical interests of the school simply did not extend to these movie reviews.[22]

Students may find the occasional court that will refuse to defer to educator judgment about legitimate pedagogical concerns; but some states have passed statutes that afford the student press additional protection. In addition to the First Amendment in the U.S. Constitution, states can provide additional protection to their citizens under their state constitution or by enacting special legislation. At least seven states—Arkansas, California, Colorado, Iowa, Kansas, Massachusetts, and Oregon—have passed statutes, sometimes called anti-*Hazelwood* laws, that provide students with added protection against administrative censorship.[23] For example, the Arkansas Student Publications Act provides that school officials must recognize student journalists' free-expression rights, but reserves the right to prohibit certain types of publications, including those that (1) are obscene to minors; (2) are libelous or slanderous; (3) constitute an unwarranted invasion of privacy; or (4) incite students and create a clear and present danger of the commission of unlawful acts on school premises or the violation of lawful school regulations or the material and substantial disruption of the orderly operation of the school. Thus the *Tinker* standard, threaded throughout the statute, becomes the standard even for school-sponsored publications.

Because of *Hazelwood*'s focus on school-sponsored newspapers, students turned toward independent underground newspapers that had no school affiliation, and test cases arose to determine how *Hazelwood* affected these publications. For example, a high school junior distributed his newspaper entitled *Outside!* on school grounds. He wrote about the "top ten things [he] would like to see happen at school . . . to the people who 'run' it." Those "things" included "feeding snake bite antidote or Visine" to someone, "deposit[ing] some very disgusting smelling liquid in the school commons," setting off "stink bombs," gluing school locks with epoxy, "blowing things up" such as school toilets, making bomb threats, usurping the school intercom system, and taking out advertisements of a pornographic nature using teachers' phone numbers and addresses. The newspaper described where the wires to the public address system were located and the equipment required to carry out an invasion of the system. It informed the reader that the components for bombs could be found in the chemistry room in the school and described other places where students could purchase ingredients. The article ended with the words "Enjoy, and I hope to see some of these employed in the near future." An article that accompanied the "top ten" list stated the names, addresses and telephone numbers of faculty members and singled out a particular hall monitor whose child apparently was a student at the school. Other articles suggested using a computer virus to disrupt computers and encouraged the use of firecrackers on school premises.

After he was expelled for distributing his newspaper, the student sued the school district. The Oregon Court of Appeals reviewed the case after the trial court had dismissed his claims.[24] The U.S. Supreme Court has not ruled on school discipline related to underground newspapers, so the Oregon court used *Tinker, Fraser,* and *Hazelwood* to inform its analysis. The common thread the court discerned in these cases was the Supreme Court's focus on the school's educational mission. Thus, the question for the court was whether distribution of *Outside!* had the potential to disrupt the mission of the school. After all, Judge Edmonds said, school attendance in Oregon is compulsory, and parents have every expectation that school officials will provide a safe and nondisruptive learning environment. The *Outside!* articles advocated specific methods for causing personal injury, property damage, and the disruption of school activities. Furthermore, they described where to obtain the necessary materials to engage in some of these acts. Thus—using the words from *Tinker*—the school district reasonably could have believed that *Outside!* would "substantially interfere with the work of the school or impinge upon the rights of other students." The court of appeals took care to distinguish *Tinker,* noting that disciplining the student in this case was not the result of an undifferentiated fear, particularly in light of the trend of increasing school violence and the specific actions urged by this student. The dissenting judge in the case saw no evidence that the student engaged in or planned to engage in the activities he wrote about, and that judge would have found the school liable for violating the student's First Amendment rights.

It is common for students (as well as many adults) to have a skewed view of the rights the First Amendment protects, without any notion of the *responsibility* that goes along with those rights. Asked for comment after the case was decided, the student writer stated, "I don't like the idea that one has to defend their speech—no matter what it is." It is that kind of ignorance about speech rights that comes into play when students do not learn the fundamentals of democratic society and are then turned loose with no grounding in what their freedoms mean. Some adolescents revel in a "take-no-prisoners" approach to journalism and enjoy their ability to denigrate teachers and other administrators. They often use words that are crude, nasty, and hateful.

The Los Angeles School District became embroiled in litigation over the content of an underground high school student newspaper called *Occasional Blow Job.* The paper insulted teachers, students, and administrators and used profane language. Five students filed lawsuits against the school district challenging the punishments they received for contributing to material that caused disruption on the high school campus. Although student-sponsored newspapers may be restricted under the rule laid down in *Hazelwood,* school officials must take a more hands-off approach—more in line with *Tinker*—in states with anti-*Hazelwood* statutes. Under the California anti-*Hazelwood* statute, students may not be disciplined for speech on a high school campus that is permitted outside of campus. Student speech can be prohibited only if it is obscene, libelous, slanderous, or if it creates a clear and present danger of substantial disruption. A federal district court allowed the school to punish four of the five students, apparently because their actions were disruptive. But the court refused to allow the school to punish the fifth student, reasoning that the student's use of the word "fuck" was not obscene since it was protected speech outside campus.[25]

Even if a school district is successful in defending its actions against student journalists, a lawsuit takes an enormous toll in economic and emotional resources. Given the time and expense of a lawsuit, a prudent school official—even in states without anti-*Hazelwood* statutes—may think it wise simply to give students free rein in their writings. But permitting student speech is not without cost. The psychological (and even physical) drain on teachers, principals, and some students who are the focus of ridicule has a corrosive effect on the learning environment. And there may even be a cost that is easier to quantify. Over the course of three months and ten issues, the writers of *Occasional Blow Job* attacked teacher Janis Adams, making her the target of jokes, calling her a porn star, and superimposing her head on pictures of nude models. Her husband described it as spoiled rich kids raping their teacher with words. Adams sued the school district and convinced a jury to award $4.35 million in damages ($3.25 million for emotional damages) for failing to protect its employee from harassment directed at her by students.[26]

The war over student press rights continues unabated, and one of the more controversial issues is the extent to which *Hazelwood* applies to institutions of higher education. In one of the most significant student press legal battles of the 1990s, *Kincaid v. Gibson,* the Sixth Circuit needed full en banc review to decide whether administrators could confiscate a yearbook that was fully funded by Kentucky State University. The yearbook, called the *Thorobred,* had only one student editor who took any interest in the project, and she took it upon herself to present a yearbook unlike any in the past. She created a foil purple cover (the school colors are green and gold) and conceived a theme for the book—"Destination Un-known." The vice president for student affairs claimed the year-book was of poor quality and objected to the cover, the theme, the lack of captions under the photos, and the inclusion of current events not relating to the university. She and the university presi-dent decided to confiscate the yearbooks and withhold them from distribution. The editor and another student who was not on the yearbook staff sued, claiming that the decision to distribute the yearbooks violated their First Amendment rights. The district court—the court that first heard the case—relied on *Hazelwood*. It found that the yearbook was not a public forum and determined that university officials refused to distribute it because they be-lieved that it was of poor quality and did not represent the school as it should was reasonable.

A divided panel of the Sixth Circuit Court of Appeals affirmed the district court, but a divided panel of all the judges in the circuit reversed. Federal courts of appeal have a procedure where the rul-ings of a three-judge appellate panel may be appealed to all of the judges in the circuit for a hearing "en banc." The standard for ob-taining such a hearing is high, so not many cases receive this review. The Kentucky State case was an exceptional one, and the court de-cided it needed further consideration. The en banc opinion was written by Judge R. Guy Cole, a former bankruptcy court judge who was appointed to the Sixth Circuit by President Clinton.

Judge Cole stated up front that the yearbook was a limited pub-lic forum (not a nonpublic forum, as in *Hazelwood*), so *Hazelwood* had "little application to this case."[27] In a limited public forum, the university could impose only reasonable time, place, and manner restrictions on expressive activity. Confiscating the yearbooks and refusing to distribute them was not reasonable, and the university had not provided any alternative for similar expression by the stu-dents. The court simply did not believe the claim that the officials did not like the *quality* of the yearbook, rather than the *content*.

The vice president had stated that she did not like the theme or the inclusion of pictures of current events. In short, the officials had no compelling reason to take the yearbooks.

But another federal circuit court, this time the Seventh Circuit, has set forth a different view of *Hazelwood* at college. The plaintiffs in *Hosty v. Carter,* were students at Governors State University who served as editors and reporters for the *Innovator,* the school newspaper, which was supported by student activity fees.[28] This case arose when the dean of student affairs called the newspaper's printer and stated that a university official needed to review any paper before it went to print. The printer wrote to the students and told them of his conversations with the dean. A printing company representative later told the students that the printer did not wish to risk printing the paper and then not get paid for its work. The students filed suit.

The district court dismissed the claims against all defendants except the dean. Because of procedural rules, the dean was able to appeal this decision and her claim that she was immune from suit before the case continued. Thus, when the case reached the court of appeals—the Seventh Circuit—needed to decide the immunity issue. The standard for this immunity is whether the law was "clearly established" that the dean's request to review and approve the issues of the *Innovator* would violate the student's First Amendment rights. The main focus, therefore, was to what extent the law regarding university student speech rights was clear at the time the conduct occurred.

The appeals court observed that for several decades courts had consistently held that the student press in colleges and universities was entitled to strong First Amendment protection. Under this view, administrators could constrain student media only if the speech was unprotected or if it would cause significant and imminent physical disruption of the campus. The court cited numerous cases that had been decided *before Hazelwood* in its analysis. Accordingly, the dean's actions, if proved, violated clear constitutional rights of the students *unless Hazelwood* "muddled the landscape to such an extent that the law has become unclear."

Does a decision about the First Amendment in a high school setting have any effect on the rights of university students? The court of appeals decided that it did not. The court determined that because the college landscape differs so much from high school, even the landmark *Hazelwood* ruling did not affect student rights in higher education. First, there are obvious differences between the two cases: in one, the newspaper was part of the curriculum, and in the other, it was an extracurricular activity. Moreover, the missions of high schools and colleges are distinct and reflect the needs of students of differing ages and maturity levels. Because only 1 percent of the students in the nation's colleges are under eighteen, they should not be treated like fifteen-year-old high school students. The court was emphatic that there was nothing in the *Hazelwood* opinion that changed the general view favoring broad First Amendment rights for university students.[29]

Two years later, the Seventh Circuit voted to hear *Hosty* en banc, and the majority of the judges came to the opposite conclusion on the identical facts. The opinion, written by Judge Frank Easterbrook, dissected the *Hazelwood* opinion and determined that age was a factor only when determining whether the school officials had a legitimate pedagogical justification for their actions. If a justification was based on the maturity level of the students, the age difference between high school and college might be important. There might be no crucial difference between high school and college students, however, if the justification was based on the quality of the written work—whether it was ungrammatical, inadequately researched, biased, or profane—or if the school wished to disassociate itself from any position other than neutrality on controversial political matters. Thus, the court stated unequivocally that *Hazelwood*'s framework applies to subsidized student newspapers at elementary schools, high schools, and colleges.[30] Using *Hazelwood* as a guide, the court then needed to decide whether this college newspaper was a public forum. Based on the facts it had before it (recall that the appeal occurred before a trial), the court ruled that the newspaper was a public forum.

Even if this part of the *Hazelwood* test is met, in lawsuits like this against public officials, they are immune from personal liability (paying money damages from their own purses) unless it should have been clear to a reasonable public official—like the dean in this case—that his or her conduct was unlawful. The court observed that decisions since *Hazelwood* had not made it clear that college administrators had to keep their hands off student newspapers. It pointed to the lack of any analysis about the issue in *Kincaid* and to a Ninth Circuit case in which the three members of the panel had articulated three distinct and incompatible views on whether *Hazelwood* applied in college settings and on how the First Amendment affected relations between college faculty and student expression. Public officials are not required to predict, at their own financial peril, how these kinds of controversies will be resolved.

Controversy indeed! Four judges vehemently dissented from Judge Easterbrook's opinion. Because high school students are less mature than college students and because the mission of the high school differs from that of higher education, the dissenters insisted that there is no reason to apply *Hazelwood* beyond the high school context. Whereas the mission of K–12 education is the inculcation of values (citing *Fraser*), the mission of the university is to expose students to the "marketplace of ideas."

The next step in the case was a petition for certiorari to the U.S. Supreme Court. Despite disagreement in the courts below, the Supreme Court denied certiorari on February 21, 2006, leaving the issue to percolate more throughout the lower courts before intervening on this important issue. Since the Court will often hear cases when there is confusion in the circuits, it seems it will only be a matter of time before a case like this gets a hearing before the high court. Other splits that have developed regarding *Hazelwood's* wingspan include the extent to which *Hazelwood* applies to a teacher's classroom speech and whether *Hazelwood* allows viewpoint-based restriction on speech (which the First Amendment generally prohibits).[31]

The Student Press Law Center, nonprofit organization based in Arlington, Virginia, may be the harshest critic of the *Hazelwood* opinion. It is a persistent advocate for anti-*Hazelwood* legislation and opposes any extension of the *Hazelwood* reasoning into other areas. Its members work with both high school and college students across the country, offering free information, advice, and legal assistance. The Center has encouraged student journalists, especially those covered by the Seventh Circuit (Illinois, Wisconsin, and Indiana) to request college administrators to designate student publications as public forums. In 2007 the Illinois legislature passed the College Campus Press Act, which essentially negates the effect of *Hosty* by declaring that all student media at state colleges are public forums.

As Judge Easterbrook aptly observed in *Hosty,* "Many aspects of the law with respect to student speech . . . are difficult to understand and apply." But is the solution to allow students unfettered freedom to publish what they will? Is there any real harm if the content and tone of school newspapers is left to the judgment of students? Ironically, without oversight, the student newspaper experience could end up painting a picture that is totally unlike that on a real newspaper. Whereas a journalist writing for a mainstream newspaper will have an editor's supervision to ensure factual accuracy and ethical commitment, the student journalist—especially on an underground newspaper—will likely have no editor or a student editor with neither the training or the incentive to rein in a peer. Where a mainstream newspaper has an economic incentive (in the form of lawsuit for defamation) to avoid statements that denigrate and humiliate others for sport, students, who have little to offer in the way of money damages, are seldom targets in lawsuits when someone's character is destroyed. Sixteen-year-old high school students (and even twenty-year-olds) do not know everything about the contours of the First Amendment or the ethics in the field of journalism. Without meaningful constraint, those within range of the student publication can become subject to a verbal flaying constrained only by the appetite of the perpetrator.

Publications that ridicule and humiliate others can cause real suffering. A high school's monthly newspaper gave senior Heide Peek the "worst reputation" award. It stated that her favorite song was "Underneath Your Clothes" and made reference to her being raped by a monkey. Peek said that she had been the victim of a rape the month before, so the words were especially painful. Peek fought back, suing the school district, the superintendent, the principal, the vice principals, and the newspaper advisor. Notably, not one student journalist was named in the lawsuit.[32] As with the lawsuit by the teacher mentioned earlier, it is the school district, not the students, who is being hauled into court to answer for student writings that denigrate others and the district taxpayers who ultimately pay the award.

College journalists sometimes demonstrate that self-restraint does not necessarily come with a couple more birthdays. Leonard Pitts, a Pulitzer Prize–winning journalist himself, asks, "What's up with student journalists today?" He berated a "white kid from Oregon State" for calling black people immoral and a student from the University of Massachusetts for writing that Pat Tillman, a former NFL player killed in Afghanistan, "got what was coming to him." He was most appalled, however, by a weekly student journal at Rutgers that published a cartoon on its cover under the headline "Holocaust Remembrance Week." The cartoon, set at a carnival, showed a bearded man sitting on the edge of a kitchen stove. The caption read, "Knock a Jew in the oven! Three throws for a dollar." Pitts expressed outrage at the purpose of the piece—the diminution and humiliation of a marginalized group while hiding behind irreverence.[33]

But irreverence is the mantra of today's popular culture, and stu-

dent journalists merely reflect what they see in the world. If mean-
ness and lack of basic humanity permeate much of popular culture,
this is what students will publish. Of course, this merely perpetu-
ates a downward spiral, as the next journalist believes the next
article must be even more outrageous and irreverent.

Justice Brennan's *Hazelwood* dissent stated that schools must
teach student journalists a civics lesson as part of their journalism
program. But civics is that branch of political science that deals with
both the rights *and* the duties of citizens. Surely it means more than
the unfettered ability to ridicule and humiliate whomever you wish,
without regard to consequences. There is an ethical component to
one's duty both as a citizen and as a journalist, and learning about
how to manage that would seem to be one of the most important
lessons any student could learn. Thus, *Hazelwood* may not necessarily be as harmful for students as its critics claim.

The last three chapters have considered the school speech cases
primarily from the perspective of the speaker—the Tinkers, Matt
Fraser, and the student journalists. Yet, as we have seen throughout
this chapter, part of the focus in these student press cases is on the
"recipient" of the speech—those who will be reading the articles in
question. For example, the *Hazelwood* Court took seriously the
high school principal's concern that parts of the articles would be
inappropriate for younger student readers. And the named plaintiff
in *Kincaid* did not work on the yearbook staff, but the court
nonetheless viewed him as protected recipient of the speech contained in that publication. In the next chapter, the focus shifts from
the person sending the speech to the person who receives it. Is
there a right to receive speech in school?

CHAPTER FIVE

Banning Books from School:
The Right to Receive Speech, or Not

shitty, goddamned, pissing, ass, goddamned be
Jesus, screwing life's ass, shit. Doris was ten and had
humped with who knows how many men in between . . . her current stepfather started having sex
with her but good . . . sonofabitch balling her

—Anonymous, *Go Ask Alice* (one of
the books removed from the school library
in the *Pico* case)

ANY DISCUSSION OF THE RIGHT to receive speech in school must include the opinions (there were seven) the Supreme Court set forth
in *Pico v. Board of Education, Island Trees Union Free School District*, certainly one of the more confusing (and confused) opinions
in the school speech milieu. The issue addressed in *Pico* was the
power of a school board to remove books from a school library and
the rights of students to receive the information in those books.
Despite its opacity, *Pico* continues to be cited often by lower courts
and even by the Supreme Court itself. Its place in the school
speech world appears to be secure, even if the clarity of its analytical framework is not as riveting as its facts.

Before examining *Pico,* let us first detach the scene for a brief de-
tour away from the schoolhouse. Certainly a state's use of power to
condemn a book "touches the central nervous system of the First

Amendment."[1] In a nation that prides itself on freedom and en-
lightenment, the specter of a state that removes certain books from
the hands of its citizens evokes dark and oppressive images. Viewed
as close kin to witch hunting, history has handed us dispiriting stories of attempts to obliterate ideas by destroying the books that contained them: the Florentines burning of Dante's *Divine Comedy,*
the Catholic Church suppressing Galileo's *Dialogo,* and the banning of Mark Twain's *Huckleberry Finn.*[2] The black-and-white film
images of Nazi youth groups burning over 20,000 books on May 10,
1933, remind us how destroying books equates with maleficence.
Author Rebecca West summed up our collective repulsion well:
"God forbid that any book should be banned. The practice is as in-
defensible as infanticide."

Restricting access to libraries is one way for despotic regimes to
regulate exposure to ideas. Former *New York Times* correspondent
Harrison Salisbury has described the iron-fisted control of the former Soviet Union over its libraries as "books enchained." He noted
that the Lenin Library, the equivalent of our Library of Congress,
had only a small number of books in the card catalog and was available only to recognized students and scholars with the proper identity cards and papers certifying their need to examine the books. A
person needed a security clearance to get to the next catalog, and
some categories of books were available only to members of the
Politburo or someone in the Kremlin.[3]

Given this background, few of us come to the issue of book banning without feeling a visceral reaction against it—no matter the
identity of the person banning the book. School board members
may not be Hitler Youth, but removing a book from the school library is likely to cause dissent from some quarter, along with the
"ensuing shouts of book burning, witch hunting and violation of academic freedom."[4] It is therefore hardly surprising that this volatile
issue would eventually make its way to the nation's highest court.

The book banning issue came before the U.S. Supreme Court in
the context of a school board's removal of library books from a

school library in Long Island, New York, in 1976. Three school board members attended a conference sponsored by Parents of New York United, a group the trial court called "conservatively oriented."[5] At the conference, the board members saw excerpts of books the group deemed objectionable. When the board members returned home, they found that nine of the books were in the high school library, one was in the junior high school library, and one was used in a high school literature course. The books in question were *The Fixer,* by Bernard Malamud, *Slaughterhouse Five,* by Kurt Vonnegut, *The Naked Ape,* by Desmond Morris, *Down These Mean Streets,* by Piri Thomas, *Best Short Stories by Negro Writers,* by Langston Hughes, *Go Ask Alice* (anonymous), *A Hero Ain't Nothing but a Sandwich,* by Alice Childress, *Black Boy,* by Richard Wright, *Laughing Boy,* by Oliver LaFarge, *Soul on Ice,* by Eldridge Cleaver, and *A Reader for Writers,* edited by Jerome Archer.

The school board's first act was to remove the books from the school libraries for review. After some criticism by teacher union leaders and some negative press, the board appointed a committee of four school staff members and four community residents to review the books and make a recommendation regarding their educational suitability, and "whether they were in good taste, appropriate and relevant." The committee recommended removing two books, retaining four, and requiring parental permission for another. The committee did not reach agreement about the remaining books. The school board then voted to retain one book *(Laughing Boy),* to retain one book on a restricted basis *(Black Boy),* and to remove the others entirely. Five high school students sued the school district claiming that the school board removed the books because certain passages in the books violated social, political, and moral tastes, not because the books, taken as a whole, were lacking in educational value.[6] The confusion that ensued demonstrates how difficult this issue was for all the judges who addressed it. The federal district court that first heard the case found for the school district. The federal appeals court, in a 2–1 split, with all three judges writing opinions, found for the students.

The division among the justices of the Supreme Court was even more remarkable. Seven of the nine justices wrote opinions in the case—everyone but Stevens and Marshall. The clerk of court should have provided a written diagram to help the reader unravel how the justices voted. The leading opinion by Justice Brennan had four votes for some sections, but Justice Blackmun refused to join one of the sections, so that section garnered only three votes. Usually Supreme Court opinions begin with the statement "Justice *X* delivered the opinion of the Court." Because of the deep disagreement between the justices, the *Pico* opinion merely states that "Justice Brennan announced the judgment of the Court and delivered an opinion, which Justices Stevens and Marshall joined and in which Justice Blackmun joined except for Part II-A(1)." Justice Blackmun wrote a concurrence, Justice White wrote another concurrence, and there were *three* separate dissenting opinions.

The structure of the "right to receive" speech in school was one of the major points of controversy for the justices, and—given the jumbled opinions that were rendered in *Pico*—it remains a bewildering concept even today. The next section explores the genesis of this intriguing theory by presenting the perspective of the *Pico* Court when it first considered the issue. I first examine the concept in a non-school context, as set forth in the U.S. Supreme Court case *Virginia Board of Pharmacy.* I then explain how federal courts interpreted the ideas stemming from that case in the school context before the Supreme Court weighed in with the *Pico* opinion.

> There seems to be a kind of order in the universe, in the movement of the stars and the turning of the earth and the changing of the seasons, and even in the cycle of human life. But human life itself is almost pure chaos. Everyone takes his stance, asserts his own rights and feelings, mistaking the motives of others, and his own.
>
> —Katherine Anne Porter

The idea of individuals possessing a First Amendment right to receive communication did not arise for the first time in the *Pico* case. The constitutional "right to receive" information began to get some traction after the Supreme Court expounded on its virtues in 1976 in *Virginia Board of Pharmacy v. Virginia Citizens Consumers Council.*[7] This case involved commercial speech directed at adults and had nothing to do with the school environment, but it laid the groundwork for the Justices when the issues from *Pico* came before them.

In *Virginia Board of Pharmacy,* the Court struck down a state statute banning pharmacists from publishing or advertising prescription drug prices. The plaintiffs in the suit were not pharmacists, and no pharmacist joined in the litigation. Rather, the plaintiffs were individual consumers and two consumer groups who claimed that the First Amendment entitled them to receive information that pharmacists wished to communicate to them regarding the price of prescription drugs. Justice Blackmun wrote for the majority: "Where a speaker exists . . . the [First Amendment] protection afforded is to the communication, to its source *and to its recipients both*" (emphasis added).

In support of this constitutional right to receive communication, Justice Blackmun cited another case, *Kleindienst v. Mandel.* The opinion in that case (which he also wrote) referred to a First Amendment right to "receive information and ideas," and stated that freedom of speech "necessarily protects the right to receive."[8] Unlike *Virginia Pharmacy,* the *Kleindienst* case had some ties to education, albeit higher education rather than K–12. The information and ideas at issue were those of Ernest Mandel, a journalist and self-described advocate of the economic, governmental, and international doctrines of world communism. He was invited to speak at several universities and conferences throughout the United States. The Immigration and Naturalization Service (INS) refused to grant Mandel a visa because it had determined that Mandel's activities on a previous trip to the United States went beyond the basis on which his visit had been authorized. The

Supreme Court was asked to decide whether the INS action in refusing to allow an alien scholar to enter the country to attend academic meetings violated the First Amendment. The rights in
question were those not of Mandel but of the American professors
who had invited him and wanted to hear what he had to say.[9]

Although recognizing that the Constitution protects the right to
receive information and ideas, the Court determined that this right
did not overcome the firmly established plenary congressional
power to make policies and rules for the exclusion of aliens and its
delegation of that power to the executive branch (including the
INS). When the executive exercises this power for a facially legitimate and bona fide reason, the courts should neither look behind
the exercise of that discretion nor test it by balancing the asserted
justification against the First Amendment interests of those who
seek personal communication with the applicant. Thus even though
the Court did not ultimately rule for the professors, the language in
the opinion set up the "right to receive" concept that found firmer
footing in *Virginia Pharmacy* (and would emerge again in *Pico*).

After the *Virginia Pharmacy* opinion built the legal framework
for the right-to-receive theory, it ventured into the schoolhouse.
The Sixth Circuit used *Virginia Pharmacy* for support in its opinion
addressing the removal of library books—*Cat's Cradle* by Kurt Vonnegut and *Catch-22* by Joseph Heller—from a high school library
in Strongsville, Ohio *(Minarcini v. Strongsville City School Board)*.
Because the school board had given no "explanation that is neutral
in First Amendment terms" for removing the books, the court of
appeals concluded that the board must have removed the books
because it objected to their content and because it believed it had
the power to remove books it found distasteful. The court concluded that this violated the First Amendment rights of the student
plaintiffs. Judge Edwards, writing for a unanimous court, pointed
out that although the Supreme Court had recognized the right to
receive in the past, this was a "more difficult concept than a direct

restraint on speech." Indeed, Judge Edwards admitted that he "might have felt that its application [in the school context] was more doubtful absent a very recent Supreme Court case"—*Virginia Pharmacy.* The court quoted Justice Blackmun's opinion at length, ending with the statement "If there is a right to advertise, there is a reciprocal right to receive the advertising." Taken together with the *Kleindienst* case (and another case about censorship of prisoners' mail), this language "firmly established" both the First Amendment right to receive speech and the standing of the students to raise the issue. The appeals court ordered the trial court judge to direct the school board to replace the books. If necessary, the board was required to purchase the books out of the first sums available for library purposes.[10]

Despite the unequivocal language from the Sixth Circuit (which handles federal appeals in Michigan, Ohio, Kentucky, and Tennessee), this First Amendment "right to receive" did not appear to be so "firmly established" for the Seventh Circuit (which handles federal appeals in Wisconsin, Illinois, and Indiana). The Seventh Circuit addressed a school board's removal of the book *Go Ask Alice* (a book that would later be at issue in *Pico*) from a high school library in Indiana. In this case, *Zykan v. Warsaw County Community School Corp.,* the court acknowledged the "qualified freedom to hear" that had emerged under *Virginia Pharmacy,* but refused to apply it in the school context.

First, the student's right to and need for such freedom is bounded by the level of his or her intellectual development. A high school student's lack of the intellectual skills necessary for taking full advantage of the marketplace of ideas engenders a correspondingly greater need for direction and guidance from those better equipped by experience and reflection to make critical educational choices. Second, the importance of secondary schools in the development of intellectual faculties is only one part of a broad formative role encompassing

the encouragement and nurturing of those fundamental social, political, and moral values that will permit a student to take his place in
the community. . . . The Constitution neither disparages the application of social, political and moral tastes to secondary school educational decisions nor specifies that such criteria are irrelevant or alien
to the legitimate exercise of educational choice.

This language reveals how these judges were grappling with
some of the themes that course through the school speech cases, including the theme of self-preservation—how does a nation teach its
young to embrace its democratic values without harming those values in the process? This court believed that students were in school
to learn and that students of a certain age do not have sufficient
cognitive development to eschew all direction from adults at school.
Some limitation of liberty while students are in school is necessary
to educate students so that they have the necessary skills to take
their place as adult political actors.

There was no hint in the complaint that the decision to remove
the books in the *Zykan* case was motivated by a desire to exclude a
particular type of thought or ideological preference. The court acknowledged that other courts, like the Sixth Circuit, had stated that
once books were admitted to the school library, they could not be
removed because school authorities objected to their content. The
court pointed to substantial authority on the other side (including
the district court opinion in *Pico* that was making its way up the
pipeline) and decided that those courts held the better view. The
Seventh Circuit made it clear that it was "rejecting the suggestion
that a particular book can gain a kind of tenure on the shelf merely
because the administrators voice some objections to its contents."[11]

As the Sixth and Seventh Circuits were reaching different conclusions about library books, the district court in *Pico* considered the
book removal by the Island Trees school board in New York. The

district court was bound by the precedent in the Second Circuit (which handles New York, Connecticut, and Vermont). Thus the district court needed to follow a case called *President's Council v. Community School Board*, which the Second Circuit had decided in 1972.[12] This case had dealt with a decision by the school board in Queens about the book *Down These Mean Streets* by Piri Thomas (another book that later found its way onto the banned list in *Pico*). The board first voted to remove copies of the book from all junior high school libraries and then voted to make it available on a direct loan basis to parents who wanted their children to read it. Because the book became part of the *Pico* litigation, the court's detailed description of it is of particular interest:

> The book . . . is an autobiographical account by Piri Thomas of a Puerto Rican youth growing up in the East Side Barrio (Spanish Harlem) in New York City. Predictably the scene is depressing, ugly and violent. The argot of the vicinage is replete with four letter and twelve letter obscenities unreported by Tom Swift or even Tom Jones. Acts of criminal violence, sex, normal and perverse, as well as episodes of drug shooting are graphically described. . . . Presumably the educational value of this work, aside from whatever literary merit it may have, is to acquaint the predominantly white, middle-class junior high school students of Queens County with the bitter realities facing their contemporaries in Manhattan's Spanish Harlem. Some parents objected to the public school library stocking the book, which they claimed would have an adverse moral and psychological effect on 11 to 15 year old children, principally because of the obscenities and explicit sexual interludes. The plaintiffs on the other hand have supplied affidavits from psychologists, teachers, and even children who claim the book is valuable and had no adverse effect on the development of the children of the District.

In its analysis, the *President's Council* court took its cue from *Epperson v. Arkansas*, which at the time was the Supreme Court's most recent pronouncement on First Amendment rights in school.[13] *Epperson* dealt with a state statute that made it unlawful to teach evolution in the public schools (discussed in greater detail in Chapter 6). While striking down the statute, the Court was careful to emphasize that "by and large, public education in our Nation is committed to the control of state and local authorities. Courts do not and cannot intervene in the resolution of conflicts which arise in the daily operation of school systems and which do not directly and sharply implicate basic constitutional values."[14]

Observing that any choice about what books might be in a school library collection was likely to meet with dissent from someone, the *President's Council* court saw no sharp implication of constitutional values in the record. The school district did not ban the teaching of any theory or doctrine, and the problems of youth in the ghetto—crime, drugs and violence—were not placed off limits for any classroom discussion. The court found that any intrusion on First Amendment rights was "minuscule" and determined that the concept of a "book acquiring tenure" was "unsupportable under any theory of constitutional law we can discover."

Given this blunt language from the court of appeals in its own circuit, the district court in *Pico* ruled for the school board. The court gave little heed to the *Minarcini* case from the Sixth Circuit. Judge Pratt viewed that decision as, in essence, having adopted the book tenure concept forbidden by *President's Council,* because it required school boards to be content-blind and allowed book removal only for space considerations or obsolescence. And the *Pico* district court paid only slight homage to *Virginia Pharmacy,* acknowledging that the students had standing to present a First Amendment academic freedom claim under its "right to receive" doctrine, but stating that there was not a sufficient showing that the students were deprived of receiving what their teachers wanted to teach. Although the court viewed the Island Tree school board's decision as misguided, the court saw its disagreement with the board about the merits of its evaluation of the books as irrelevant to the question whether a constitutional violation had occurred. In deciding what books to place in a school library, a school board "not only may, but must choose on the basis of content."[15] There was no restriction on class discussion, no student was denied either silent or open speech, and thus there was no "sharp and direct infringement of any First Amendment right." The court granted the school district summary judgment (i.e., the district won without the need of a trial).

By the time the *Pico* case was argued before the Second Circuit Court of Appeals, eight years had passed since that court's pronouncement in *President's Council.* Four new judges had been added to the Circuit. None of the judges from the *President's Council* panel—Medina, Lumbard, and Mulligan—were on the *Pico* panel, which consisted of Mansfield, Newman, and Sifton. Unlike the unanimous twelve-page opinion in *President's Council,* the *Pico* opinion is twenty-eight pages, with strong disagreement among the judges, all of whom wrote opinions. Judge Sifton voted to decide the case in favor of the students. Judge Mansfield voted to decide the case in favor of the school board. Judge Newman believed that there was a sufficient claim of a constitutional violation, but he voted to require a trial to determine if the facts of the case would support the claim.

Judge Sifton took issue with the criteria (or lack thereof) for the books' removal, stating that the terms the school board members used, including "anti-Christian" or "anti-American," suffered from "excessive generality and overbreadth."[16] He described the board's process for removal as "erratic, arbitrary and free-wheeling." There had been several irregularities, and he thought the whole operation seemed calculated to create public uproar. These irregularities included: (1) the board's reasons for removing the books were incoherent; (2) the matter had been pursued in a dilatory and informal manner over three months; (3) the book review committee's determinations had not been followed; (4) professional personnel, including the superintendent, strongly opposed the board's procedures; and (5) the books were written by "generally recognized authors."

Judge Sifton was not opposed to board members using their own personal views when making decisions. But decisions based on these beliefs, when coupled with irregularities in procedure, raised the inference that the school board had asserted its political views and personal tastes with the intent of establishing them as the correct views in the community and not because it was in the best interest of the children. Thus the board had failed to establish that the manner of—if not the motive for—their actions did not violate the First Amendment.

In the second opinion, Judge Newman acknowledged that if the case had been about government prohibition of a book because of its political content, the decision would have been unanimous for the plaintiffs. But the case was not so simple. Although the removal of the books was alleged to have been motivated—at least in part—by their political content, the books had not been prohibited; they had merely been removed from one location—a *school* library. Schools are specialized environments devoted to a process of inculcation of both knowledge and social values in children. Our society has decided to grant school authorities considerable discretion in determining how that process will occur. This usually involves informal, day-to-day judgments that are inappropriate for legal supervision.[17] Nonetheless, those in the school community have a right to be free from official conduct that, in addition to conveying the message that an idea is unsound, conveys the message that it cannot be aired within the school community. When school officials take "clearly defined and carefully planned action to condemn an idea" and do so because they are motivated by their own opinions about "the proper way to organize and run a society in general," then this action "merges into impermissible suppression." Judge Newman agreed with Judge Sifton that there was a sufficient claim that a constitutional violation may have occurred, but he was unable to tell for sure from the record as it stood. Their votes together meant that the case would be remanded for trial to allow the fact finder (either judge or jury) to determine what happened.

Judge Mansfield found the *Pico* case indistinguishable from the *President's Council* case, and he would have affirmed the district court's summary judgment ruling for the school district. In his view, the best evidence whether the books were suitable for the education of secondary schoolchildren is the text of the books themselves. Although the other judges studiously avoided discussing the books' contents, Judge Mansfield believed that all but one contained "indecent matter, vulgarities, profanities, explicit sexual descriptions or allusions, sexual perversions or disparaging remarks about Blacks, Jews or Christ."[18] The important question is not whether the removal was politically motivated—"whatever that means"—but whether it threatened to suppress the discussion of ideas. Absent some evidence that speech or ideas were likely to be suppressed, "this court should keep its hands off."

The three panel opinions were not the last word from the court of appeals. The school board filed a petition for rehearing en banc that resulted in five judges voting to hear the case and five voting to deny the rehearing. By court rule, a failure to obtain a majority vote in favor of a rehearing means that the petition is denied. One can surmise that there was some biting discussion throughout the chambers while the petition was being considered, as both Judges Newman and Mansfield wrote forceful separate opinions concurring and dissenting in the denial. Judge Mansfield pointedly stated that the panel's decision was inconsistent with the *Zykan* decision from the Seventh Circuit. This was a clear signal to the Supreme Court that certiorari would be appropriate to resolve this conflict.

After the Supreme Court decided to hear the case, the litigants honed their arguments. Once again the battle over the mission of the public schools was at the core of the controversy. The school district maintained that the Island Trees community had a legitimate and substantial interest in promoting respect for authority and traditional values in its schoolchildren. The public school, through its curriculum, is an instrument of socialization, and this prescriptive effort at inculcating community values distinguishes secondary schools from universities, where the analytical model that governs is the "marketplace of ideas." The school board had been elected to serve as stewards of the schoolchildren and to make difficult and sensitive decisions regarding the educational suitability of library materials. Part of this responsibility encompassed deciding whether these library materials were consistent with the basic values of the community that elected the board members.[19]

This argument had some foundation. The marketplace metaphor did stem from the higher education world. Justice Brennan used the "marketplace of ideas" metaphor in *Keyishian v. Board of Regents,* which was set in the university environment: "The classroom," he wrote, "is peculiarly the 'marketplace of ideas.' The Nation's future depends upon leaders trained through wide exposure to that robust exchange of ideas which discovers truth out of a multitude of tongues, rather than through any kind of authoritative selection."[20] (*Keyishian* addressed a challenge by two professors at the University of Buffalo to a state law that required them to sign a certificate that they were not communists.) To be sure, transplanting portentous concepts from higher education to the K–12 world presents some knotty problems.

Even the brief submitted for the students acknowledged that the book removal issue was "complicated by the fact that it takes place in an institution—the public schools—where content-based judgments about books and ideas are unavoidable and where one of the recognized institutional goals is the transmittal of certain societal values." The First Amendment does not forbid school officials "from affirmatively emphasizing certain values as part of the school's inculcative function."[21] But the students maintained that the board went beyond this acceptable line because the intent of the book removal was to exclude unpopular viewpoints and values. If allowed, this conduct would embolden a transient majority to use the education system to exclude ideas and values other than those in favor, whether the current orthodoxy is religious, cultural, or political.

Neither the briefs for the students nor for their supporting amici were clear about exactly what idea or viewpoint the board had been trying to suppress, and there was no allegation of a comprehensive pattern of excluding from the school all material inconsistent with a particular ideology. Recall that Judge Mansfield had read all of the books and stated that all but one contained "indecent matter, vulgarities, profanities, explicit descriptions of sexual relations, or some perverted or disparaging remarks about Blacks, Jews, or Christ."[22] Would the Court allow removal of books on the basis of the "idea" that a school could choose not to put its imprimatur on works containing lurid prose? Or does the First Amendment's broad scope in areas outside the schoolhouse trump the ability of the school board in its attempt to inculcate social values?

As noted, when the *Pico* case arrived at the Court, there was sharp disagreement among the different circuit courts and among the three judges who had heard the case. It is therefore hardly surprising that the nine justices had difficulty finding a consensus on how to deal with the issue. Justice Brennan announced the judgment of the Court. The Court's judgment merely states the outcome for the parties, that is, who wins. Justice Brennan divided his opinion into sections; he garnered three other votes for one part of his opinion and only two other votes for another part.

The Brennan opinion discussed the tension between the needs of the school and the liberty of the student. School officials need to be able to exercise discretion in performing their mission, but at some point the imperatives of the First Amendment put limits on that discretion. Four Justices agreed that a First Amendment violation had occurred (1) if the board's actions were motivated by the intent to deny access to ideas with which they disagreed; and (2) if that intent was the decisive factor in the removal decision. School boards must not exercise their discretion in a "narrowly partisan or political manner." But there would not be a constitutional violation if the books were removed because they are "pervasively vulgar" or if the decision was based on "educational suitability." Justice Brennan cautioned that the *Pico* decision did not affect the discretion of school boards regarding the *acquisition* of library books; it applied only to the discretion to *remove* books. The four Justices in the plurality also agreed that the evidentiary record showed that there was a genuine issue of fact regarding the motivation behind this school board's decision, and the case was remanded to the district court for a trial on this issue. Since no part of Justice Brennan's opinion garnered a majority of the votes, the analysis he crafted has dubious value as precedent. This has not stopped courts from quoting and citing *Pico*—even the parts where only three justices agreed—as if it were the law of the land. Part I-A-1 of the opinion, which claimed that the Constitution protected a student's right to receive information and ideas, garnered only three votes. Nevertheless, courts cite *Pico* for that very proposition.[23]

Interestingly, Justice Blackmun, the author of two of *Pico*'s predecessors, *Kleindienst* and *Virginia Pharmacy*, refused to join in the part of the Brennan opinion that stated, "the *right to receive ideas* is a necessary predicate to the recipient's meaningful exercise of his own rights of speech and political freedom" (emphasis added). So this concept had the support of only three justices. Nor did Justice Blackmun agree that the school library was an especially appropriate environment for the recognition of students' First Amendment rights.

Like Justice Brennan, Justice Blackmun recognized the tension between the socializing function of the public school and the First Amendment proscription—from *Tinker*—that schools may not attempt to "foster a homogeneous people." Outside the schoolhouse, a general principle had emerged from the Supreme Court's First

Amendment cases that a state may not suppress exposure to ideas absent a compelling state interest. This principle applies, Blackmun said, albeit in a limited way, to public education.

Justice Blackmun was nonetheless concerned that the "right to receive" espoused by Justice Brennan could be viewed as an affirmative obligation to provide students with information and ideas. Rather than focus on the right to receive information, Justice Blackmun emphasized the problem of discrimination *between* ideas. In his view, the state should not deny access to an idea because state officials disapprove of the idea for partisan or political reasons. He would, however, allow school boards to refuse students access to a book because it had offensive language, because it was "psychologically or intellectually inappropriate for the age group," or because the ideas advanced were "manifestly inimical to the public welfare." Justice Blackmun did not elaborate on just what he meant by "manifestly inimical to the public welfare," but one can well imagine the flood of litigation that would ensue aimed at obtaining a clarification of exactly what that term would include.[24]

In Justice White's view, the Supreme Court should have remanded the case to the trial court to determine the reasons the books were removed. Depending on what the trial court found, the case might end then and there. Until that factual record was developed, he saw no need for the Supreme Court to weigh in on the extent to which the First Amendment limits the discretion of the school board. If the books were removed because they were vulgar, there might be no appeal, and the Supreme Court would have been premature in deciding the issue.

Chief Justice Burger, much like Justice Black's dissent in *Tinker*, saw the plurality opinion as a misguided expansion of rights that would allow public schools to be administered by federal courts and teenage pupils. The plurality had fashioned the previously unheard-of right of access to certain books in a school library with no basis in the First Amendment or in previous Supreme Court cases.

By taking over the role of the elected school board, the court disrupted this "democracy in a microcosm." Parents rightfully have the largest voice in how their children are educated, and it is they who participate in school board elections. A school board is not a giant bureaucracy; it consists of accountable elected officials who either respond to their constituents or are removed from office.

Similarly, Justice Powell's dissent emphasized the basic concept in public education that locally elected school boards should have the responsibility for determining the educational policy of the public schools. He pointed out that no single agency of government is closer to the people it serves than the typical school board. He was dismayed at the Court's opinion because the resolution of policy decisions through litigation and the exposure of school board members to liability for their decisions would corrode the authority and effectiveness of school boards. In his view, judges are rarely as competent as school authorities to decide about the educational worth of a book, and judges are not responsive to the parents and other people in the school district. This decision "symbolizes a debilitating encroachment upon the institutions of a free people."

Justice Rehnquist was not appointed Chief Justice until 1986, so he wrote his dissent in *Pico* while still an associate justice. He acknowledged that the books that were removed certainly contained "ideas," but it was also apparent that eight of the books contained demonstrable amounts of vulgarity and profanity and that the ninth contained nothing partisan or political. Certainly if the government had tried to prohibit the sale of these books by private booksellers, there would be a First Amendment problem. But the government in that situation would have been acting in a different capacity from that in this case. The government may act as a sovereign, a property owner, or an employer, and it has different authority in each case. Here, the government (the school board) was acting as *educator*, engaged in inculcating social values and knowledge to impressionable young people. Acting in this role, the government is subject to fewer strictures than when it is acting as sovereign over the general citizenry.

Thus it is permissible and appropriate for local boards to determine that a particular book, a particular course, or even a particular area of knowledge is not educationally suitable for inclusion in the body of knowledge that school seeks to impart. Justice Rehnquist saw no basis in past Court opinions for Justice Brennan's position that high school and junior high school students have a right to receive ideas in school. This new "right" appears to exist only in the school library and only if the idea appears in a book the school had previously acquired. There is no constitutional right for authors to have their books placed in school libraries. Without this right of the sender to send, the Court's prior decisions would not recognize this right to receive information. Moreover, even if there is a constitutional right to receive information, basing a First Amendment violation on the improper motive of the school board makes no sense. Removal for bad motives and good motives both deny access to the book removed.

Finally, Justice O'Connor weighed in, emphasizing that the government in the *Pico* case was acting in its special role as educator. Although she personally disagreed with the decision with respect to some of the books, she stated that it was not her function to make decisions that had been relegated to elected school boards. She saw no reason why a school board—if it can set curriculum, select teachers, and determine what books to purchase—cannot determine which books to discontinue or remove, "so long as it does not interfere with the right of the students to read the material and to discuss it."

With this confusing mosaic as a guideline, the case was remanded to the lower court for trial. School officials throughout the country were left with yet another decision with nearly incomprehensible rules, once again plunging them into a sea of uncertainty. The *Pico* trial never came to pass, as the parties reached a settlement

whereby the books were restored to the school library.[25] Nat Hentoff
reports that the school board first requested that the library send a
notice to parents when a student checked out one of the books.
Lawyers for the New York Civil Liberties Union objected, and the
school board eventually allowed all the books back on the shelves.
Yet—since curriculum is still in the hands of the school board—the
Island Trees board refused to allow *The Fixer*, by Bernard Malamud, to be taught in the classroom.[26]

> If you don't know where you are going, any road will
> get you there.
>
> —Lewis Carroll

Despite the numerous theories about how this issue should be resolved, the justices agreed about one thing: Even Justice Brennan
emphasized that the school curriculum was not at issue in the case.
One commentator said that this amounted to throwing a "pall of orthodoxy" over one part of the school (the classroom) and allowing
broad freedom under the First Amendment in another (the library),
calling this "a new form of school segregation."[27] And however illog-
ical it might have been, the Brennan opinion was careful not to include the *selection* of books in its ambit. Despite the prediction at
the time that the Court would use *Pico* to move on to these other areas, except for the cases about the teaching of evolution (discussed
in Chapter 6), the Court has stayed away from any expansion or re-
duction of the "*Pico* power" for over twenty-five years.

This failure to alter or elucidate the concept any further certainly
is not due to the clarity of the doctrine the Court set forth. All books
have "ideas," and most books have many. Does this mean that
adults can never remove a book from a school library because they
disagree with a particular idea the book contains? At least four justices in *Pico* believed that the school board could not remove a book
merely because it disagreed with the board's "political" views. Of

course, one of the difficulties with using the word "political" is that the term can take a protean form that refers to any characteristic of politicians, the role of government, or social and cultural thoughts. In the context of an elected school board acting in the course of its representative duties, it is hard to separate out politics in its broadest form.

The transmission of knowledge and the values deemed essential to a republic—all part and parcel of what happens at school—will likely often be bound up with "politics." The lawyers for the students admitted as much in stating that "ideas and language are so inextricably bound together that it is impossible to separate the school board's putative concerns about language from their predominant ideological concerns."[28] As the Supreme Court itself has observed, in *Ambach v. Norwick,* "Although the findings of scholars who have written on the subject are not conclusive, they generally reinforce the common-sense judgment, and the experience of most of us, that a teacher exerts considerable influence over the development of fundamental social attitudes in students, including those attitudes which in the broadest sense of the term may be viewed as political."[29]

Even if the term "political" could somehow be narrowed, the difficulty of ascertaining the true motivation for people's conduct makes *Pico* hard to apply in practice. As the attorneys for the students observed in their briefs, "Often, of course, the intent to impose orthodoxy will not be clear."[30] There are also practical limitations of time, shelf space, and resources.[31] Even if an impermissible motive is present, there may be so many other factors involved that it will be hard to isolate.[32] What happens when the motives are mixed? Does the mixed-motive analysis used in employment law apply? The Supreme Court has stated that when a discharge from employment may have been prompted by both protected and unprotected conduct, the employee must show that he or she would not have been fired "but for" the exercise of protected

First Amendment rights.[33] The analogue here would be if the books were removed not just because of vulgar language/explicit sex but also because of disagreement with the ideas in the books. The students would have to show that the books would not have been removed "but for" the ideas expressed therein.

This assumes that the permissible motive can be separated from the impermissible motive. It seems like a formidable task to try to separate a permissible motive of removing books with vulgar language (recall the Court and Matt Fraser in Chapter 3) from an impermissible motive of removing books with ideas that are *conveyed* by that language. (The *Pico* case was decided before the *Fraser* opinion held that schools could prohibit vulgar language.) Moreover, having the motivation of the board members serve as the linchpin also allows savvy officials to circumvent the rule simply by asserting a motivation that will pass muster.

Justice Brennan allowed that a removal decision based on the "educational suitability" of the book or because it was "pervasively vulgar" would be "perfectly permissible." But how much objectionable material must there be in a book before it reaches a "tipping point" so that it is unsuitable? How does one page of *really* objectionable material (say, profanity of the most offensive type) stack up against a book that eschews that kind of language but has an objectionable theme (perhaps racial hatred) that permeates the book?

To what extent should school boards be influenced by outside reviewers like *Library Journal, School Library Journal,* or *Booklist,* all of which stated that these books (with the exception of *A Reader for Writers,* which was not evaluated) were educationally suitable for high school students? (Not all of the books were reviewed favorably. Amicus Long Island Library Association Coalition quotes a review of *The Naked Ape* in *Contemporary Authors* as saying that the author's treatment of man's behavioral patterns "leaves much to be desired," the book was "unevenly written," and some chapters were "very badly written.") Does the focus on the influence of a national outside reviewer take away from the cultural diversity in each community? Does this permit another type of orthodoxy to prescribe how best to transmit values to children?

Any decision-making group, from the U.S. Congress to the town school board, seldom speaks with one united voice, and members often will cast a yea or nay vote for various reasons. One Island Trees board member said that students should not be reading books in classrooms that contained words that they would not be able to use in classrooms. Another said that a few expletives in a story might not be a problem, but if a book seemed to be written for the purpose of using expletives or contained deviant behavior or explicit sex scenes, this was enough to remove it from the school setting.

Even though thirty-odd years have passed, the notion of removing books still raises hackles in a country that prides itself on self-criticism and tolerance of diverse viewpoints. It strikes at the very core of our cherished freedoms when officials attempt to bury ideas simply because the ideas are unpopular or they disagree with them. The factual hurdle the school board in *Pico* had to climb was the students' claim that the board was not as concerned about explicit sex and profane language as about the other ideas in the books. In *A Hero Ain't Nothing but a Sandwich,* a black teacher in a black school calls attention to the fact that the "hero" George Washington owned slaves. The lawyers for the students brought out facts that showed that board members had received pamphlets (at the conference they attended before removing the books) that said that Eldridge Cleaver's book was full of anti-American material and that an essay in *A Reader for Writers* "equates Malcolm X, considered by many to be a traitor to this country, with the founding fathers of our country." A school board press release stated that some of the books were "anti-Christian" and "anti-Semitic."

It is a testament to the changing nature of our cultural values that the concerns expressed in Long Island, New York, in 1976 about George Washington, Eldridge Cleaver, and Malcolm X would hardly raise an eyebrow in many, if not most, communities today. But all books contain "ideas." A school board member who wanted to remove a book because it is racist, homophobic, or misogynist would be disagreeing with the "ideas" it contained, too.

So before we totally denounce the school board for its actions, let us unpack this examination just a bit more. The presentation of the board's argument was clumsy, and its motivations might well have been the inappropriate ones asserted by the students, but there is a kernel of a vision in there—perhaps unbeknownst to the board members themselves—that might make a bit more sense if it were set forth in another configuration.

Interestingly, long before the term took on the political patina it has come to possess in the context of affirmative action, both sides in the *Pico* case used the concept of "diversity" as a way to shore up their argument. Each side loaded the term from a different perspective. The lawyers for the students argued that the book removal harmed diversity by imposing an orthodoxy on the individual student and classroom. They supported their argument with a quotation from *Keyishian v. Board of Regents.* The *Keyishian* opinion was crafted in the context of higher education, and it stated: "the First Amendment . . . does not tolerate laws that cast a pall of orthodoxy over the classroom."[34] Using this quotation, the students and their amici emphasized the need for heterogeneity—diversity— in the nation's public schools and suggested that school board decisions about library books would harm that ideal. As we saw in Chapter 4 (recall the uproar when courts used the *Hazelwood* doctrine in higher education), the concepts that courts develop in one tier of public education may not always transplant well when placed in another tier.

The lawyers for the school board came at diversity from a different perspective, and quoted a report of the U.S. Commission on

Civil Rights entitled *Toward Quality Education for Mexican-Americans:* "Curriculum is neither neutral nor impartial. It necessarily reflects value judgments that significantly affect the child's perception of himself and society in general. The school shapes the culture and values of its students by presenting favorably certain styles and customs."[35] According to this argument, it is federal court interference with local school districts that will cast a *national* orthodoxy over the classroom, not the individual school boards representing the different communities they serve.

Because the 14,383 public school districts in the United States differ in their cultural and socioeconomic makeup, the values that are important to some districts will be deemed less important in others.[36] When elected school board members represent those who elected them, there will be a difference in perspectives. This difference between community values in one place and those in another underscores the rich diversity in our national fabric. It would be ironic indeed if the *Pico* opinion resulted in more orthodoxy in public schools because school boards refuse to purchase books recognizing cultural differences or anything else out of the ordinary because it would be too risky to remove them later.

As one commentator noted in the *Harvard Law Review,* "Public opinion strongly supports local control, apparently because local responsibility tends to insure that educational policies reflect the needs of the individual community."[37] Justice Powell, a strong supporter of local control, has pointed out that different localities can tailor local programs to fit local needs, resulting in a pluralism that affords "opportunity for experimentation, innovation and a healthy competition for educational excellence."[38] Perhaps some of the judicial opinions in *Pico* merely masked a contempt for the input of the "provincial" (and, as the court described them, "conservative") citizens in Island Trees who did not have the education, the wisdom, or the broad perspective of the judges overseeing the educational system in their community.

One interesting facet of the case is the homogeneity of the writers of the amicus briefs. (These are "friend of the court" briefs by a person or organization who is not a party to the litigation, but who believes that the decision may affect its interests.) All of the amicus briefs for the students were written by law firms in New York City; the two briefs for the school board were written by firms in Texas and Arizona.

Despite the rhetoric surrounding the question of access to ideas, the *Pico* opinion was fairly narrow. There was no question whether adults should have full access to all of the ideas and all of the language in the books at issue. There was not even a question whether children might have access to these books outside of the school library at the public library or bookstores. Like the public school, the public library serves an important function. It provides its users with ready access to a wide selection of all kinds of information and viewpoints, and it allows for a free and mostly unencumbered portal into a different world. Public libraries that want to receive federal funds have had their own "right to receive" issues with regard to pornography and obscenity. In 2003, Chief Justice William Rehnquist wrote for a plurality that the Children's Internet Protection Act did not violate the First Amendment rights of public library patrons when it required libraries to install filters to block out pornographic and obscene images on library computers if the library wanted to received federal funds.[39]

But the issue in *Pico* did not concern books in a public library. Rather, *Pico* addressed whether an institution that has *education* as its mission could choose to remove books in the *school* library. It is the location of the library—within the inculcative institution that is the public school—that might allow for exploration of a subtle distinction that was lost in the morass of high-flown language in the opinions and the briefs.

One goal of secondary schooling is to transmit basic information using established pedagogical techniques. Because students are not

fully mature intellectually or emotionally, the pedagogical techniques are established based on their needs. Students are not afforded the same open forum as adults, who usually are already
"habituated to social restraints [and so] exchange ideas on a level of
parity."[40] Where adults are concerned, it is often argued that the
cure for troublesome speech is "more speech." Yet when a student
checks out a book from a school library, the opportunities for "more
speech" are diminished. The student reads the book, with all its
"ideas," skewed or otherwise, with no opportunity for reasoned discussion or debate about their truth or complexity.

Public school students are not adults. They are still developing
cognitively and emotionally. They often make impulsive decisions,
and sometimes they make bad decisions about their health and
their future. They have not yet learned how to distinguish truth
from fiction or debate from demagoguery. Some students may not
be sophisticated enough to understand—without guidance from a
teacher or another adult—that allegory is not meant to be taken lit-
erally. They may not understand that satire portrays behavior the
writer actually deplores. And they may not comprehend that neutral description of reprehensible behavior can illustrate moral com-
plexities. If psychologists are correct that children learn moral
judgment by assimilating stories, educators in the school setting
may wish to ensure that the stories presented in that setting are set
forth in a way that enables the students to think critically and carefully about the presentation, as well as the content. After all, "schools
must play a central role in preparing their students to think and analyze and to recognize the demagogue," and demagoguery comes at
students from all sides.[41]

What if one of the books had claimed that the State of Israel is illegal and the result of a Zionist conspiracy, that affirmative action is
a plot to keep deserving Caucasians from opportunity, or that evolution and natural selection are myths, or that homosexuality was
condemned in the Bible? These topics certainly are not inappropri-

ate for high-school-aged children, but a conscientious educator knows that these are complex topics that deserve sensitive and careful discussion of the facts and historical context. This kind of critical examination may very well be missing in a book with one agenda.

A conscientious educator may believe that when students obtain such serious information *in a school setting* like the school library, it is important for the educative mission of the school that the students see the entire context in which the information exists. A careful educator might argue that presenting only one side of an issue or presenting vulgar and sexually explicit materials the school setting without explanation and discussion could leave students with a distorted impression. Moreover, the books in a school library, which are selected by school personnel, may leave another kind of impression. Some courts have reviewed the contents of books in school libraries when addressing challenges to school curriculum in the *classroom.* If the material—or even something the court deems similar—can be found in the school library, it sends a signal that this material could be acceptable for the classroom. For example, one court decided that a teacher who was dismissed for making students read *Welcome to the Monkey House,* by Kurt Vonnegut, in class after administrators asked her to cease was punished under a standard what was too vague, since "the school library contains a number of books with controversial words and philosophies."[42] In another case, a court reviewing the dismissal of a teacher for writing the word "fuck" on the board observed that the word was contained in books in the school library.[43]

Thus there is a more nuanced argument—one not articulated in *Pico* by the parties or the Court—that sees school board members trying in good faith to fulfill their school's educative mission, even in the indeterminate realm of "politics" and "ideas." Although this perspective did not come to light in the *Pico* opinion, a slight hint of it appeared in the *student's* brief, of all places. The brief asked, "If the language in these books is degrading to blacks or women, could an effective lesson in the use of non-racist and non-sexist language not be built upon such passages?"

Certainly, the answer is yes. But this lesson is difficult to accomplish as a practical matter when many different issues appear throughout many books. Schools have limited time to teach, and they must teach certain subjects and core material pursuant to state and federal mandates. Just working through the issues presented in the ten books presented in this case could take up an entire semester, or more. Since the books could be checked out any time by students at various grade levels, there would be no way to tell when the books with material that needed the "effective lesson" and "more speech" would be read by students, as different students using the school library would read them at different times.

Viewed through this lens, the pedagogical goal is not to suppress ideas but to structure the way students are exposed to ideas *while they are within the school setting.* The Island Trees school board made it clear that "no teacher has been instructed not to discuss the books which were removed or to refrain from discussion or comment upon the ideas and positions they represent."[44] Indeed, the board recognized that it had no authority to remove any books in an effort to "'aid or oppose' a particular religion, to prohibit the teaching of a 'theory which is deemed antagonistic to a particular dogma' or to prohibit a teacher from mentioning 'the very existence of an entire system of human thought.'"[45] Even though there may be some leeway to allow school boards to regulate books in the school library, the board must have a process with standards to avoid arbitrary and capricious removal. The problem is that it is difficult to set objective principles to implement community standards, which are by their nature subjective and dependent on the makeup of the community itself. One thing that is clear, however, is that it is not useful to approach this issue armed only with slogans and sound bites that merely obscure the complexity of the issue and paralyze critical analysis.

> Censorship is the strongest drive in human nature. Sex is a weak second.
>
> —Phil Kerby, former editor of the *New York Times,* quoted by Nat Hentoff in *Free Speech for Me, but Not for Thee* (1993)

Challenges to books in school libraries have continued unabated since the *Pico* case. Some of the focus of these challenges, however, has changed. Where the cases were about profanity and sex in the 1980s, fantasy stories have joined these books on the most not-wanted list.[46] According to the American Library Association, J. K. Rowling, author of the Harry Potter series, was fourth among the top ten challenged authors of 1999–2004, and in some years she was the most challenged author of all.[47] Fantasy stories like the Harry Potter series trouble some parents because they believe it makes witchcraft exciting for children. They worry that the books teach an earth-centered spirituality, and fear that there is no place for God in the world of wizards.

Most librarians and teachers will not acknowledge that they self-censor, but it is easy to understand how it can happen if they are aware that a book may cause trouble. Indeed, the uproar about Harry Potter caused one school superintendent in Michigan to direct teachers not to read the books aloud, to restrict their use in the library without parental permission, and to refrain from ordering them in the future.

Mark Twain's *Adventures of Huckleberry Finn* and John Steinbeck's *Of Mice and Men* are usually somewhere on the list of book challenges. But lately books that contain homosexuality or non–

nuclear family lifestyles have been at or near the top of the list and seem most likely to raise the ire of parents. The book *Families,* by Meredith Tax, was the subject of a case in Virginia when the Christian Coalition of Fairfax claimed that it glorified divorce and told about a lesbian couple. The most challenged book in 2006 was Justin Richardson and Peter Parnell's book *And Tango Makes Three,* about two male penguins parenting an egg from a mixed-sex penguin couple.

Many, if not most, of the parents who challenge books at school do so because they believe that their children's exposure to these books will undermine family religious beliefs. These parents argue that their children have a right *not* to receive certain information from a state-sponsored school, because it interferes with their constitutional right to exercise their religion and their constitutional right to raise their children as they see fit. And so we come to the issue of religion in school.

.✦.

Religious Speech: On a Wing and a Prayer

THIS SUBJECT IS, IF ANYTHING, even more complex and intricate than previous chapters. It deserves its own volume (or a multivolume treatise), for it is difficult to set forth an in-depth examination of religious speech in school in one chapter. Nonetheless, a book on school speech would not be complete without addressing this fascinating issue.

The preceding chapters have worked through the complex balancing exercise that occurs when the school and the student clash over speech rights. The issue of religious speech adds a new layer to the analysis, and a new section of the First Amendment enters into the equation. The First Amendment addresses religion in one sentence that deals with two concerns—the "establishment" of religion and the "exercise" of religion—the establishment clause and the free exercise clause. The establishment clause says: "Congress shall make no law respecting the establishment of religion," and the free exercise clause adds, "or prohibiting the free exercise thereof." Although the text of the amendment refers only to laws by Congress, the Supreme Court—starting in the 1930s—made some rulings that fundamentally changed the way the Constitution worked.

(There were some isolated cases earlier, but scholars generally count the 1930s as the time when the Court began to develop a more consistent approach toward what was to be known as the doctrine of incorporation.) Before that time, the Court had consistently ruled that the first ten amendments were drafted as a check only on the federal government and were not applicable to the states. Thus federal courts could not control *state* law by using the *federal* Constitution.

The Fourteenth Amendment was passed after the Civil War, and that changed everything, although these changes did not occur for decades. The Fourteenth Amendment provides that no *state* "shall deprive abridge the privileges or immunities of citizens of the United States" or "deprive any person of life, liberty or property without due process of law." Beginning in the 1930s, the Supreme Court decided that some of the provisions of the Bill of Rights were "incorporated" into the word "liberty" in the Fourteenth Amendment. Thus some of the provisions of the Bill of Rights are also applicable to the states. The degree to which this doctrine of selective incorporation changed the balance of power between state and federal courts and state and federal government is incalculable. For the purposes of this discussion, all of the provisions of the First Amendment, including the religion clauses, have been incorporated into the Fourteenth Amendment and made applicable to the states. The Supreme Court has held that the Second Amendment right to bear arms, the Fifth Amendment clause that guarantees criminal prosecution only on a grand jury indictment, and the Seventh Amendment guarantee of a jury trial in a civil case are not applicable to the states.

So the First Amendment is a check on both state and federal government, and it "protects speech and religion by two different mechanisms."[1] Nonreligious speech is protected even when government participates, "for the very object of some of our most important speech is to persuade the government to adopt an idea as its own."[2] But "the method for protecting freedom of worship and freedom of conscience in religious matters is quite the reverse. In religious debate or expression, the government is not a prime participant, for the framers deemed religious establishment antithetical to the freedom of all. The free exercise clause embraces a freedom of conscience and worship that has close parallels to the speech provisions of the first amendment, but the establishment clause is a specific prohibition on forms of state intervention in religious affairs with no precise counterpart in the speech provisions."[3]

The tension between these two clauses and the free speech clause, which appears in the text immediately after them, has proved a fertile ground for conflict in the public schools. The conflicts come in numerous guises—states requiring speech that is at odds with a religion; students desiring religious speech in the form of prayer or proselytizing; parents requesting curriculum changes that better comport with their religion; students distributing religious materials—the list goes on and on. Organizations exist to generate test cases and to help fund individual plaintiffs as they litigate. Thus there is no dearth of claims or cases regarding religion in school, and in many instances these claims have been at the center of a cultural firestorm.

> That's me in the spotlight; I'm losing my religion.
>
> —"Losing My Religion," by Berry, Buck,
> Mills and Stipe, REM (*Out of Time*, 1991)

Religious claims entered the schoolhouse gate long before the Tinker children donned their black armbands. The Pledge of Allegiance, which has lately been an accelerant in the incendiary culture wars of the early twenty-first century, caused a problem that first reached the Supreme Court even before the midpoint of the twentieth century. Unlike *Tinker* or *Fraser,* this was not a case where students wished to speak but where students wished to remain silent. The issue arose when states required students to recite the Pledge of Allegiance, and Jehovah's Witness students did not wish to do so.

The stirring language in *West Virginia v. Barnette,* has stood as the watchtower for diversity for over six decades, and it shows no sign of losing its luster over time.[4] Justice Jackson reproached those who would require convention in religious practice. But his rhetoric reached more than religion when it scorned orthodoxy in politics, nationalism, and "other matters of opinion"—remarkable words to be written by any jurist while the nation was in the midst of World War II. Coming as it did years before the civil rights movement, it forged a path for the justices on the Warren Court to follow, and these words have been quoted many times in many cases.

The potent language in *Barnette* is all the more remarkable because it came only three years after the Supreme Court had decided another Pledge of Allegiance case with a diametrically opposite result. Comparing the opinions of *Minersville School District v. Gobitis*[5] and *West Virginia v. Barnette* reveals how *Barnette* was attempting to chart a course of tolerance in a nation that was struggling with its cultural identity. Tracing the "Pledge" litigation gives us insight into what has changed and what has remained the same since that first challenge gained such notoriety.

At its core, the litigation about the Pledge of Allegiance echoes the oft-repeated theme of self-preservation. Those who argued to make the pledge mandatory for all students believed that daily pledges by young people in school would help to ensure that the nation continued with the ideals found within the pledge's language. Although *Gobitis* and *Barnette* are the two cases that are often viewed as the genesis of the pledge speech issue, the Supreme Court was asked to review pledge cases four times before it decided to hear *Gobitis* in 1940. There was no suggestion in those cases that the plaintiffs would ever prevail. In 1937 the Georgia Supreme Court unanimously dismissed an appeal by a twelve-year-old Jehovah's

Witness student who was expelled from public school for refusing to recite the pledge. One of the tenets of Jehovah's Witness belief is a literal understanding of the commandment in the Book of Exodus: "Thou shalt not make unto thee any graven image, or any likeness or anything that is in the heaven above, or that is in the earth beneath, or that is in the water under the earth; thou shalt not bow down thyself to them nor serve them." They consider the flag an "image" and refuse to salute it.

The Georgia court explained that the pledge of allegiance was not a religious rite. "[Saluting] the flag of this country is just a part of a patriotic ceremony, an act of respect to the institutions and ideals of the land that is affording them a free education and a safe and bountiful place to live, and is not a bowing down in worship of an image in the place of God."[6] The court saw no federal or state constitutional violation, finding the pledge requirement reasonable in keeping with the policy of the state that the schools were to instruct its youth in the study of and devotion to American ideals. The U.S. Supreme Court dismissed the case for want of a substantial federal question. When an appeal is dismissed for want of a substantial federal question, it means that every question the appeal brings to the court is "so clearly not debatable and utterly lacking in merit as to require dismissal for want of substance."[7]

That same year, the Court was asked to hear another appeal from the Supreme Court of New Jersey, which had stated, "It is little enough to expect of those who seek the benefits of the education offered in the public schools of this state that they pledge their allegiance to the nation and the nation's flag," and "Those who do not desire to conform with the commands of the statute can seek their schooling elsewhere."[8] Again, the Supreme Court dismissed the appeal in a one-sentence order because of the lack of a substantial federal question. When the Supreme Court of California was faced with a similar question, it noted the two dismissals by the U.S. Supreme Court and stated, "By reason of [those decisions], the question as to whether the flag saluting requirement violates the Due Process Clause of the Fourteenth Amendment to the federal Constitution, or any other provision of the federal Constitution, is no longer open."[9] The U.S. Supreme Court again dismissed the appeal and the same day summarily affirmed a federal court in Massachusetts that had upheld the Massachusetts statute requiring the pledge against a Jehovah's Witness challenge.

Four courts, four rejections, four dismissals by the U.S. Supreme Court. No hint of success for the student plaintiffs, until one federal district judge started the change that would crack and later rend open the wall that had protected the Pledge of Allegiance from these silent students. The case arose in Schuylkill County, Pennsylvania, when the Gobitis children were expelled from school for their failure to salute the flag in November 1935. The attorney for the students, a Jehovah's Witness from Brooklyn, New York, had been looking for a flag salute case where he could gain a plaintiff's victory. District Judge Albert Branson Maris, a descendent of Quaker colonists and a member of the Society of Friends, seemed like a judge who would understand the problems of a minority religion. He did indeed.

When the case first appeared before him, Judge Maris was newly appointed to the district court bench by President Roosevelt. He refused to dismiss the case and set it for trial. By the time the case came to trial in early 1938, war was imminent in Europe, and Jehovah's Witnesses were often being harassed for what others saw as disloyalty to the United States. When Judge Maris's ruling was released on June 18, 1938, he had just been elevated to the Third Circuit Court of Appeals. (In contrast to the confirmation process today, Judge Maris was appointed by President Roosevelt on June 14 and confirmed two days later on June 16.) In a brief opinion, he simply stated that it was clear from the evidence that the refusal of "these two earnest Christian children to salute the flag cannot even remotely prejudice or imperil the safety, health, morals, property or personal rights of their fellows."[10] Judge Maris acknowledged that other state courts had disagreed with his assessment, but he believed "the courts which decided these cases overlooked the fundamental principle of religious liberty . . . namely, that no man, even though he be a school director or a judge, is empowered to censor another's religious convictions or set bounds to the areas of human conduct in which those convictions should be permitted to control his actions, unless compelled to do so by an overriding public necessity which properly requires the exercise of the police power."[11] A few short years later, Justice Robert Jackson drew on these very words in *Barnette* when he asserted that "no official, high or petty can prescribe what shall be orthodox in politics, nationalism, religion, or other matters of opinion or force citizens to confess by word or act their faith therein."

Judge Maris was especially impressed with the "earnestness and sincerity of [the plaintiff's] convictions," and he was entirely satisfied that they believed that the salute was an act of worship. Once again, context was important to the judge writing the opinion. This was 1938, as Hitler was building his Nazi war machine. Judge Maris wrote, "We need only glance at the current world scene to realize the preservation of individual liberty is more important today than ever it was in the past. The safety of our nation largely depends upon the extent to which we foster in each individual citizen that sturdy independence of thought and action which is essential in a democracy."[12] Without any mention of the fact that the Supreme Court had dismissed appeals on the issue, the district court granted the plaintiffs an injunction restraining the school district from requiring that they salute the flag.

The case was appealed to the Third Circuit, which set forth an opinion that barely disguised its contempt for those who would force "false patriotism" of "flag worship" on children.[13] The term "flag worship" had been used by a Colonel James Moss, who, the court reminded those who had served in "World War No. 1," had been "our staff of life." Moss had written training manuals and a book entitled *The Flag of the United States, Its History and Symbolism,* which the court quoted at length, decrying "blind and excessive adulation of the Flag." The court also sprinkled numerous quotations throughout the opinion, ranging from Roger Williams to Thomas Jefferson to Cicero. The opinion writer, Judge William Clark, even used one of the most famous biblical quotations about children to great rhetorical effect. ("Suffer little children, and forbid them not, to come unto me: for of such is the kingdom of heaven"; Matthew 19:14.)

If the opinion reads more like a lawyer's brief or an op-ed piece, it was successful as such. A federal court of appeals unmistakably told the world that there was strong opposition to what heretofore had been slam-dunk wins for state power. This opinion, because it ran counter to several per curiam dispositions of the Supreme Court, set a high probability that the Court would take on the issue. When it did, the Court's focus on the issue gave it a higher profile, resulting in even more publicity from the nation's press and critiques from the nation's scholars. This lone appeals court insisted that a forced show of ceremonial patriotism was a poor substitute for understanding the values the flag symbolizes. It paved the way for the arguments in the *Barnette* case four years later, and gave others both the incentive and the courage to sustain arguments against flag regulations. Although the plaintiffs lost this battle in Pennsylvania, they later won the war in West Virginia.

The first sentence of the Third Circuit opinion left no doubt as to how the case had been decided. Judge Clark, who had been confirmed to the Third Circuit the same day as Judge Maris, evoked the imagery of a large bully intimidating a little child and inserted a biblical reference to remind the reader "what Jesus would do": "Eighteen big states have seen fit to exert their power over a small number of little children ('and forbid them not')." And later, "These little children ('suffer them') are asking us to afford them the protection of the First Amendment to the Constitution and to permit them the "free exercise" of their "religion." The court described the "little girl of 13" and "little boy of 14" as members of a group known as Russellites, Earnest Bible Students, or Jehovah's Witnesses. Despite its questionable relevance, Judge Clark explained what Adolf Hitler thought of the sect: "I consider them quacks. I dissolve the 'Earnest Bible Students' in Germany; their property I dedicate to the people's welfare; I will have all their literature confiscated."[14]

Using a phrase reminiscent of the "clear and present danger test," the court found no connection between failure to salute the flag and harm to the nation—"departure from a recently evolved ritualistic norm of patriotism is not a clear and present assurance of future cowardice or treachery." Showing how legal commentators influenced his analysis, Judge Clark pointed out and cited to numerous law reviews that contained criticism of judicial protection of the flag salute and praise for the *Gobitis* district court opinion.

The court of appeals still had the Supreme Court dismissals to contend with, and it did so by attempting to distinguish the flag regulations at issue in the different cases. In *Gobitis* the school board had promulgated the pledge regulation under a state law that merely required the teaching of civics. The other cases had a different pedigree that the court thought was important: The state legislature had declared and the state's highest court had affirmed the policy of flag saluting. When a state legislature passes a statute and the highest court in the state upholds it, there is a stronger connection between the refusal to salute and harm to the public welfare. So the Third Circuit affirmed Judge Maris and ruled for the plaintiffs.

The Jehovah's Witness free exercise victory was short-lived, as the U.S. Supreme Court, with only one dissent, reversed the Third Circuit seven months later. Justice Felix Frankfurter wrote the Court's opinion, and he framed the question as follows: When does the constitutional guarantee of free exercise (of religion) compel exemption from doing that which society thinks necessary for the promotion of some great common end? Basically, his analysis focused on whether religious belief could exempt a person from a generally applicable law that was not directed at a particular religion. The Court determined that "the mere possession of religious convictions which contradict the relevant concerns of a political society does not relieve the citizen from the discharge of political responsibilities." Legislatures needed to able to pass laws they deemed necessary to "secure and maintain that orderly and tranquil society, without which religious toleration itself is unattainable."

Note the parallel here to other school speech cases. One argument for some constraints on students is that to obtain a serious education and the tools to speak (and to listen and weed out demagogues) students need to have a skill and knowledge set that is unattainable without some "order and tranquility" in the community of learning. The *Gobitis* Court was unwilling to constrain the hand of legislatures on this issue because, as Justice Frankfurter emphatically stated, "National unity is the basis of national security."

The cornerstone of the opinion was Frankfurter's view that "The ultimate foundation of a free society is the binding tie of cohesive sentiment." Transmitting this sentiment from generation to generation creates "that continuity of a treasured common life which constitutes a civilization." Without this unifying sentiment, there ultimately will be "no liberties, civil or religious." Again note the parallel with some arguments in other school speech cases: without the discipline of focused study, students do not learn the tools that it takes to put First Amendment freedoms into practice.

Justice Frankfurter pointed out that there is a great diversity of psychological and ethical opinion regarding the best way to train children for their place in society (a fact that certainly remains true today), and the courts are not the arena for debating educational policy. Instead, leaving the issue to be debated in the forum of public opinion and decided by elected legislatures would "vindicate the self-confidence of a free people."

There was only one dissent, that of Justice Harlan Stone, who at the time was just one year away from being named chief justice. The crux of the issue for him was that these schoolchildren had been compelled to make public affirmations that violated their religious conscience. The very essence of constitutional liberty, in his view, was an individual's freedom from compulsion as to what he will think or what he will say. Moreover, to leave the issue to the democratic process merely "surrenders the constitutional protection of the liberty of small minorities to the popular will."

In retrospect, even though the Supreme Court overruled Judge Maris's decision, his opinion in *Gobitis* was the beginning of a sea change. As Justice Frankfurter pointed out, the *Gobitis* case "was brought [to the Supreme Court] because the decision of the Circuit Court of Appeals for the Third Circuit ran counter to our rulings."[15] And the Third Circuit affirmed Judge Maris after his opinion had been lauded in many circles. Although the plaintiffs ultimately lost in *Gobitis,* there was a dissent by an influential justice, and the issue was played out before a much larger audience. Long before the days of twenty-four-hour news and Internet access, a decision of a state supreme court or even a federal circuit court of appeals was unlikely to attain much national attention, except in certain newspapers. But a decision by the Supreme Court focused national attention on the issue, along with the criticism of commentators and legal scholars. Thus *Gobitis,* which is often ignored because it was soon overruled by an opinion filled with the intoxicating prose of Justice Robert Jackson, played an important role in the religious speech story.

> But I am constant as the Northern Star.
> Of whose true, fixed and resting quality
> There is no fellow in the firmament.
>
> —William Shakespeare, *Julius Caesar,*
> act 3, scene 1

The battles pitching Jehovah's Witness schoolchildren against the Pledge of Allegiance were far from over. Two years later, three Supreme Court justices who had sided with Justice Frankfurter and the majority in *Gobitis* told the world that they had made a mistake. In an astonishing move, Justices Black, Douglas, and Murphy used another Supreme Court opinion to make this announcement. The case that allowed them to do so, *Jones v. Opelika,* had nothing to do with the Pledge of Allegiance. Rather, it affirmed the conviction of four Jehovah's Witnesses who had violated a city ordinance forbidding the selling of books or pamphlets without a license.[16] Justice Murphy wrote a dissent, joined by Justices Black, Douglas, and Stone (who by now was the chief justice). At the end of the Murphy dissent, the three justices set forth a single paragraph to proclaim that things had changed in the two years since the ruling in *Gobitis:* "Since we joined the opinion in the *Gobitis* case, we think this is an appropriate time to state that we now believe that it was wrongly decided." This unmistakable invitation to rehear the pledge issue would not go unanswered.

The year after *Gobitis* was handed down, the West Virginia legislature directed the state board of education to prescribe courses of study "for the purpose of . . . perpetuating the ideals, principles and spirit of Americanism." The board passed resolutions filled with quotations from the *Gobitis* opinion and ordered that the flag salute become a regular part of the public school program. Students could be expelled for failure to comply, treated as delinquents, and their parents could be prosecuted and subject to a fine or jail. At first the resolution required the common flag salute at the time—extended raised right arm with palm up—but it changed to the right-hand-on-breast salute when groups like the PTA, the Red Cross, and the Girl and Boy Scouts objected that the salute looked too much like Hitler's.

A group of Jehovah's Witness citizens brought suit in federal court claiming that the West Virginia regulation was an unconstitutional denial of free speech and freedom of religion and that it denied due process and equal protection of the law. Because of a procedural rule (not especially relevant to this examination), the case came before a panel of three district court judges on October 6, 1942. Recall that *Gobitis* had been in the books for only two years before the issue arose again in West Virginia, just the blink of an eye in Supreme Court time. Recall, too, that the country was in the midst of a major war effort in Europe and the South Pacific and that the flag was the symbol of what American soldiers were fighting for. Virtually every town had soldiers who had joined the war effort, and many towns had lists of missing and dead. Patriotism was at a fever pitch throughout most of the country.

Given the clear precedent by the Supreme Court—precedent that unquestionably bound the lower court—the lower court had little choice but to refuse to grant the injunction, whether it agreed with the Supreme Court or not. Yet it refused to do so. Instead, in a stunning move, this court essentially overruled the *Gobitis* case and granted the injunction requested by the plaintiffs (*Barnette v. West Virginia*, 47 F. Supp. 251 [S.D. W. Va. 1942]). The district court judges tried to explain this remarkable decision by stating that they believed that things had changed. Developments since the *Gobitis* case had been decided, they maintained, gave them the choice not to accept *Gobitis* as binding precedent. It is true that two new justices were on the Court, James F. Byrnes and Robert H. Jackson. Moreover, Justice Stone, the lone dissenter in *Gobitis*, was now chief justice. Of the seven justices currently on the Court, the district court observed, four had publicly stated that the opinion was unsound, and three others had made a special point of disowning *Gobitis* in *Jones*. Apparently making a head count of the current justices, the district court decided that it could treat *Gobitis* as if it had already been overruled. The district court thereupon set its own standard for constitutionality and determined that there had to be a clear and present danger to the community for a state to override a person's religious scruples. Because the flag salute has only an indirect influence on national safety, and there is no clear and present danger if schoolchildren refrain from saluting it, the plaintiffs prevailed.

It is highly unusual for the Supreme Court to ignore stare decisis and overrule one of its own opinions. It is even more unusual to do so after only three years. The district court panel must have felt vindicated when the Supreme Court affirmed its decision and ruled for the Jehovah's Witness plaintiffs. Given the fact that the district court had decided to rule for the plaintiffs despite the binding *Gobitis* precedent, the district judges must have even felt a bit relieved when no justice remarked on their willingness to ignore a previous ruling by the Supreme Court.

Justices today might not be as forgiving as the *Barnette* Court was in 1943. In *Agnostini v. Felton* (1997), the Court overruled an opinion from twelve years earlier in which it had stated that public schoolteachers could not provide remedial instruction to students in a religious school on the premises of the religious school.[17] Justice O'Connor pointed out that stare decisis does not prevent the Supreme Court from overruling a previous decision when there has been a significant change or subsequent development in constitutional law. She was clear, however, that other courts should not conclude on their own that more recent cases have, by implication, overruled an earlier precedent. Justice O'Connor cautioned, "If a precedent of this Court has direct application in a case, yet appears to rest on reasons rejected in some other line of decisions, [the courts below] should follow the case which directly controls, leaving to this Court the prerogative of overruling its own decisions." The trial court in such a case may hear the plaintiff's motion, "but it must be denied *unless and until this Court [has] reinterpreted the binding precedent.*" A lower court today would be risking a severe reprimand if it acted like the district court in *Barnette*.

To be sure, Justice Jackson also had some "splaining" to do in his

opinion overruling *Gobitis. Gobitis* had been written by no less a lu-
minary than Felix Frankfurter in his first year as an associate justice. The call for judicial restraint that sounds throughout the
Gobitis opinion became his theme throughout his career. Highly
regarded for his keen intellect, Frankfurter had helped to form the
American Civil Liberties Union and had joined efforts to save the
lives of the anarchists Sacco and Vanzetti before President Franklin
Roosevelt—for whom he had served as an advisor—nominated him
to the Supreme Court. He was no stranger to issues relating to discrimination based on religion. Born in Vienna, he had lived in that
city's Jewish quarter, and he was only the third Jewish justice to sit
on the high court. Although he came to the Court as a liberal political progressive, he was heavily influenced by his friend and men-
tor Oliver Wendell Holmes regarding the importance of judicial
restraint—judges refraining from placing burdensome limits on the
elected legislative and executive branches. Losing the votes of Justice Hugo Black and William O. Douglas such a short time after the
Gobitis opinion was a bitter blow, and it was the start of a rift that
took years to heal between Frankfurter and Black. The fracture
never healed between Frankfurter and Douglas.

In fact, the *Gobitis* repudiation was the beginning of a long slide
of declining influence for Justice Frankfurter. Harlan Stone and
Fred Vinson both served for a time as chief justices, and then came
Earl Warren. Chief Justice Warren headed a Court that much of the
time eschewed Justice Frankfurter's firm convictions about judicial
restraint. (Despite this divergence of opinion about the role of the
courts, Justice Frankfurter, an ardent opponent of segregation,
joined the per curiam opinion in *Brown v. Board of Education*.)

Justice Robert Jackson, the writer of the *Barnette* opinion, joined
the Court after *Gobitis* had been decided, in June 1941, just six
months before the Japanese attack on Pearl Harbor. It is somewhat
surprising that Justice Jackson was tapped to write *Barnette*. After
all, Harlan Stone had been the lone justice who dissented in *Gobitis*,

and he was now chief justice. This meant that he determined who would write every opinion in which he was in the majority. It must have been tempting to Chief Justice Stone to keep the opinion for himself. Perhaps he chose Jackson, who had served as U.S. Attorney General before joining the Court, because he thought it would be less shocking if an opinion striking down the compulsory flag salute were written by someone who had held that high office. Perhaps he was trying to obtain and hold Justice Jackson's vote. Whatever the reason, Justice Jackson, who will now be forever linked with the powerful prose in the *Barnette* opinion, must have been grateful that he got the call.

Like Justice Frankfurter, Justice Jackson had come to the Court with impressive credentials, having served as Solicitor General and Attorney General. He later took a leave of absence for the 1945–1946 term to serve as chief U.S. prosecutor at the Nuremberg Trials. President Franklin Roosevelt had promised Jackson that he would become Chief Justice, but President Harry Truman was in the Oval Office when Chief Justice Stone resigned in 1946. Factions formed between those who supported Jackson for the position and those who supported Justice Hugo Black. The contest turned vicious, and it was played out before a dismayed public audience.

But the year in Nuremberg and the feud with Black was still to come in 1943 when Jackson penned the words in *Barnette* that may be his most enduring legacy. His opinion first pointed out that the plaintiffs' behavior was peaceful and that they did not interfere with the rights of others to participate in the flag salute. And the compulsory flag salute, unlike a required study of U.S. history, demands affirmation of a belief and an attitude of mind.

But there still was the matter of *Gobitis*. Jackson claimed that the analysis in the *Gobitis* opinion simply had started in the wrong place. The opinion *assumed* that the state had the power to impose the flag salute on students generally. Starting with that assumption, the *Gobitis* opinion merely examined whether students could be exempt from this general rule for religious reasons. Justice Jackson refused to assume that this power existed in the first instance, and he spent the rest of the opinion explaining why it did not.

First, educators are educating the young for citizenship, "reason for scrupulous protection of Constitutional freedoms of the individual, if we are not to strangle the free mind at its source and teach youth to discount important principles of our government as mere platitudes."[18] He pointed out that the very purpose of the Bill of Rights was to remove certain subjects from the "vicissitudes of political controversy" and to put them beyond the reach of officials and away from the outcome of elections. First Amendment freedoms may be restricted only to prevent "grave and immediate danger" to interests the state may lawfully protect.

Perhaps most important, Justice Jackson took issue with the *Gobitis* opinion's emphasis on national unity. Although national unity might be fostered by example and persuasion, he insisted that the Constitution does not allow it to be coerced. The cause of unity could result in bitter strife regarding "whose unity it shall be." "Probably no deeper division of our people could proceed from any provocation than . . . choos[ing] what doctrine . . . public education officials shall compel youth to unite in embracing." The Constitution was designed to avoid this by setting up a government of consent by the governed, and the Bill of Rights denies those in power the ability to coerce that consent.

A euloguim to what we now call diversity, *Barnette* contains a powerful sentence that has not garnered the same fame as other parts of the opinion. Now that our nation has become more heterogeneous than even Justice Jackson could have dreamed when he penned these words in the spring of 1943, this statement embodies our hopes for the future: "We apply the limitations of the Constitution with no fear that the freedom to be intellectually and spiritually diverse or even contrary will disintegrate the social organization." Of course, this sentence was really an ideal, rather than a description of the American mindset. Fear of contrariety has been at the root of many sharp political and cultural divisions, from the time of Senator Joseph McCarthy (not too many years after *Barnette*) to current controversies over the place of religion in public life and over illegal immigration. Nonetheless, this aspiration, expressed in Jackson's stirring prose, bolsters the perception that the principles on which the Constitution was built are strong enough to withstand nonconformity.

The two sentences that would make an indelible mark on how the First Amendment would be viewed for decades to come appear near the end of the opinion:

> If there is any fixed star in our constitutional constellation, it is that no official, high or petty, can prescribe what shall be orthodox in politics, nationalism, religion, or other matters of opinion or force citizens to confess by word or act their faith therein. If there are any circumstances which permit an exception, they do not now occur to us.

With that, the *Barnette* opinion, with Justice Jackson at the helm, charted a course for a nation. It planted the seeds that would germinate over twenty years later in *Tinker*, and it energized the individualist in religion and politics. We can only speculate what the United States would have been like under a regime that kept *Gobitis* in place, but it most certainly would be a different place from the country we know today. There is no question that the change from *Gobitis* to *Barnette* was a monumental hour in the history of the Constitution and the Supreme Court.

Justices Black and Douglas, both of whom had joined the now-reversed majority opinion in *Gobitis*, wrote together to explain why they had changed their minds. They said that they had joined *Gobitis* because they were reluctant to make the Constitution a rigid bar against state regulation of conduct that the state believes is inimical to the public welfare. They still believed that "No well-ordered society can leave to the individual the right to make final decisions, unassailable by the State, as to what they will or will not do." The First Amendment does not protect even religious conduct that presents a grave and imminent danger. But refusal to say the pledge does not create a grave danger to the nation, and enforced ceremony is inconsistent with the plan and purpose of the Constitution.

Justice Murphy also wrote a concurrence, echoing much of the theme set forth by Justice Jackson. The freedom to believe and to worship one's Maker according to the dictates of conscience is a right the Constitution specifically shelters. Justice Murphy wrote that he had no loftier duty or responsibility as a judge "than to uphold that spiritual freedom to its farthest reaches."

Justices Roberts and Reed remained faithful to *Gobitis*, but they did not write a dissent. The only written dissent in *Barnette* was that of Justice Felix Frankfurter. The tone of his dissent reveals his feeling of anger and personal resentment of the rejection of his *Gobitis* opinion. His first sentence reminded the Court and the nation that, as a Jew, he knew all about discrimination based on religion. "One who belongs to the most vilified and persecuted minority in history is not likely to be insensible to the freedoms granted by our Constitution." Although he personally agreed with the views in the Court's opinion, he was emphatic that it was not his personal opinion that mattered. What mattered was whether reasonable legislatures could have enacted a law for a legitimate end—promotion of good citizenship. "Mr. Justice [Oliver Wendell] Holmes went to the very essence of our constitutional system when he wrote that 'it must be remembered that legislatures are the ultimate guardians of the liberties and welfare of the people in quite as great a degree as the courts.' Our only role is to determine if legislatures have exercised a judgment for which reasonable justification can be offered."

The controversy surrounding *Barnette* generated submissions from two amici, the American Civil Liberties Union (ACLU) and the American Bar Association (ABA) Committee on the Bill of Rights. The ACLU wrote that "compulsion in this country has never been the handmaiden to patriotism" and that courts are not powerless "to exorcise the whiplash of tyranny over a religious minority from our national scene." The ABA reported that of the twenty-two law reviews that had commented on the *Gobitis* decision, eighteen agreed with the dissent, two agreed with the majority, and two did not take sides. The brief then quoted passages from some of the reviews that supported the plaintiffs' position. Harvard law professor Thomas Reed Powell wrote an essay stating that he had great sympathy for the schoolchildren, "however misguided the teachings and compulsions of their simple-minded, unintelligent parents." In addition, the ABA pointed out how flag regulations operated after *Gobitis:* children who were expelled obtained a piecemeal education from their parents, were sent to a religious school far away from their families, or were placed in institutions for juvenile delinquents. Alluding to Justice Frankfurter's writing in *Gobitis,* "These ugly facts have made glowing abstractions about loyalty and national unity seem increasingly remote from the enforced statute." The language in the briefs and in the *Barnette* opinion—on both sides of the question—was uncompromising and at times impassioned, if not overwrought. Issues that evoke such strong feelings are unlikely to leave the national consciousness permanently. Far from being extinguished, issues surrounding the pledge have continued to surface decades after *Barnette* and are currently on some court dockets as I write this book.

One Nation, under God, with Liberty?

The Pledge of Allegiance had its genesis in 1892 in a national magazine called the *Youth's Companion* and its commemoration of the four hundredth anniversary of the landing of Christopher Columbus. The magazine suggested that pupils recite the affirmation "I pledge allegiance to my Flag and the Republic for which it stands. One Nation, indivisible, with Liberty and Justice for all." (At that point, less than thirty years after the end of the Civil War, the word "indivisible" was probably the most likely to cause argument.) In the midst of World War II, Congress adopted rules and regulations regarding the display and use of the flag. The pledge, with some word changes, was included. Congress added two words to the pledge in 1954 that are at the heart of the more recent controversy.

At the time of the Cold War, when many saw communism as the next ideological battleground, Congress added the words "under God" to the pledge to show how the United States differed from countries under the communist governments (and perhaps to seek divine blessings). The legislative history accompanying this change makes clear that this change occurred to insert the notion of a deity into the pledge language. The House report stressed "the belief that the human person is important because he was created by God and endowed by him with certain inalienable rights which no civil authority may usurp. The inclusion of God in our pledge therefore would further acknowledge the dependence of our people and our government upon the moral directions of the Creator."[19] Even outside the school context, issues about the flag often evoke deep emotion. It was the focus of strident debate in 1989, when the Supreme Court invalidated a state law in Texas (similar to that in forty-eight other states) that prohibited the desecration of the American flag. Five justices agreed that the act of burning the flag was protected speech.[20]

But the Pledge of Allegiance issue was not dead, and it once again took center stage in 2002 when a federal appeals court ruled, in *Newdow v. U.S. Congress*, that the mere *recitation* of the pledge in public schools was unconstitutional. The opinion set off an uproar of almost primal force. Unlike the earlier pledge cases, this one was filed by an atheist. In March 2000, Michael Newdow, an emergency room physician and father of a school-aged daughter, filed a lawsuit claiming that the school district policy of reciting the pledge with the words "under God" in his daughter's kindergarten class was unconstitutional. The California policy allowed those with religious objections to refrain (as it must under *Barnette*), but Newdow nonetheless objected that his daughter was exposed to others reciting a pledge that invoked God. Both a magistrate judge and a district court judge determined that the pledge does not violate the establishment clause and dismissed the complaint.

The Ninth Circuit reversed in a 2–1 opinion that held that the school district policy was unconstitutional.[21] The court determined that the policy coerced a religious act. Just being present in the classroom while other students recite the pledge has a coercive effect. It puts students in the position of either participating in an exercise with religious content or protesting.

Perhaps a federal court opinion that ruled that the Pledge of Allegiance was unconstitutional would have caused a furor at any time. This opinion, however, came only nine months after the attacks of September 11, 2001, and only one week before the nation's first Independence Day celebration since the attacks. After 9/11, many people in the country flew the flag for the first time. The song *God Bless America* was heard at public gatherings ranging from car rallies to baseball games. The level of patriotism was at its highest in decades, and it was as if people believed that the sight of the flag would ward off evil. When the Ninth Circuit decision was delivered, the outcry breached the political aisle, with Democratic senator Tom Daschle labeling the decision "nuts" and President George W. Bush calling it "ridiculous." Members of Congress rushed to the steps of the Capitol to recite the pledge in unison. The next day both chambers let other business wait as the Senate (99–0) passed a bill that reaffirmed the pledge (and the national mottos "In God We Trust") and the House (416–3) passed a resolution denouncing the court's decision.

If ever there was a time in recent history when—to paraphrase the words of Justice Frankfurter—national security seemed bound up with national unity, this was it. ("National unity is the basis of national security"—*Gobitis*, 310 U.S. 586, 596.) The Supreme Court granted certiorari "in light of the obvious importance of the [Ninth Circuit] decision." There were forty-eight amicus briefs filed, from the Associated Pantheist Groups to the Christian Legal Society. The numbers on each side were fairly evenly divided, with those supporting the school system having a slight edge. The appetite of the press was insatiable.

With such a high-profile case, there is always a charged atmosphere in the courtroom the day that it becomes apparent the opinion will be read. With all the hoopla surrounding the case, the Supreme Court's resolution did not live up to the billing. It simply failed to answer the pledge question at all. As it turned out, Newdow did not have legal custody of his daughter. The child's mother, Sandra Banning, had legal custody, and she filed a motion stating that neither she nor her daughter objected either to reciting or hearing others recite the pledge. In an opinion written by Justice John Paul Stevens, the Supreme Court ruled that Michael Newdow did not have standing (the legal right to initiate a lawsuit) to challenge the school district's policy. The Court reversed the court of appeals, but it never reached the First Amendment issue.

Chief Justice Rehnquist, joined by Justices O'Connor and Thomas in part (Justice Scalia did not participate in the case) concurred that the Ninth Circuit opinion should be reversed, but they would have reached the merits of the First Amendment issue. The chief justice set forth numerous examples of patriotic invocations of God that have occurred throughout the nation's history, including Washington's first inaugural address, his Thanksgiving proclamation, the Gettysburg Address, Lincoln's second inaugural address, Woodrow Wilson's request of Congress for a declaration of war, the statements of other presidents, the national motto, and the opening words for each meeting of the Supreme Court itself, "God save the

United States and this honorable court." These events strongly suggest that "our national culture allows public recognition of our Nation's religious history and character." These three justices maintained that reciting the pledge or listening to others recite it is a patriotic exercise rather than a religious one; the pledge affirms fidelity to the flag, not to God or any church. This is not an "establishment" of religion at school. Moreover, unlike *Barnette*, the students were not compelled to recite the pledge on pain of expulsion, but could opt out if they wished without consequence.

In addition to joining the chief, both Justice O'Connor and Justice Thomas wrote separate concurrences. Justice Thomas's opinion is of particular interest, as he is likely to be on the Court if the issue arises again in the next few years. He used this concurrence to set forth his view that it was time to rethink the establishment clause. Justice Thomas stated unequivocally that the pledge policy was unconstitutional under current Supreme Court precedent. He would, however, revisit the Court's establishment clause jurisprudence, which he said was in "hopeless disarray" and led to results that "can only be described as silly." He argued that the First Amendment establishment clause should not have been subject to incorporation under the Fourteenth Amendment at all. If Justice Thomas's view gains adherents under a new configuration of justices on the Court, the establishment clause could be in for a massive overhaul.

But the Court left that issue for another day. The opinion was rather anticlimactic after such a huge buildup. *Newdow* was—as the district court called it—a "cause celebre in the ongoing struggle as to the role of religion in the civil life of this nation." The issue was unlikely to stay buried, and it arose again like a hydra monster when Newdow was joined by two sets of parents who had no custody issues to muddy the waters. The question they raised was whether the Supreme Court's reversal based on standing left the Ninth Circuit's opinion on the establishment clause intact. The district court determined that the Supreme Court reversed the case because Newdow lacked prudential standing rather than because he lacked article 3 standing. The intricacies of standing analysis are not important here; what is important is that the remaining portion of the *Newdow* opinion (the part about the establishment clause) was still binding on the district court and on the states in the Ninth Circuit.

In the wake of *Newdow*, pledge policies in other states have also come under scrutiny. The state of Virginia successfully defended its pledge statute (requiring daily voluntary recitation of the pledge in public schools) before the Fourth Circuit Court of Appeals.[22] The court determined that the pledge did not threaten an establishment of religion and was not a religious exercise. The pledge is far less of a threat to established religion than legislative prayer, President Washington's prayer of thanksgiving, and the words of the Declaration of Independence (stating that all men were "endowed by their creator"), none of which was an establishment of religion either.

The court of appeals pointed out that justices denouncing other religious exercises had been careful to exclude the pledge from being implicated. For example, Justice Brennan stated that the reference to God in the pledge was a form of "ceremonial deism" that had lost its religious content by rote repetition.[23] (It seems ironic that Justice Brennan thought the reference to God was acceptable because it was *meaningless*. The fact that constant repetition of religious words in school makes them meaningless, perhaps even degrading religion, could be an interesting part of the school prayer discussion.)

Put simply, the Fourth Circuit viewed the recitation of the pledge, despite the insertion of the phrase "under God," as a patriotic exercise that acknowledges the ideals the flag symbolizes. The pledge does not constitute a personal communication between the individual and his or her deity. As such it is not a religious exercise and is "of no moment under the establishment clause."

Although there is no record that the plaintiff appealed this case to the Supreme Court, this split between two circuit courts of appeal (the Ninth and Fourth Circuits) is just the kind of thing that gets the attention of the Court when a petition for certiorari is filed. Given today's climate of litigation on the pledge of allegiance, it is likely that the Supreme Court will have the chance to revisit the issue before long.

> Of all the issues the ACLU takes on—reproductive rights, discrimination, jail and prison conditions, abuse of kids in the public schools, police brutality to name a few—by far the most volatile issue is that of school prayer. Aside from our efforts to abolish the death penalty, it is the only issue that elicits death threats.
>
> —Parish, "Graduation Prayer Violates the Bill of Rights," *Utah Bar Journal* (June–July 1991), quoted in *Lee v. Weisman* 505 U.S. 577 (1992) (Blackmun, J., concurring).

There may still be some argument about whether the words "under God" in the Pledge of Allegiance make it a religious exercise, but there is little question whether prayer in school amounts to a religious exercise. Nonetheless school prayer was an integral part of the school day for most schoolchildren throughout the nation until the mid–twentieth century. There were some early challenges. Toward the end of the nineteenth century, questions arose whether these religious exercises were acceptable under various *state* constitutions. (At this time the Supreme Court had not yet stated that the First Amendment applied to state action.) Of the eighteen state courts that considered the issue, six had determined that compulsory religious exercises in the public school violated their state constitutions.[24] Of course, after the First Amendment was incorporated into the Due Process Clause of the Fourteenth Amendment, issues like school prayer were fair game for the federal courts and the federal constitution. The Supreme Court has addressed a number of cases dealing with student prayer in school settings and has yet to decide that the prayer at issue was acceptable.

The first case that reached the Supreme Court was filed in 1959—only five years after Congress added the words "under God" to the Pledge of Allegiance. In 1951 and again in 1955 the New York Board of Regents recommended that all local school boards require an "act of reverence to God" joined with the Pledge of Allegiance at the start of each school day. The recommended "act of reverence" consisted of reciting the following:

> Almighty father, we acknowledge our dependence upon Thee, and we beg Thy blessings upon us, our parents, our teachers and our country.

The parents of ten students in New Hyde Park, Long Island, New York, filed a lawsuit challenging a school district regulation requiring the recitation of this prayer. The issue reached the U.S. Supreme Court in 1962, in *Engel v. Vitale*.[25] It traveled to the Supreme Court by way of the New York state courts, which upheld the state's power to use the prayer, as long as students could be excused if their parents objected.

From the very first sentence of the Supreme Court's analysis, there was no doubt how Justice Hugo Black, the author (soon to gain more fame for his dissent in *Tinker*), felt about prayer in school: "We think that by using its public school system to encourage recitation of the Regent's prayer, the State of New York has adopted a practice wholly inconsistent with the Establishment Clause." Unlike the pledge cases, there was no question that this was a religious activity—"a solemn avowal of divine faith and supplication for the blessings of the Almighty." Justice Black's opinion made it clear that "it is no part of the business of government to compose official prayers for any group of the American people to recite as part of a religious program carried on by government." He discussed the historical roots that had made the nation's founders so wary of the dangers of a union between church and state, especially the strife that ensued when government put its stamp of approval on one form of worship or religious service.

The fact that the prayer was nondenominational and that students who objected were excused did not make it acceptable, Black wrote. The establishment clause was based on the belief that "a union of government and religion tends to destroy government and degrade religion." Religion is too personal and sacred to allow it to be corrupted by government officials. Nonetheless, Justice Black was quick to point out that the opinion was not meant to affect the recitation of historical documents or the singing of anthems that include a profession of faith in a Supreme Being or "many [other] manifestations in our public life of belief in God." These bore "no true resemblance" to the "unquestioned religious exercise" New York had sponsored with this prayer.

Justice Potter Stewart, the lone dissenter, began with a counterargument that would reverberate for decades to come. First, "We are a religious people whose institutions presuppose a Supreme Being."[26] The relevant issue was the history of the religious traditions of the nation's people, reflected in the countless practices of the institutions and officials of the government. These spiritual traditions of the nation are "deeply entrenched and highly cherished," and they are not part of the establishment of a state church.

Forcing change in a tradition, especially one that is "deeply entrenched and highly cherished," ignites the passion of press and people. "A wave of protest against the Supreme Court decision . . . swept the country" right after the case was decided.[27] School districts declared they would defy the Court's ruling, members of Congress proposed a constitutional amendment to undermine the decision, and church leaders railed against it.[28] Many called the opinion a victory for communism.

Not all reaction from religious communities was negative, as some rabbis and some Unitarian Universalist ministers approved of the ban. President John Kennedy tried to calm the waters by explaining that the decision would stimulate the private practice of faith.[29] The Supreme Court was inundated with mail about the decision, reportedly the most mail received in the Court's history. The Court keeps the content of these letters secret, so there was no report about how the writers viewed the decision.[30] In what was called "an extraordinary spectacle," Congress put aside all its serious business for several days while its members denounced the Supreme Court.[31] Of course, the Court is supposed to rise above the influence of public emotion. But Court-watchers worried that its broad opinion in *Engel* would undermine its leadership at a crucial time for race relations and other important social issues.[32]

Despite this reaction to *Engel* (or perhaps because of it), the Court accepted another school prayer case the next year.[33] In this case, *School District of Abington Township v. Schempp,* the Court invalidated Bible reading in schools. The *Schempp* case was heard with a companion case, *Murray v. Curlett,* which helped to make a celebrity of one of the litigants. *Schempp* involved a Pennsylvania law requiring daily Bible readings; *Murray* involved a Maryland law requiring a Bible reading or the recitation of the Lord's Prayer.

The plaintiff, Bill Murray (no relation to the actor) was a fourteen-year-old whose mother filed suit with him as his "next friend." Her name was Madalyn Murray at the time, and she was later known as Madalyn Murray O'Hair. The Schempps kept a low profile, but O'Hair became a champion of atheism and a pariah of the prayerful. She was a lightning rod for much of the high emotion that ruled the day, and in 1964 *Life* magazine called her "the most hated woman in America."[34]

During World War II, Madalyn Mays had enlisted and served in the Women's Auxiliary Army Corps, where she had met Bill's father, William Murray. Murray denied he was the child's father, and Mays sued him to prove paternity and obtain child support. Murray was Catholic, and O'Hair's son William has speculated that Murray's refusal to divorce his wife (although perhaps not solely because of the Church) may have provoked his mother's antipathy to all things religious. O'Hair had two additional children with other men; she never married. Although she maintained that she was not a communist, she joined the Socialist Labor Party and the Socialist Workers Party, and she applied for Soviet citizenship in 1959. William Murray has claimed that his mother filed the school prayer case in a reaction to her failed attempt at defection.

After she won the case, O'Hair, working out of a Baltimore row house, ran the Freethought Society of America, which promoted atheism, and Other Americans, Inc., which instituted lawsuits against religious intervention in the secular world. She also published a monthly magazine called the *American Atheist.* One writer stated that he "had never seen anyone with such a breathtaking willingness to endure public hatred."

This life filled with controversy had an ending nothing short of bizarre. In 1995, Madalyn Murray O'Hair disappeared, along with her son Jon and granddaughter Robin. A former employee had abducted them, forced them to withdraw over $500,000 from their bank accounts, murdered them, dismembered their bodies, and buried them in shallow graves. He led authorities to the bodies years later in 2001. It can only be termed an exquisite irony that her son William, the student plaintiff in the landmark case, had become a born-again Christian. He buried his mother near Austin, Texas. There was no prayer at the burial.[35]

It is yet another ironic twist that though O'Hair achieved great notoriety, the Supreme Court case that helped to foster it does not bear her name. Instead the case is known by the name of the quiet and reserved Edward Schempp who, with his wife, Sidney, and his children claimed that the doctrines in school Bible readings were contrary to their religious beliefs and familial teachings under the Unitarian faith. The Supreme Court used the *Schempp* case to fashion a test to use to when analyzing state legislation dealing with religious belief or expression. "The test may be stated as follows:

What are the purpose and primary effect of the enactment? If either is the advancement or inhibition of religion, then the enactment exceeds the scope of legislative power as circumscribed by the Constitution." Thus to be valid under the establishment clause, state legislation must have a secular purpose, and it must have a "primary effect that neither advances nor inhibits religion." This is the genesis of what is now known as the *Lemon* test (from *Lemon v. Kurtzman,* 403 U.S. 602 [1971], in which the Court invalidated a Rhode Island statute that gave a salary supplement to teachers in private parochial schools).

The Court's application of the test seems a bit perfunctory. With regard to the purpose of the state legislation, the Court determined that even though the Bible could be used for secular purposes—to promote general good moral values and to teach literature—this was not the situation here. The Bible was used as an instrument of religion, and the ceremonies had a "pervading religious character." After analyzing the purpose prong, the Court did not go further to explain how Bible reading had the primary effect of advancing religion. It simply stated that the state was requiring religious exercises in school and that "such exercises are being conducted in direct violation of the rights of [the Schempps and the Murrays]."

The Court ended by pointing out that its ruling actually protected religion, rather than demeaned it. The author of the opinion, Justice Tom C. Clark, likened religion to a citadel that needed to be made safe from government intrusion. "The place of religion in our society is an exalted one, achieved through a long tradition of reliance on the home, the church and the inviolable citadel of the individual heart and mind. . . . [I]t is not within the power of government to invade that citadel, whether its purpose or effect be to aid or oppose, to advance or retard."

Justice William Brennan's concurrence was almost three times as long as the majority opinion Justice Clark wrote. This may have been because Brennan was originally assigned the majority opinion but could not obtain four more votes. He also may have felt pressure as a member of the Roman Catholic Church to explain himself in detail. His opinion is of interest not only because of its length, but because it set forth two scenarios that were taken up by legislatures and the courts in the future. First, Justice Brennan suggested that a moment of reverent silence could be an acceptable substitute for prayer. He cited editorials from the *Washington Post* and the *New York Times* that discussed starting the school day "with a quiet moment that would still the tumult of the playground and start a day of study." Twenty years later, the Court was faced with an establishment clause issue regarding a moment of silence in Alabama schools, in *Wallace v. Jaffree* (discussed later).

Justice Brennan also discussed at great length provisions that allowed students to excuse themselves from prayer. He expressed concern that refraining from prayer was tantamount in the eyes of teachers and classmates to professing disbelief or nonconformity, and this might deter children from exercising their constitutional right to be excused. This situation subjects these students to a "cruel dilemma," as children might be reluctant to be "stigmatized" as atheists or nonconformists. As Edward Schempp pointed out in his testimony, at that time, the word "atheist" was often tied to "atheistic communism" and had a bad connotation in the minds of children and many adults. Justice Brennan emphasized that children are disinclined to flout peer-group norms, and he inserted a lengthy note citing various behavioral science studies attesting to the susceptibility of schoolchildren to peer-group pressure. Almost thirty years after *Schempp*, this issue came to the forefront when the Supreme Court decided *Lee v. Weisman* (also discussed later).

Justice Stewart was again the lone dissenter. He chided the majority for its failure to recognize that religion and government "must necessarily interact in countless ways." He expressed concern that the refusal to permit these religious exercises was based not on state neutrality but on a preference for a "religion of secularism" or government support of those who believe that religious exercises should be conducted only in private.

> "The inviolable citadel of the individual heart and mind."
>
> —Justice Thomas C. Clark, *School District of Abington Township v. Schempp,* 374 U.S. 203 (1963)

Given Justice Brennan's invitation in his *Schempp* concurrence, it is not surprising that some states passed statutes requiring a moment of silence at the start of the school day. A challenge to a law passed by the state of Alabama gave the Court another chance to address the issue of religion in the public school. A tortuous litigation that lasted over six years began in 1982 when an agnostic parent, Ishmael Jaffree, filed a lawsuit on behalf of his three children challenging the constitutionality of three Alabama statutes: the "meditation" statute (enacted in 1978 and authorizing a one-minute period of silence "for meditation"; the "meditation or prayer" statute (enacted in 1981 and authorizing a period of silence for "meditation or voluntary prayer"); and the "prayer" statute (enacted in 1982 and authorizing teachers to lead willing students in a prescribed prayer to "Almighty God").

In the first stage, the district court had to decide whether the plaintiffs were entitled to an injunction to keep the school district from implementing the prayer until a trial could occur that would decide the case on the merits. The governor of Alabama, Fob James, together with the state's attorney general, maintained that the federal courts had no jurisdiction over the case because prayer flowed from the Almighty and no court has power over the requirements of the Lord or the prayers of his people. Some private citizens also joined the case, claiming that denying a citizen the right to the free exercise of their religion in the public schools was itself unconstitutional.

The district court countenanced no argument regarding its jurisdiction and said so plainly. One of the considerations in granting an
injunction is whether the plaintiffs are likely to prevail on the merits of the issue at trial. The court stated clearly and unequivocally
(the importance of this will become apparent later) that the First
Amendment was incorporated by the Fourteenth Amendment.
Moreover, the "clear import of [the] controlling decisions [of the
Supreme Court is] . . . that the state shall not involve itself in either
prescribing or proscribing religious activity."

As noted, in the years since *Engel* and *Schempp*, the Supreme
Court had crafted a test, known as "the *Lemon* test," of any law
challenged on establishment grounds. Under this test, the law in
question must (1) clearly reflect a secular purpose; (2) have a primary effect that neither advances nor inhibits religion; and (3)
avoid excessive government entanglement with religion. This test
has been the subject of much controversy. Despite calls for its removal, the *Lemon* test is still alive as of this writing.

The district court concluded that there was nothing wrong with
the meditation statute, but that the plaintiffs were likely to prevail
regarding the meditation-prayer statute and the prayer statute.
Both statutes failed the first prong of the *Lemon* test, as they did not
reflect a clearly secular purpose. The legislative preamble to the
prayer statute stated that its purpose was to provide for prayer in
the public schools, and the sponsor of the prayer-meditation statute
stated that its purpose was to return voluntary prayer to the Alabama schools. The court stated that it was obligated to follow the
"binding precedent" of *Engel* and *Schempp*. Since the plaintiffs
seemed likely to prevail on the merits at trial, the court issued the
injunction to keep the two statutes from being implemented until a
trial could occur. The court did not enjoin the meditation statute,
since it prescribed only that "a child in school shall have the right to
meditate in silence and there is nothing wrong with a little meditation and quietness."

Despite his willingness to follow the case law handed down by the Supreme Court—at least at this point—Judge Brevard Hand could not resist adding his own view to the opinion: that courts reviewing these issues had ignored "the totality of what is religion." The word "religion" simply means a value held to be of supreme importance. Courts have failed to scrutinize atheism, materialism, agnosticism, communism, and socialism, all of which are ardently adhered to and advanced in the teachings presented to schoolchildren. The nation's laws are based on a Judeo-Christian ethic, and the courts have somehow decided that Christianity is the religion to be proscribed. The Constitution also prohibits the establishment of a "secular religion." Judge Hand asked the question "If the state cannot teach or advance Christianity, how can it teach or advance the Antichrist?"[36]

Judge Hand answered that question five months later after the trial on the merits. He not only changed his mind and ruled for the defendants but he attempted to turn the postincorporation world of constitutional law on its head. He declared that the Supreme Court had been in error in *Engel* and *Schempp* because the establishment clause could not be used against the states. He reviewed the history of the Bill of Rights through the lens of two legal scholars, James McClellan and Robert L. Cord and determined that the state of Alabama was free to establish religion as it saw fit.

The lawyers for the defendants put forth volumes of historical evidence and scholarly argument that ultimately convinced Judge Hand that much of the Supreme Court's jurisprudence in recent decades was built on a groundless premise. McClellan testified at the trial itself, and Judge Hand quoted him liberally throughout the opinion. McClellan asserted that the First Amendment guaranteed to individuals that the federal government would not impose a national religion, and to states that they were free to deal with the establishment issue under their own laws. Professor Cord might as well have been present in person, for his writings were also very much a part of the decision.

The analysis has two prongs. First, the meaning of "establishment" has nothing to do with a wall of separation between church and state. Second, the establishment clause applies only to Congress, not to state legislatures. With respect to the first prong, Judge Hand found "reasonable" Cord's views regarding James Madison and Thomas Jefferson—the two First Amendment framers generally believed to have been the most adamant about the separation of church and state. Cord believed that this traditional view is "historically faulty, if not virtually unfounded," and that the historical record paints a different picture.

For example, Cord pointed out that Jefferson proposed a treaty with the Kaskaskia Indians providing for federal money to be used to support a Catholic priest and to build a church. Drawing on Cord's views, Judge Hand stated, "One thing which becomes abundantly clear after reviewing the historical record is that the founding fathers . . . and the framers . . . never intended the establishment clause to erect an absolute wall of separation between the federal government and religion." The high and impregnable wall Justice Black had described in *Everson v. Board of Education* is "revisionary literary flourish."[37]

After determining that the meaning of "establishment" in the First Amendment was circumscribed, Judge Hand went on to conclude that it had never been incorporated by the Fourteenth Amendment in the first place. This time he relied on another professor, Charles Fairman, and an article he published in the *Stanford Law Review* in 1949 ("Does the Fourteenth Amendment Incorporate the Bill of Rights?"). There has been much scholarly debate, sometimes heated, about whether the sponsors of the Fourteenth Amendment intended to make the Bill of Rights applicable to the states. After reading many articles on the subject, Judge Hand decided that "the weight of the disinterested scholars supports the analysis of Professor Fairman." (He discounted the writings of one professor, William Crosskey, because his analysis was merely ad hominem attacks on Fairman and appeared to be result-oriented.)[38]

Along with Professor Fairman, Judge Hand found that the historical record conclusively demonstrated that (1) the debates in Congress did not show that Congress intended to incorporate the Bill of Rights against the states; (2) the popular sentiment (evidenced by review of contemporary newspapers) did not understand that incorporation was part of the Fourteenth Amendment; (3) members of Congress did not refer to incorporation in their campaign speeches in the fall after the Fourteenth Amendment was passed; (4) there was no evidence that state legislatures had understood that the Bill of Rights was incorporated when they debated ratification (and many states would have had to radically change their state laws regarding rights like jury trials to comply with the federal Bill of Rights); and (5) Supreme Court decisions of the time showed that the justices did not believe that the Fourteenth Amendment incorporated the Bill of Rights. For example, in 1875, nine years after Congress passed the Fourteenth Amendment, James Blaine of Maine proposed what became known as the Blaine Amendment at the request of President Ulysses Grant: "No STATE shall make any law respecting an establishment of religion or prohibiting the free exercise thereof." Twenty-three members of that Congress had also been members when the Fourteenth Amendment had been passed. Although the Blaine Amendment ultimately did not pass, no one even hinted that the Fourteenth Amendment had covered this issue, as the Congressmen would surely have done if it had incorporated the First Amendment. In fact, some Congressmen instead had stated that the amendment would deprive states of powers they currently possessed.

Having demonstrated that the Supreme Court got it wrong when it started applying the Bill of Rights to the states through the Fourteenth Amendment, Judge Hand's next step was to note that a judge had to remember "above all else that it is the Constitution which he swore to support and defend, not the gloss which his predecessors may have put upon it" (quoting an article by none other than William O. Douglas, "Stare Decisis," in the *Columbia Law Review*).[39] According to Judge Hand, "the United States Supreme Court has erred in its reading of history." There may have been "pebbles on the beach of history," but scholars and judges had used those pebbles to establish a beachhead. Their conclusion had been based on faulty analysis and interpretation of history. Acknowledging that his opinion might amount to "no more than a voice crying in the wilderness," Judge Hand nonetheless marched on, vowing to give no future generation a way to use more pebbles to build a beachhead.

Although Judge Hand's opinion ultimately was not accepted (our country would certainly be very different today if it had), it demonstrates the considerable weight such a historical argument still carried, and both the confusion and fervor that still surrounds any discussion of religion in school. Less than a month after Judge Hand dismissed the constitutional challenge, Justice Powell entered a stay that stopped Judge Hand from dissolving the preliminary injunction, and the Eleventh Circuit took up the appeal.

The Eleventh Circuit Court of Appeals reversed Judge Hand, but its opinion did little to determine the true meaning of the establishment clause. The court acknowledged that there were two views on the matter and explained that Judge Hand agreed with historians who maintained that the clause prohibits only Congress from establishing a religion. Without citing any historical record that contradicted this contention, the appeals court merely stated: "The Supreme Court, however, has carefully considered these arguments and rejected them."

The court of appeals then cited and quoted Supreme Court cases that took a broader view of the establishment clause—cases that looked at the historical context from the perspective of the framers. For example, *Engel* pointed out that history showed there was a widespread awareness among Americans of the danger of a union of church and state. The *Engel* opinion did indeed make this point, but it did not cite or quote any historians for support. The appeals court quoted *Engel*'s pronouncement that "Under [the First Amendment's] prohibition against governmental establishment of religion, as reinforced by the provisions of the Fourteenth Amendment, government in this country, be it state or federal is without power to prescribe by law any particular form of prayer which is to be used as an official prayer in carrying on any program of governmentally sponsored religious activity."[40] The Eleventh Circuit certainly quoted the *Engel* opinion correctly, but a review of the *Engel* opinion itself shows that it contained no citations from previous cases or from historical documents to support this proclamation about state government power.

The Eleventh Circuit did not attempt to determine which argument was more persuasive. Instead, it said, "The important point is: *the Supreme Court has considered and decided the historical implications surrounding the Establishment Clause.* The Supreme Court has concluded that its present interpretation of the first and fourteenth amendments is consistent with the historical evidence."[41] Thus the salient issue was the Supreme Court's conclusion, not whether that conclusion is correct. Indeed, the Eleventh Circuit panel stressed this point: Judge Hatchett stated, "If the Supreme Court errs, no other court may correct it." Justice Thomas's dissent in *Newdow* suggests that at least one justice would like to reconsider the issue.

Once it determined that the First Amendment applied to the case, the court of appeals analyzed whether the prayer statute or the meditation-prayer statute passed the *Lemon* test, and determined that both statutes failed it. The intent of the prayer statute was to advance religious beliefs, and the intent of the meditation-prayer statute was to return prayer to the public schools. "We do not decide today whether prayer in school is the proper policy to follow. This court merely applies the principles established by the Supreme Court."

That body was the next one to explore the issue of prayer and meditation in Alabama's public schools. It summarily affirmed the court of appeals with regard to the prayer statute. The parties never contested Judge Hand's ruling that there was nothing wrong with the meditation statute. Thus the only question before the Supreme Court was whether the meditation-prayer statute passed constitutional muster. Justice John Paul Stevens delivered the opinion for the Court, joined by Justices Brennan, Marshall, Blackmun, and Powell, and determined that the statute could not stand. (By this time, Governor George Wallace had replaced Governor Fob James, so the case became known as *Wallace v. Jaffree*.)[42] Justice Stevens addressed what he called Judge Hand's "remarkable" conclusion that the establishment clause did not apply to the Alabama case. He pointed out "how firmly embedded in our constitutional jurisprudence is the proposition that the several States have no greater power to restrain the individual freedoms protected by the First Amendment than does the Congress of the United States." Justice Stevens stated that the Fourteenth Amendment imposed the same limitations on the states that the First Amendment had put on Congress. "This Court has confirmed and endorsed this elementary proposition of law time and time again."

Of course, confirming a proposition, no matter how many times it happens, does not mean that the proposition was correct at the outset. Judge Hand would say that this merely meant that the Court had turned a few pebbles on the beach into a beachhead. Justice Stevens's basis of support came from past Supreme Court cases, starting with *Cantwell v. Connecticut*.[43] But tracing back the proposition's pedigree yields little insight for rigorous analysis. In *Cantwell*, Justice Roberts stated that the word "liberty" in the Fourteenth Amendment ("no state shall deprive any person of life, liberty or property without due process of law") included the liberties that were guaranteed by the First Amendment. Justice Roberts cited *Schneider v. State* (308 U.S. 147 [1939]) for support. *Schneider* stated that the First Amendment applied to the states and cited *Gitlow v. New York.* In *Gitlow,* Justice Edward Sanford wrote, "For present purposes we may and do assume that the freedom of speech and of the press—which are protected by the First Amendment from abridgement by Congress—are among the fundamental personal rights and 'liberties' protected by the Due Process Clause of the Fourteenth Amendment from impairment by the States." But it is that very assumption that Fairman and others questioned. Merely repeating the statement without explaining *why* this is so does little to support the argument and fails to counter Fairman's point that those who passed the statute and the contemporary polity did not intend to have the word "liberty" carry the entire Bill of Rights on its back.

The Court left this complex issue for another day. Justice Stevens quoted Justice Jackson's famous "fixed star" passage from *Barnette,* and cautioned: "The State of Alabama, no less than the Congress of the United States, must have respect for that basic truth." As for the issue of meditation or prayer, the statute failed the first prong of the *Lemon* test, because its purpose was to advance religion. The sponsor of the bill left no doubt that its purpose was to return voluntary prayer to the public school, and the state did not present evidence of any secular purpose.

Justice Sandra O'Connor's concurrence began with the emphatic statement "Nothing in the United States Constitution as interpreted by this Court or in the laws of the State of Alabama prohibits public school students from voluntarily praying at any time before, during, or after the school day." This is reminiscent of the old canard that many teachers recite, "There will be prayer in school as long as we give math tests." Justice O'Connor suggested a refinement of the *Lemon* test—an examination whether the government's purpose is to endorse religion and whether the statute in question actually conveys a message of endorsement. Under this test, even if a statute stated that a student could choose to pray in a quiet moment, the state has not encouraged or endorsed prayer over other alternative thoughts that the student might have. Nonetheless, the legislative history and the text of this statute from Alabama showed that its purpose was to endorse prayer in the public schools.

Although three justices dissented from the opinion, none of them joined hands with Judge Hand (sorry) in his determination that the Fourteenth Amendment did not apply the establishment clause to the states. Justice Rehnquist (not yet chief) made much of the historical argument about the meaning of the establishment clause, however. He used historical writings from the time of the Bill of Rights and from early legal scholars that undercut the idea of a "wall of separation" between church and state. The phrase came from a letter Thomas Jefferson wrote to the Danbury Baptist Association fourteen years after the Bill of Rights was passed by Congress. The Supreme Court used it in an 1879 case dealing with the free exercise clause and a Mormon challenge to federal polygamy law *(Reynolds v. United States)*, and it has been an enduring metaphor ever since.[44] Like Judge Hand, Justice Rehnquist maintained that the Court had built constitutional doctrine around a mistaken understanding of constitutional history, and he insisted that the establishment clause was designed to prohibit the designation of a national church or any preference for one sect over another.[45]

> The task of separating the secular from the religious in education is one of magnitude, intricacy and delicacy.
>
> —Illinois ex rel. *McCollum v. Board of Education,* 333 U.S. 203 (1948) (Justice Jackson, concurring).

After prayer was erased from the daily routine in the classroom, it still remained in the public schools. Prayer was a routine part of many graduation ceremonies, and this issue reached the Supreme Court in 1992 in *Lee v. Weisman*. The case arose in Providence, Rhode Island at a middle school graduation. Perhaps in an effort not to show preference for one church over another, as suggested in Justice Rehnquist's *Wallace* dissent, the City of Providence, Rhode Island had a practice of inviting clergy from various religions to speak at school graduations. The clergy were provided with a pamphlet, written by the National Conference of Christians and Jews entitled "Guidelines for Civic Occasions," that recommended prayer at nonsectarian civic occasions be conducted with "inclusiveness and sensitivity." At a graduation ceremony at Nathan Bishop Middle School, Rabbi Leslie Gutterman of the Temple Beth El in Providence conducted the following prayers.

INVOCATION

God of the Free, Hope of the Brave: For the legacy of America where diversity is celebrated and the rights of minorities are protected, we thank You. May these young men and women grow up to enrich it. For the liberty of America, we thank You. May these new graduates grow up to guard it. For the political process of America in which all its citizens may participate, for its court system where all may seek justice we thank You. May those we honor this morning always turn to it in trust. For the destiny of America we thank You. May the graduates of Nathan Bishop Middle School so live that they might help to share it. May our aspirations for our country and for these young people, who are our hope for the future, be richly fulfilled. AMEN

BENEDICTION

O God, we are grateful to You for having endowed us with the capacity for learning which we have celebrated on this joyous commencement. Happy families give thanks for seeing their children achieve an important milestone. Send Your blessings upon the teachers and administrators who helped prepare them. The graduates now need strength and guidance for the future, help them to understand that we are not complete with academic knowledge alone. We must each strive to fulfill what You require of us all: To do justly, to love mercy, to walk humbly. We give thanks to You, Lord, for keeping us alive, sustaining us and allowing us to reach this special, happy occasion. AMEN

Deborah Weisman and her father brought a lawsuit seeking an injunction barring the public schools in Providence from inviting the clergy to give invocations and benedictions at graduation ceremonies. The district court ruled that the practice violated the establishment clause *Lemon* test because it created an identification of governmental power with religious practice and endorsed religion.[46] The court of appeals affirmed.[47]

When the case reached the Supreme Court, the city of Providence hired Charles J. Cooper, a young, confident appellate litigator. He had recently been hired at Shaw, Pittman, Potts and Trowbridge, a staid Washington law firm best known for its real estate and banking practice. Many of the attorneys at Shaw Pittman had been together for decades, working their way up from new associate to partner. Cooper was hired to inject some energy into the firm's litigation practice. He was a consummate showman; arguing a Supreme Court case that had garnered national attention was right up his alley.

Cooper was proud of the time he had spent as a law clerk to then Justice William Rehnquist, and he displayed a large signed photograph of all the justices on the wall—just to the left—as you entered his office. Associates at Shaw Pittman vied for the opportunity to work with Cooper, as the work he brought in was interesting, and he was generally good-humored. They called him "Little Eddie" behind his back, because his hair was combed back from a widow's peak like the character in the television show *The Munsters,* but the appellation was used more in affection than derision. Some partners at the firm, however, were suspicious of litigation generally and particularly suspicious of this new flamboyant presence.[48]

Cooper's written brief to the Court covered all the necessary points, but he seemed to enjoy his preparation for the oral argument the best. He planned his time before the court like a military attack, trying to work out a plan for every contingency and every possible question a justice might ask. He held moot court arguments with people like Jay Sekulow and Michael Carvin. Sekulow later became the chief counsel for the American Center for Law and Justice, and *Time* magazine named him "The Almighty's Attorney at Law" and one of the twenty-five most influential evangelicals in America.[49] He reappears when he argues the next big school prayer case before the Supreme Court, *Santa Fe Independent School District v. Doe* in 2000 (discussed later). Michael Carvin, a brilliant attorney, would later garner a measure of fame when he argued for the Bush campaign before the Florida Supreme Court during the 2000 election controversy.

The Supreme Court justices do not convene in the courtroom every day, and excitement is always in the air on oral argument day. Oral argument before the Supreme Court is a dignified and serious event surrounded by pomp and tradition. The large hall leading up to the courtroom and the courtroom itself are imposing structures; even the architecture contributes to the solemnity of the occasion. The public is admitted, but no one but the press (seated in the front behind columns on the left) and the justices' law clerks (seated behind columns on the right) is allowed to take notes or write during the argument. No television cameras are allowed. If anyone in the audience looks as though he or she is dozing off, a marshal will quickly walk over and give them a push to wake them up.

The black-robed justices enter the courtroom by walking through dark red curtains that hang behind the bench. As they enter, the Court's marshal cries out:

The Honorable, the Chief Justice and the Associate Justices of the Supreme Court of the United States. Oyez! Oyez! Oyez! All persons having business before the Honorable, the Supreme Court of the United States, are admonished to draw near and give their attention, for the Court is now sitting. God Save the United States and this Honorable Court!

The attorney who is arguing steps before the bench and stands at a podium. Some say it is the loneliest place in the world. The podium has lights that tell the attorney when the time allotted is up. Woe unto anyone who keeps talking after the red light flashes!

On November 6, 1991, the courtroom was packed. Chuck Cooper was set to lead off as attorney for the petitioner. He was to be followed by the solicitor general of the United States. The United States had submitted a brief as amicus curiae supporting the school district, and the solicitor general's office had petitioned the court for time at oral argument. It was a signal that the case was significant because the solicitor general had decided to argue the case himself rather than assigning it to a staff member. Thus Solicitor General Kenneth Starr was at the attorneys' table in the front of the courtroom. He was only a few years away from gaining the spotlight as the Independent Counsel investigating President William Clinton. One of his staff members who joined him on the government's brief was John G. Roberts, who would become Chief Justice of the Supreme Court after Chief Justice Rehnquist died fifteen years later. Also in the courtroom audience was the mayor of Providence, Vincent "Buddy" Cianci. Known as "the Prince of Providence," he was just a few years away from criminal indictment on racketeering, conspiracy, extortion, witness tampering, and mail fraud. Convicted of one count of conspiracy, he was sentenced to five years in prison.

Veteran Supreme Court watchers know the general question pattern of the justices. With this bench, for instance, the first question would usually come from Justice O'Connor or Justice Stevens, and Justice Kennedy was also likely to ask some questions early in the argument. Justice Scalia was always an avid questioner whose jabs could sometimes be scathing. Chief Justice Rehnquist might get up out of his chair in the middle of argument and leave the courtroom to walk back behind the curtain if his back was bothering him. Justices Thomas and Blackmun rarely asked questions at all.

As the argument began, Justice Blackmun surprised even those who knew him well. He seemed especially energized by this case, and Cooper hardly had introduced himself before he started peppering him with questions that seemed to throw Cooper off his game. Cooper barely said "may it please the Court" before Justice Blackmun interrupted him, asking "How old were these youngsters?" Cooper seemed surprised at the question and asked Justice Blackmun to repeat it. After hearing the question again, Cooper answered that the students were graduating from middle school to high school and were just completing the eighth grade. Justice Blackmun was not satisfied, "Well, how old were they is my question. You haven't answered me." Cooper seemed at a loss in the face of what might have been an easy factual question. He looked in confusion over at the attorneys sitting at his table, one of whom was frantically trying to signal something to him on a large piece of white paper. "Your Honor, I think—" At this point Justice Blackmun chimed in, "About thirteen or fourteen, aren't they?" "Yes, your Honor."

Cooper seemed relieved that he had finally satisfied Justice Blackmun, but it had knocked him off balance. He tried to focus on his argument that the "elegantly simple" graduation invocation was less of a threat to the establishment clause than the words "God save this honorable Court" in the Court's own opening ritual. He argued that the *Lemon* test should be reconsidered (he meant overruled) and a new test fashioned that asked whether there was government coercion of religious sentiment. Since the parents and students had stipulated to the fact that attendance at the graduation ceremony was voluntary, there was no coercion here.

Cooper's argument got into a tangle when one justice pressed him on how it would play in context with the free exercise clause (no law prohibiting the free exercise of religion). If Cooper was arguing that the establishment clause merely requires no government coercion and no government preference for one religion over another, "it wouldn't have a content different from the free exercise clause would it?" Cooper answered, "Your Honor, I believe that is an accurate statement." This is where he may have lost the vote of Justice Souter, who brought up this point in his concurrence: "[A] literal application of the coercion test would render the Establishment Clause a virtual nullity, as petitioner's counsel essentially conceded at oral argument."[50]

Cooper quoted language from an opinion by Justice Kennedy where he had expressed concern about "exhortations of religiosity that amounts to proselytization." Justice Kennedy had observed that this particular kind of prayer "may well cross the threshold of mere expression to coercion." But Cooper asserted that this kind of sectarian prayer was not at issue, because the prayer in the Providence schools "was clearly nondenominational." At that point he asked to reserve the balance of his time for rebuttal.

But Justice Blackmun wanted something clarified. "Mr. Cooper, let me ask you a question. You say it was nondenominational. I read from the benediction: 'We must each strive to fulfill what you require of us all, to do justly, to love mercy, to walk humbly.' That's lifted almost verbatim from the sixth verse of the eighth chapter of the prophet Micah, isn't it?" Again, Cooper seemed knocked off balance by the question. "Your Honor, I—I believe that you're right. Yes." "You *believe* so?" queried Justice Blackmun. Cooper replied, "I will not argue with that." Cooper maintained that he did not see how one could compose a prayer that did not include some phrases that had been used by different sects. As long as a prayer had phrases from different sects, it should still be considered a nonsectarian prayer.

Solicitor General Starr was next on the podium. He asked the Court to look to history and tradition in interpreting the establishment clause. He argued that the invocation and benediction in this case was "a far cry from practices that the founding fathers meant to stop." Answering a question Justice Stevens posed, Starr acknowledged that the same prayer in the classroom would be coercive and thus unconstitutional, since it was part and parcel of compulsory attendance laws and an instructional program with a teacher in control. By contrast, graduation is a ceremonial event without the type of coercion that is present in the classroom.

Sandra Blanding, of Revens and DeLuca, a small firm in Warwick, Rhode Island, argued the case for the Weismans. Blanding was experienced in dealing with the constitution and religion; she had been the ACLU attorney for a lawsuit on behalf of the Hmong family whose son's body had been autopsied against their religious beliefs and for *Donnelly v. Lynch,* a challenge to a nativity scene erected under the auspices of the city of Pawtucket, Rhode Island.[51] The *Donnelly* case had also reached the highest court in the land. After the lower federal courts ruled that the display violated the establishment clause, the Supreme Court reversed. Blanding had been listed on the Supreme Court brief for that case, but she did not argue it before the Court. Now—with *Lee v. Weiman*—she had her chance.

Whereas Starr and Cooper had sought to distinguish the classroom from the graduation ceremony, the crux of Blanding's argument was on the distinction between prayer in a public school setting and other ceremonial invocations of religion, like that at the beginning of the Court sessions. She claimed that under any establishment clause test that had been proffered by the justices, this prayer did not meet constitutional muster. This included the *Lemon* test, the endorsement test Justice O'Connor favored, and the coercion test Justice Kennedy had set forth in a separate opinion in *County of Allegheny v. ACLU* (dealing with holiday displays).[52]

As Cooper had used up his rebuttal time answering Justice Blackmun's question about the Book of Micah, the Chief Justice thanked Blanding, and the case was submitted. The Court did not render its opinion in the case until the last week in June, over six months later. This is the final week before the Court recesses for the summer, and it is often when the opinions in the most contentious cases are finally handed down.[53]

If Chuck Cooper had been able to choose which justice would write the opinion, he would likely have chosen either Justice Scalia or Chief Justice Rehnquist, or perhaps Justice Thomas, all of whom read the Constitution as allowing school prayer that does not favor one religion over another. But Cooper had fashioned his argument to appeal to Justice Kennedy and the coercion test Kennedy had set forth in *Allegheny*. If Cooper had received word that Justice Kennedy had been assigned to write the opinion, he still would have anticipated a victory. When he learned of the 5–4 decision for the Weismans, Cooper walked into his office and turned his signed picture of the Supreme Court justices to the wall.

Justice Blackmun was the senior justice in the majority, and he could have kept the opinion for himself. Instead, it appears that he assigned it to Justice Kennedy, who was joined by Blackmun, Stevens, O'Connor, and Souter. (Justice Blackmun wrote a separate concurrence, and it is possible that he intended this to be the majority opinion, but it did not garner enough votes. The concurrence does not read as if it was a "lost majority" attempt, however; it merely argues that coercion, although sufficient for an establishment clause violation, is not necessary.)

At the outset of the majority opinion Justice Kennedy expressly declined the invitation to reconsider *Lemon,* but he did not mention *Lemon* again.[54] This obvious unwillingness to apply *Lemon* led some commentators to wonder if *Lemon* had been implicitly cast aside for some newer framework. If so, it is hard to discern exactly what it would be, as the opinion never precisely sets forth the test it is applying.

The opinion first discussed the degree of school involvement in the prayer: the principal deciding to have a prayer, deciding who would give it, and then giving the rabbi guidelines advising how to make the prayer nonsectarian. Turning to the experience of the students, the opinion noted that "there are heightened concerns with protecting freedom of conscience from subtle coercive pressure in the elementary and secondary schools."[55] In the context of a school graduation, students are under public pressure and peer pressure to stand or to maintain respectful silence. Justice Kennedy cited research in psychology showing that adolescents are susceptible to pressure from peers toward conformity and that this is strongest in matters of social convention.[56]

Justice Kennedy was not persuaded that attendance at the graduation was voluntary. To argue that a teenager had a real choice not to attend "one of life's most significant occasions" was "formalistic in the extreme."[57] Referring to *Marsh v. Chambers,* in which the Court had upheld a prayer at the opening of a state legislature, he noted that the influence and force of a formal exercise at a school graduation was much greater than that over adults at a legislative session.[58] Here, where young graduates who object to a religious exercise are induced to conform, there is a violation of the establishment clause.

Even those justices who joined Justice Kennedy's opinion were not entirely convinced by it. Justice Blackmun wrote a separate concurrence, joined by Justices Stevens and O'Connor, and Justice Souter wrote a separate opinion, also joined by Justices Stevens and O'Connor. Justice Scalia wrote a scathing dissent, joined by Chief Justice Rehnquist and Justices White and Thomas. Justice Scalia's opinions are often sarcastic and caustic, but this dissent was particularly so.

The dissent began with a quote from Justice Kennedy himself in *Allegheny.* He had said there that the meaning of the establishment clause should be determined by reference to history, but his opinion here was "conspicuously bereft of history." Instead, with a "bulldozer of social engineering," Justice Kennedy's opinion invented a "boundless" test of "psychological coercion."[59] Justice Scalia stated that it was "a sufficient embarrassment that Establishment Clause jurisprudence regarding holiday displays has come to 'requir[e] scrutiny more commonly associated with interior decorators than with the judiciary'" (quoting Judge Frank Easterbrook in a Seventh Circuit opinion). "But," says Justice Scalia, "Interior decorating is a rock-hard science compared to psychology practiced by amateurs." The argument that students were coerced to take part in the invocation and benediction at their graduation is "not to put too fine a point on it, incoherent." To assert that a student who sits and remains silent could be perceived as joining in prayers is "nothing short of ludicrous." Even if a student chooses to stand up, this merely signifies respect for the views of others.

Justice Scalia argued that the concept of coercion should not be expanded beyond "acts backed by threat of penalty—a brand of coercion that, happily, is readily discernible to those of us who have made a career of reading the disciples of Blackstone, rather than of Freud." Although Justice Scalia was pleased that the majority had ignored *Lemon* (hoping that this meant the "internment of that case"), replacing it with the new "psycho-coercion" test was "a jurisprudential disaster."

As with the other Supreme Court opinions on these complex issues, *Lee v. Weisman* left many questions unanswered, and it was up to the lower federal courts to use the opinion as a guideline for cases addressing the same issue with different facts. What if the person reciting the prayer was a student, instead of a religious leader selected by the school? What if the occasion was something that lacked the solemnity and importance of a graduation ceremony?

The school district of Santa Fe, Texas, a small community in the southern part of the state, became the focus in the next case in which the Supreme Court began to answer these questions. The plaintiffs—several schoolchildren and their parents—alleged that the school district engaged in several proselytizing activities, including promoting attendance at revival meetings, encouraging membership in religious clubs, distributing Gideon Bibles on school premises, and chastising children because of nonmainstream religious beliefs. The complaint also alleged that the district allowed students to read Christian invocations and benedictions at graduation ceremonies and to deliver Christian prayers over the public address system at home football games. The district court issued an interim order requiring the school district to establish policies to deal with "manifest First Amendment infractions of teachers, counsellors, [sic] or other District or school officials or personnel."

The district then formally adopted a series of policies. The graduation policy provided that students would hold two elections: first to decide whether a nonsectarian, nonproselytizing invocation and benediction should be part of the graduation ceremony, and if so, second, to decide which students would deliver them. Two months later the school district eliminated the nonsectarian, nonproselytizing requirement but provided a fallback provision to reinsert it if a district court so ordered.

The football policy, entitled "Prayer at Football Games," passed a month later, and provided for the same procedure as that for graduation. According to the court record, the students held an election and "chose to allow a student to say a prayer at football games." A week later they elected a student "to deliver the prayer at varsity football games." The school district made one more change after that, omitting the word "prayer" from the policy title and adding the words "statements" and "messages." It is that policy that was at issue in the case.

The district court in *Santa Fe* had some guidance beyond the *Lee* opinion. After *Lee*, but before *Santa Fe*, the Court of Appeals for the Fifth Circuit (which includes Texas) had ruled (in *Jones v. Clear Creek*) that allowing a student-selected, student-given, nonsectarian, nonproselytizing invocation at a high school graduation ceremony did not violate the establishment clause.[60] Because the football policy did not contain the "nonsectarian and nonproselytizing" limitation, the district court ordered that the alternative policy be implemented. Since it required the prayer to be nonsectarian and nonproselytizing, it was consistent with the *Clear Creek* case and therefore constitutional. With regard to the school district's liability for other past practices (i.e., other than at graduations and football games) the court granted summary judgment for the plaintiffs and proceeded to a trial for damages. At that trial the court determined that the incidents in question were isolated and not attributable to a policy or custom of the school district and that even if they were, there was no compensable harm.[61]

When the court of appeals heard the case, it confirmed that a "nonsectarian and nonproselytizing" limitation was necessary for a prayer policy to be constitutional. The majority opinion maintained that sectarian and proselytizing prayer changes the tenor and the focus of the event away from the student to the religious content of the speaker's prayers. It transforms the character of the occasion and by its polarizing and politicizing nature might even disrupt it. This kind of prayer fails both the purpose and the primary effect prongs of the *Lemon* test. It also violates the endorsement test, because it conveys the message that government endorses religion *and* a particular form of religion.[62]

But inserting the requirement for nonsectarian, nonproselytizing prayer was not enough to preserve prayer at football games. Although a prayer that is nonsectarian and nonproselytizing may be permissible to solemnize an annual high school graduation, the court of appeals ruled that high school football games are not "the sober type of annual event that can appropriately be solemnized by a prayer."[63] At this point, then, in the states in the Fifth Circuit, a student-led prayer that was nonsectarian and nonproselytizing was permissible at high school graduations, but no prayer at all was allowed at football games.

Regarding the damages for the other incidents the plaintiffs complained of, the appeals court agreed with the district court that there was no compensable harm to the plaintiffs—no specific, discernible injury to their emotional state.

Judge E. Grady Jolly dissented. Since the school policy involved merely speech by students, the state was not involved, and the court should not have placed a "judicial curse" on sectarian religious speech. Judge Jolly believed that *Lee* had "largely abandoned" the *Lemon* test, and he chastised the majority for using it. Oh, the tangled web of school prayer!

A concern that *Lee* was being misunderstood in the circuits might have prompted the Supreme Court to grant certiorari on the following question: "Whether [the school district] policy permitting student-led student-initiated prayer at football games violates the Establishment Clause." In a 6–3 opinion written by Justice Stevens, the court determined that it did.[64] The Court based much of its opinion on the language in *Lee*, but also made clear that reports of the demise of the *Lemon* test had been greatly exaggerated (at least for the time being).

Perhaps to ensure that he kept the votes of Justices Kennedy and O'Connor, Justice Stevens's opinion quoted *Lee* extensively and also inserted the endorsement test favored by Justice O'Connor. The school district had argued that *Lee* did not apply here because the speech/prayer at issue was private speech that by definition could not be government coercion. With invocations authorized by government policy and taking place on government property at a government/school-sponsored event, the Court majority was not persuaded by this argument.

According to the majority, the school policy involved both perceived and actual endorsement of religion. The school board chose to permit an invocation. The election was supervised by the school. The invocation was to have been given at a school-sponsored event over the school public address system, which school officials controlled. The team, the cheerleaders, and the band, as well as members of the crowd, are clothed in the traditional indicia of school sporting events. In this context, the audience would perceive this pregame message as a public expression of the views of a majority of the student body delivered with approval of the school administration. Moreover, the election was flawed because it ensured that minority views would never prevail and would effectively be silenced. Fundamental rights must not be subject to a majoritarian vote.

The Court was also unimpressed with the school district's argument that there was no coercion since attendance at a football game is voluntary. Although attendance was not required for all students, the Court noted that some students, like football players, cheerleaders, and band members, might be required to attend and even receive course credit for participation. Moreover, to assert that high school students do not feel immense social pressure to attend or that some do not have a truly genuine desire to be involved in this extracurricular event is, in the words of the *Lee* Court, "formalistic in the extreme." (I suspect that readers from certain parts of the country may be thinking that in some school districts the high school football game may be a more significant event than the graduation ceremony.)

At the very end of the opinion, the *Lemon* test got a reprieve. Because the football policy had been challenged before it went into practice, the claim against it was that it was unconstitutional on its face. That is, the policy as written would inevitably violate the establishment clause. Justice Stevens quoted Chief Justice Rehnquist's statement in another case that the test to use in facial challenges on establishment clause grounds is "the three factors in *Lemon v. Kurtzman.*" (This was a clever ploy by Justice Stevens, since Rehnquist was writing the dissent in *Santa Fe.*)

The football policy did not pass the purpose prong of *Lemon:* "We refuse to turn a blind eye to the context in which this policy arose, and that context quells any doubt that this policy was implemented with the purpose of endorsing prayer." Even if no student offered up a prayer, the government endorsement of religion was

enough. In addition, the election scheme turns the school into a forum for religious debate and lets the majority subject the minority
to constitutionally improper messages. This encourages divisive-
ness along religious lines and threatens coercion on students not
wishing to participate in a religious exercise. This procedure is enough
to find a constitutional violation.

The majority undoubtedly knew its holding would cause an uproar. In an effort to soften the blow, the opinion tried to make it
clear that it was not prohibiting all prayer in school. "Thus, nothing
in the Constitution as interpreted by this Court prohibits any public school student from voluntarily praying at any time before, during or after the school day. But the religious liberty protected by the
Constitution is abridged when the State affirmatively sponsors the
particular religious practice of prayer."

As noted, Chief Justice Rehnquist dissented, claiming that the
opinion "bristles with hostility to all things religious in public life."
He was joined by Justices Scalia and Thomas.

Concern about the cultural conditions that surrounded the students in this small southern Texas community surely must have affected some of the justices as they wrestled with this case. Unlike
the Weismans in Providence, Rhode Island, the plaintiffs (one
family was Mormon, the other Catholic) requested that they be allowed to proceed anonymously. The district court allowed their
names to be kept out of the public eye because of "the sensitive nature of the action."[65]

The parties jointly stipulated to other incidents that had occurred
in addition to the graduation and football prayer. A seventh-grade
student (called Jane Doe II for purposes of anonymity) was in her
history class when her teacher handed out fliers advertising a Baptist
religious revival. She asked if non-Baptists were invited to attend,
which prompted her teacher to ask about her religious affiliation.
When he heard that she was a member of the Church of Jesus Christ
of Latter-Day Saints (Mormon), he "launched into a diatribe about
the non-Christian, cult-like nature of Mormonism and its general

evils." This inspired classmates to tell Jane Doe II that her religion sounded evil and to make derogatory comments about it: "Gee . . . it's kind of like the KKK, isn't it?"[66] When her mother reported the teacher, he was reprimanded and ordered to apologize to the class for not acting in accordance with district policy.

Other proselytizing practices that the plaintiffs objected to included encouragement to join religious clubs and distributing Gideon Bibles on school premises. There were also media reports that a teacher sent a Catholic child from the room after his mother objected to a religious song being sung before meals. In a radio interview one district student said that a prayer by a Muslim or a Jew would be okay, as long as there was a prayer to Jesus, while another said that she would not like it. "That's not my faith and we believe there's only one true God."[67]

The district court's order for anonymity apparently did not stop some in the community from trying to ascertain the plaintiffs' identities. About one month after the complaint was filed, the district court threatened the "school administration, officials, counsellors, [sic] teachers, employees, or servants of the School District, parents or students or anyone else" with contempt of court. The court demanded that all attempts to covertly or overtly ferret out the identities of the plaintiffs by means of "bogus petitions, questionnaires, individual interrogation or downright 'snooping'" cease immediately. Judge Samuel B. Kent threatened "the harshest possible contempt sanctions" and criminal liability. He stated that the case would be addressed on the merits, "not on the basis of intimidation or harassment" of the participants. In addition, at the damages stage, the district court had to decide whether to have an open trial on damages where the parties would be recognized. The court observed that the plaintiffs had set forth exhibits that "demonstrated the possibility of ostracization and violence due to militant religious attitudes" and permitted the trial to be partially closed when a minor plaintiff was testifying.[68]

As with other school prayer cases, religious groups were bitterly disappointed with the decision. Some students and parents started to recite the Lord's Prayer spontaneously at football games.[69] As of this writing, *Santa Fe* is the Court's most recent ruling on prayer in public schools, but it will certainly not be the last word. Conflict over religious speech in school shows no signs of abating. Federal courts have grappled with the contours of *Lee* and *Santa Fe* regarding students at graduation who give a speech with a religious message and reached different conclusions. The Eleventh Circuit has stated that the *Santa Fe* Court did not say that every religious message at graduation violated the establishment clause. Thus a speech given by a student without the review of a school official was not state-sponsored.[70] The Ninth Circuit has taken a different tack, holding that even with a disclaimer or "hands-off" approach to a valedictory speech, there would still be the "coerced participation of dissenters attending the graduation ceremony."[71]

In addition to prayer at graduation ceremonies, prayer generally is an integral part of the baccalaureate services held in some areas to celebrate high school graduation. The baccalaureate service probably started with an Oxford University statute, which required each bachelor to deliver a sermon in Latin as part of his academic exercise. The colleges in this country were founded primarily to educate ministers, so the British practice of a baccalaureate service was transplanted here. The baccalaureate high school service is an occasion of thanksgiving prayer and celebration for the graduates. This ceremony, too, has come under fire. One school district in Arkansas was subject to an injunction prohibiting prayer at the school graduation or baccalaureate ceremonies. When, even in the face of the injunction, the school district held a baccalaureate ceremony with an invocation and benediction given by local ministers, the district judge held the school district in contempt of court. The judge was none other than Judge Susan Webber Wright, who was often in the public eye during the administration of President Bill Clinton. She presided over the sexual harassment lawsuit of Paula

Jones and ultimately granted summary judgment for Clinton. She also handled several issues that arose from the Whitewater scandal, a failed real estate investment that involved both Bill and Hillary Clinton. The Eighth Circuit Court of Appeals affirmed that Judge Wright could hold the school district in contempt for hiring school employees who planned the ceremony.[72]

There is little doubt that the highly emotional and contentious issue of prayer in school will continue to be litigated, along with other issues like distribution of religious materials and other forms of proselytization. The composition of the Supreme Court has changed since *Santa Fe* was decided. Chief Justice Roberts has replaced Chief Justice Rehnquist; Justice Alito has replaced Justice O'Connor; and more changes are certain to come. As school districts set forth new policies to deal with these issues, the new justices will undoubtedly get a chance to place their own marks on the ever-evolving doctrine of religion speech in school.

> It is not the strongest of the species that survives,
> nor the most intelligent that survives. It is the one
> that is the most adaptable to change.
>
> —Charles Darwin

For many in the United States, the mention of a controversy over the teaching of evolution may conjure up nothing more than the image of Spencer Tracy and Frederic March in the 1960 film that fictionalized the 1925 "Scopes Monkey Trial." Arguments about whether evolution can be taught in school might seem more like a history lesson than a current crisis. But evolution is still on the front burner for some people in the United States, and legislators and school boards continue to institute policies to undercut its influence on students.

As we move through the early years of the twenty-first century worried about issues like international terrorism and nuclear proliferation, it is difficult to imagine how stunned people were in the mid-nineteenth century when Charles Darwin's writings challenged their most fundamental beliefs about man and God. Some people still sincerely believe that Darwin's statements about the origin of life undermine Christianity and faith, which is the most important focus of their lives. It is beyond the scope of this chapter to analyze the science of evolution and whether it contradicts Christianity. I merely start with the premise that many American citizens fervently believe that the teaching of evolution in school is harmful to the eternal soul of their children.

Scopes v. State was called "the trial of the century" because it pitted two legal lions, Clarence Darrow and William Jennings Bryan, against each other on an issue that seared into the traditional social patterns of the day.[73] The Tennessee Supreme Court determined that the law forbidding the teaching of evolution was constitutional, and the issue never reached the Supreme Court. Indeed, it was over forty years before the Court accepted its first case about the teaching of evolution. Opposition to it had not dimmed in the intervening years.

The case arose in Arkansas, which had adopted a statute similar to that in Tennessee, prohibiting the teaching of evolution. The state had never attempted to enforce the statute; but a high school biology teacher named Susan Epperson sought a court declaration that the statute was void. Although the trial court found that the statute interfered with freedom of speech and thought protected by the First Amendment, the Arkansas Supreme Court disagreed. In a two-sentence opinion, it stated that the statute was within the state's power to specify the curriculum in its public schools.[74] Justice Abe Fortas (who would write the majority opinion in *Tinker* a year later) wrote the Supreme Court opinion in *Epperson v. Arkansas*. Three Justices wrote concurrences. No one dissented.

The majority opinion found that the statute violated the First Amendment religion clauses because it selected "from the body of knowledge a particular segment which it proscribes for the sole reason that it is deemed to conflict with a particular religious doctrine; that is, by a particular interpretation of the Book of Genesis by a particular religious group."[75] There is no doubt, Justice Fortas stated, that "the First Amendment does not permit the State to require that teaching and learning must be tailored to the principles or prohibitions of any religious sect or dogma."

Justice Stewart agreed that the statute was invalid, but he thought that it should have been struck down because it was too vague. Justice Black (who set forth his passionate dissent against Justice Fortas in *Tinker* one year later) agreed. He believed that striking down the statute on First Amendment grounds was too intrusive into state and local matters, and expressed his doubt that "sitting in Washington, [this Court] can successfully supervise and censor the curriculum of every public school in every hamlet and city in the United States. I doubt that our wisdom is so nearly infallible." Justice Harlan thought the lack of analysis from the Supreme Court of Arkansas was "deplorable" and chastised that court for "passing the buck" to the Supreme Court.

The issues surrounding the teaching of evolution did not go away just because the Supreme Court issued its ruling in *Epperson*. About twenty years after *Epperson*, the Supreme Court struck down another statute from the state of Louisiana. The Balanced Treatment for Creation-Science and Evolution-Science in Public School Instruction (the Creationism Act) was not an anachronistic throwback, like the Arkansas statute that had been passed back in 1928. It was passed by the Louisiana legislature in 1981 and required that the public schools in the state give "balanced treatment" to "creation-science" and "evolution-science" in classroom lectures, textbooks, library materials, and other educational programs. The state of Louisiana claimed that the statute had a secular purpose (recall the first prong of the *Lemon* test): to protect academic freedom. The trial court that first heard the case decided that the statute violated the establishment clause because it required the teaching of creation science with the purpose of advancing a particular religious doctrine. The court of appeals affirmed.[76] Justice Brennan wrote the Supreme Court opinion in *Edwards v. Aguillard*, but by this time the Warren Court had become the Rehnquist Court. Although, as in the *Epperson* case, there were four written opinions, this time two justices dissented.[77]

Did the Creationism Act have the purpose of protecting academic freedom? The state of Louisiana argued that it did, because academic freedom is rooted in basic fairness, that is, teaching all of the evidence. But Justice Brennan stated that the phrase could also be understood as enhancing the freedom of teachers to "teach what they will." The Creationism Act does not further that goal, or even the concept of basic fairness. Instead, the statute diminishes the notion of academic freedom by removing the ability to teach evolution without teaching creation science. Because the legislature's purpose in passing the statute was to embrace a particular religious doctrine, the Act failed the first prong of the *Lemon* test, and violated the establishment clause.

Justice Powell, a former chairman of the Richmond (Virginia) School Board, was always concerned when the Court reduced the power of local school boards. He was joined in his separate concurrence by Justice O'Connor, who agreed with him that the statute was unconstitutional. Nonetheless, interference with locally elected officials is warranted only if the purpose for their curriculum decisions is clearly religious. Other uses of religion in school—teaching the Bible for literary or historic value, for instance—would be acceptable. Justice White also wrote a short concurrence. Justice Scalia and Chief Justice Rehnquist dissented.

Justice Scalia argued that the *Lemon* test was not a good test for establishment clause analysis since *Lemon*'s "theme of chaos" gave no guidance to lower courts. But even under that test, the statute passed muster. The Louisiana legislature had articulated a sincere secular purpose for it. The Supreme Court does not sit to judge the wisdom of the legislature, but its sincerity in stating a secular purpose. The majority did not ascertain the true meaning behind the legislature's concern about academic freedom. For the legislature, academic freedom meant "*students*' freedom from indoctrination." Moreover, the Supreme Court has repeatedly affirmed that it will presume that democratically elected legislatures act in a constitutional manner, and there was nothing here that rebutted that presumption.

Justice Scalia cautioned that the facts and the legend surrounding the Scopes trial had caused an intellectual predisposition to believe instinctively that any requirements bearing on the teaching of evolution must be a manifestation of Christian fundamentalist repression. The Court's position, he said, was the repressive one, since the Court was unwilling to let the people of Louisiana present in their schools whatever scientific evidence exists against evolution science.

In the years since *Aguillard,* the teaching of evolution has continued to generate controversy. Since 1999, the Kansas State Board of Education has wrangled over references to evolution in the state science standards. Even Congress got into the fray when the No Child Left Behind Act Conference Report stated in 2001 that students should understand the full range of scientific views that exist when "controversial topics" like evolution are taught. Parents sued the school district in Cobb County, Georgia, just north of Atlanta, when the county placed stickers on its science textbooks that stated, "This textbook contains material on evolution. Evolution is a theory, not a fact, regarding the origin of living things. This material should be approached with an open mind, studied carefully, and critically considered." Federal district judge Clarence Cooper ordered that the stickers be removed, stating that they were an unconstitutional endorsement of religion that falsely suggested that evolution is a "hunch," rather than a widely accepted theory.

The latest argument over the teaching of evolution centers around the concept of "intelligent design." Although the vast majority of scientists believe that overwhelming evidence supports Darwin's theory, advocates of intelligent design—including even some scientists—argue that natural forces alone cannot explain the complexity of living things. Only an "intelligent designer" with a "higher power" could have started the process by which a lifeless molecule became a living cell that would change into the organisms that populate the planet today. In 2005 a federal judge in Pennsylvania ruled that intelligent design was religion masquerading as science and could not be taught in the classroom. In 2006, when a member of the Ohio Board of Education advocated curriculum standards that would encourage students to challenge the theory of evolution, seventy-five science professors at Case Western Reserve University dove into the political arena and signed a letter endorsing her opponent.

It seems that the forces opposed to the teaching of evolution are as relentless as the process of natural selection that Darwin espoused, and remain undaunted in the face of court rulings and impervious to public scorn. The self-preservation theme animates those who argue fervently against teaching evolution and those who argue fervently for prayer, but in a slightly different way. They understand the force of what Professor Joseph Tussman called the state's teaching power. As I pointed out in Chapter 3, Professor Tussman viewed this power as even more fundamental to the state than its war power. Through this power the state establishes and directs the institutions necessary to ensure its continuity—its schools. Those who argue against evolution and for prayer see this power as a tool to ensure their salvation. Any infringement on their ability to save themselves and others, they feel, cleaves and mutilates an essential part of their makeup. It is unlikely that they will give up their fight any time soon.

The two evolution cases from the Supreme Court give us a springboard to the next chapter's area of interest. In *Aguillard,* the Court grappled with the elusive concept of academic freedom.

Justice Brennan viewed it as emanating from the teacher—enhancing the right of the teachers to teach what they will. Justice Scalia viewed academic freedom as a right of the student to be free from indoctrination in the classroom. This view gained notoriety early in the twenty-first century, when writer and activist David Horowitz founded the Students for Academic Freedom and wrote what he called the Academic Bill of Rights. Aimed primarily at speech in higher education, Horowitz is a harsh critic of professors who, he claims engage in political indoctrination in the classroom. The next chapter explores the speech rights of teachers and the contours of academic freedom.

.⋆.

Teacher Speech and the "Priests of Our Democracy"

MUCH OF THE MATERIAL in the previous chapters deals with the speech rights of students. But students are not alone in their desire for expression. Teachers and administrators are also "speakers" in educational settings. After all, *Tinker* intoned, "It can hardly be argued that either students *or teachers* shed their constitutional rights to free expression at the schoolhouse gate."[1] The speech rights of teachers are protected, but not in the same fashion as those of their students. Indeed, it may surprise many to learn that in some circumstances, students seem to have broader speech rights than their teachers. The issue is also complicated by the notion of academic freedom, which although not explicitly a part of the First Amendment, is nonetheless woven—often in a haphazard fashion—through analyses of an educator's right of expression.

Speech rights for educators consist of an elaborate web that links the right to teach controversial subjects with the right to speak out about matters of public concern. The issue concerns not only the right of individual expression, but also the right of expression for educational institutions. And floating around with all the First Amendment analysis is the critical, but indeterminate, issue of the nature of academic freedom, a concept most scholars agree is both "poorly understood and ill-defined."[2] Academic freedom, however defined, is generally considered customary for educators in higher education, yet its protection is uncertain for teachers in elementary and secondary schools.

Teachers are educators, but they are also employees. If they are teaching in a public school or university, they are employees of the state, and any state action is constrained by the First Amendment. But the government as employer has a broader power to restrict the speech of its employee than it has over the public at large. In the late nineteenth century Justice Oliver Wendell Holmes believed that the power of the state as employer was very broad indeed. In 1892, rejecting the right of one employee to criticize his employer while keeping his job, he remarked (in *McAuliffe v. Mayor of New Bedford*), "The petitioner may have a constitutional right to talk politics, but he has no constitutional right to be a policeman. There are few employments for hire in which the servant does not agree to suspend his constitutional rights of free speech as well as of idleness by the implied terms of his contract. The servant cannot complain, as he takes the employment on the terms which are offered him."[3] Thus, the speech rights of the employee were a function of his employment contract and, not surprisingly, employees (and other individuals) found it hard to prevail under this regime.[4] Although this view prevailed for many years, the Supreme Court gradually eroded the rights/privilege dichotomy espoused by *McAuliffe*. Then, in the mid–twentieth century, the Court made it more obvious that it had changed course.

> By academic freedom I understand the right to search for the truth and to publish and teach what one holds to be true. This right also implies a duty; one must not conceal any part of what one has recognized to be true. It is evident that any restriction

> of academic freedom serves to restrain the dissemi-
> nation of knowledge, thereby impeding rational
> judgment and action.
>
> —Albert Einstein

In the late 1940s and 1950s, the government instituted sweeping efforts to root out subversive teachers, and the courts began a dialogue about the importance of freedom in the community of learning. Interestingly, the Supreme Court considered academic freedom protection before it expressly decided that teachers were protected by the First Amendment at all.

Scholars and commentators have written volumes about the contours (or lack thereof) of the elusive concept of academic freedom, in confusing and overwhelming variety. Nonetheless, it is important to understand the basic ideas surrounding the concept, if only to clarify and avoid some of the misunderstandings about it. Although it has roots in the German principles of *Lehrfreiheit* ("teaching freedom") and *Lernfreiheit* ("learning freedom"), the genesis of the concept of academic freedom in the United States was in 1915, when a committee of fifteen professors, chaired by the Columbia economist E. R. A. Seligman, wrote *The General Report of the Committee on Academic Freedom and Academic Tenure for the American Association of University Professors* (AAUP). This document contained the AAUP's Declaration of Principles stating that academic freedom has "three elements: freedom of inquiry and research; freedom of teaching within the university or college; and freedom of extra-mural utterance and action."[5] The third element was of particular concern since the AAUP had recently investigated five cases where at least one of the issues had been "the right of university teachers to express their opinions freely outside the university or to engage in political activities in their capacities as citizens."[6] Thus the idea of professorial academic freedom, *Lehrfreiheit,* was nurtured by the Seligman committee, but the student-centered freedom, *Lernfreiheit,* was omitted from the equation. "Once excised from the profession's concept of academic freedom, *Lernfreiheit* would never be restored."[7]

Although the AAUP drafted a "cautious" statement about student rights in the 1960s, "it has always assumed that student freedom is not an integral part of academic freedom, but is something different—and something less."[8] Of course, chickens that are left out *will* come home to roost. It is this omission of students from the umbrella of academic freedom that the writer David Horowitz and others who espouse the controversial Academic Bill of Rights seek to exploit. They believe that their proposals will shore up students' rights to academic freedom by making universities more intellectually diverse and protecting students from indoctrination in the classroom.

Whatever their views about student academic freedom, the AAUP professors voted themselves "a comprehensive shield."[9] The final draft not only included two principles transplanted from Germany, the freedom to teach and to inquire, but also "extramural freedom." This meant that a professor could speak beyond the walls of the university and was not bound by "the warranty of a professional task or an acknowledged expertise."[10] This concern about "extramural" speech was rooted in professorial protest against administration. On the basis of his investigations in 1915, committee member Arthur O. Lovejoy, a philosophy professor first at Stanford University and later at Johns Hopkins University, had gathered evidence that professors "were more likely to pay for outspokenness when they criticized campus officials than when they challenged anyone else."[11] He reported on mass faculty dismissals and resignations at the University of Utah, in an "eye-opening documentary on how the most devastating storms could be aroused by the academy's teapot controversies."[12] According to Walter Metzger, a historian of academic freedom, since 1916 the AAUP academic freedom docket has been dominated by extramural freedom cases, which "far outnumber disputes involving teaching or research." Metzger claims that there was another reason for the committee's declaration of freedom for extramural utterance and action—the fact that nowhere in the Western world was there "such an elaborate machinery of onsite nonacademic control, as in America." Unlike universities elsewhere, higher education in the United States was controlled by governing boards; administrators and presidents were deputies of governing boards, and university presidents held delegated power from these boards.[13]

The 1915 Declaration of Principles was warmly embraced throughout higher education circles. It has been endorsed by academic societies and incorporated into handbooks of colleges and universities across the United States. As Metzger has observed, "It has become the standard creed of the American academic profession."[14] The Declaration of Principles conspicuously omitted any reference to academic freedom in K–12 education, implying that schoolteachers were excluded from membership in the club. As discussed below, schoolteachers would need to press their claims in court through their own organizations.

Scholars disagree about why it took so long for the courts to pay attention to academic freedom.[15] The concept had been adopted by the academic community, and professors were not loathe to enter the courtroom on other matters, like breach-of-contract claims.[16] But professors in private colleges and universities lacked the state action required for a constitutional claim, and the long tentacles of Justice Holmes's pronouncement about rights and privileges in *McAuliffe* held professors in public colleges fast in its grip. In short, a legal theory simply did not exist that seemed like it would work to address a violation of academic freedom.[17]

Just as the Vietnam War protest movement would change how courts viewed student expressive rights, the McCarthy era changed how courts viewed academic freedom. In 1952 public schoolteachers claimed that their First Amendment rights had been violated by a New York statute called the Feinberg law that made any person ineligible for employment who was a member of an organization that the state Board of Regents declared advocated the overthrow of the government by illegal means. This case, *Adler v. Board of Education,* was in no way a victory for the teachers. Six Supreme Court justices rejected their claim using the Holmesian analysis, that still held sway after so many years.[18] The majority opinion stated that public schoolteachers had the right to speak, think, and believe as they pleased, but they had no right to work in the state school system under their own terms. The school system could set forth reasonable terms for employment, and the teachers could retain their beliefs and work elsewhere if they so chose. "Has the state thus deprived them of any right to free speech or assembly? We think not."[19] The majority opinion, written by Justice Sherman Minton, focused on language from the text of the First Amendment itself ("speech and assembly") in defining the teachers' rights, such as they were: the right to believe what they liked and the right to quit work if they did not like the state rules about membership in the Communist Party or affiliated organizations.

But Justice Douglas, joined by Justice Black in dissent, argued that teachers are special actors when considering First Amendment protection. "The Constitution guarantees freedom of thought and expression to everyone in our society . . . [but] none needs it more than the teacher" because "the public school is in most respects the cradle of our democracy."[20] Then Justice Douglas injected a new term into Supreme Court discourse: He maintained that the Feinberg law "cannot go hand in hand with *academic freedom.*"[21] Used for the very first time in *Adler,* "the term was to make its way into the judicial vocabulary of both liberals and conservatives on the Court within a decade."[22] Justice Douglas then stated simply, "There can be no real academic freedom in that environment." Justice Douglas made no attempt to define academic freedom, real or otherwise. In that regard, too, this dissent proved prophetic, for no later opinion has ever taken on that task.

The next convert for the academic freedom apologists was Justice

Frankfurter (of *Gobitis* fame in Chapter 6). In *Wieman v. Updegraff*, the Court unanimously struck down an Oklahoma law that made persons ineligible for all state employment if they would not swear that they did not belong to an organization listed by the U.S. attorney general as subversive or a communist front.[23] Some faculty and staff at Oklahoma Agricultural and Mechanical College refused to take the oath, and Paul Updegraff sued as a citizen-taxpayer, asking the courts to order the state not to pay faculty and staff wages. (The faculty and staff were allowed to intervene in the case and were also part of the lawsuit.) The Supreme Court held that the statute offended the Fourteenth Amendment Due Process Clause because it excluded even persons who were ignorant of the subversive goals of the organizations in question.

Justice Frankfurter wrote a separate concurring opinion extolling the virtue of freedom for teachers protected by the Constitution because of the societal role they play in protecting the Constitution itself. "In view of the nature of the teacher's relation to the effective exercise of the rights which are safeguarded by the Bill of Rights and by the Fourteenth Amendment, inhibition of freedom of thought, and of action upon thought, in the case of teachers brings the safeguards of those amendments vividly into operation."[24] Frankfurter lauded the "free play of the spirit which all teachers ought especially to cultivate" in light of the special task teachers have to "foster open-mindedness and critical inquiry as they help to shape responsible citizens." This eulogium to teachers reached its zenith when Justice Frankfurter proclaimed, "To regard teachers—in our entire educational system, from the primary grades to the university—as the priests of our democracy is therefore not to indulge in hyperbole."

More cases concerning the expressive rights of teachers followed *Adler* and *Wieman*, and the concept of some kind of constitutional dimension for academic freedom began to take hazy form. In *Sweezy v. New Hampshire*, the Court addressed the contempt con-

viction of Paul Sweezy, a Marxist economist and socialist, for refusing to answer questions put to him by the New Hampshire attorney
general, who was investigating subversive persons under powers
delegated to him by the state legislature.[25] Some of the questions
concerned the content of a guest lecture Sweezy had given at the
University of New Hampshire.

The Supreme Court plurality opinion, written by Chief Justice
Earl Warren, was not based on the right of academic freedom. Instead, the Court ruled that the questioning violated Sweezy's due
process rights, because the state legislature had not clearly defined
the power it had delegated to the attorney general.[26] As Peter Byrne,
another noted scholar of academic freedom, has observed, "This
odd holding, which imposes federal separation of powers limitations
on the state, has had no subsequent legal career."[27] He posits that
the plurality's reluctance to base the decision on a clear positive right
of academic freedom may have been a result of the Court's focus at
the time on broad legislative investigations, the main inquisitorial
vehicle for McCarthy-type probes. That same day, later known as
"Red Monday," the Supreme Court also handed down six other
opinions that made it more difficult for Congress, administrative
agencies, and state legislatures to ferret out allegedly subversive persons.[28] In this context—limiting the federal and state power of other
branches on a subject that had engendered much emotion and patriotic fervor—the Court's task is at its most delicate, and its own
power is at its most vulnerable. The Court may have believed it
needed to proceed with caution and thus refrained from the appearance of imposing any novel right of academic freedom.[29]

Yet the seeds of constitutional academic freedom were present in
the opinion. It pointed out that legislative investigations must be
carefully circumscribed when they tend to impinge on freedom of
speech, "particularly in the academic community." The right to lecture is a constitutionally protected freedom. "We believe that there
unquestionably was an invasion of petitioner's liberties in the areas

of academic freedom and political expression—areas in which the government should be extremely reticent to tread." Moreover, this freedom is essential to the survival of the nation. "The essentiality of freedom in the community of American universities is almost self-evident. No one should underestimate the vital role in a democracy that is played by those who guide and train our youth. To impose any strait jacket upon the intellectual leaders in our colleges and universities would imperil the future of our Nation. . . . Teachers and students must always remain free to inquire, to study and to evaluate, to gain new maturity and understanding; otherwise our civilization will stagnate and die." Nevertheless, the Court declared that it did not need to decide the case on these grounds, and it proceeded in another direction.

Justice Frankfurter concurred separately once again, this time joined by Justice Harlan. His opinion, which has become more influential than that of the plurality, focused on freedom in the academic realm as a positive right, comparing it to freedom in the political realm: "In the political realm, as in the academic, thought and action are presumptively immune from inquisition by political authority."[30] The part of the opinion that proved most enduring is Frankfurter's discourse on the "four essential freedoms of the university—to determine for itself on academic grounds who may teach, what may be taught, how it shall be taught, and who may be admitted to study."

As grand as these words may sound, they did little to clarify the contours of academic freedom and the First Amendment. In fact, they may have muddied the waters (which were already cloudy enough). First, both the plurality and the concurring opinions had analyzed the case as explaining the rights afforded to Sweezy as against the government—the right of the individual faculty member to be free from government constraint. To be sure, there was also a threat to the University of New Hampshire, even though it was not a party to the case. This statement by Justice Frankfurter— the one that endures from the opinion—addresses the rights of the *university* as an *institution* when faced with government intrusion. This is surely an important idea, but it was not especially relevant to the facts of the case or concordant with the First Amendment's protection of individual rights. Indeed, once this period of hunting communists passed, controversy about individual faculty freedoms often focused on interference from administrators in the university institution itself—deans, presidents, and other administrators.

In addition to adding institutional academic freedom to the mix, the opinion looked to sources outside the United States and outside the law for its description of this freedom. (This consideration of international attitudes occurred long before the Supreme Court caused a stir in 2005 when it looked to international law in an opinion regarding the execution of juveniles.)[31] The statement about the "four essential freedoms," which has been quoted ever since to support claims of academic freedom under the United States Constitution, came from a plea by academics from the University of Cape Town and the University of Witwatersrand the same year Sweezy was decided. The professors were reacting to a proposal to impose racial apartheid in educational institutions.[32] Before that date "no federal court or law journal commentator had even mentioned the concept of institutional academic freedom, much less suggested that a college's or a university's academic freedom could override or trump [a] faculty member's academic freedom."[33] Justice Frankfurter was probably merely trying to boost the idea of academic freedom generally, rather than endorsing institutional academic freedom over that of individual faculty members.[34] In all fairness, he had practical reasons to go far afield for his definition since "the words 'academic freedom' had no meaning apart from their usage in academic contexts."[35] Even so, the rhetoric in the opinion was simply not backed up by any explanation of whether or how this translated into positive legal rights that educators could depend on to vindicate their free expression.[36] Indeed, as time has passed this rhetoric has contributed to competing claims of academic freedom, when, "in response to professors suing over alleged institutional violations of academic freedom, universities have asserted their own academic freedom as a barrier to judicial review."[37]

The ambiguity about individual and institutional academic freedom raised concerns for those advocating strong professorial academic freedom rights. In fact, the AAUP itself was not sure how to deal with judicial involvement in the issue. Some members wanted professors, rather than judges, to set the norms for academic life. Others worried that once courts become involved, academic freedom would survive only at the pleasure of judges.[38] While sympathetic judges in the McCarthy era might strengthen academic freedom rights, other less sympathetic judges in a different political context might weaken them.

Just two years later, the Court was less sympathetic to the claims of a former graduate student and teaching fellow at the University of Michigan who was investigated by the House Un-American Activities Committee regarding his activities while teaching there. This case, *Barenblatt v. United States,* often receives less attention in modern commentary than *Sweezy* or *Keyishian* (which in 1967 overturned the Feinberg law that had been at issue fifteen years earlier in *Adler*). But *Barenblatt,* yet another 5–4 opinion, was significant because the Court substantially upheld the investigation of the House committee and explicitly recognized the right of a government to self-preservation, one of the recurring themes in the school speech story. In addition, the opinion, in distinguishing *Sweezy,* explained the activities that it would protect under the rubric of academic freedom and those it would not.[39]

The House Committee was investigating communist infiltration into the field of education. Barenblatt refused to answer questions whether he was a member of the Communist Party, and he challenged his contempt conviction on the grounds that his right of association under the First Amendment had been infringed. The Court allowed the contempt conviction to stand. It explained its position by distinguishing the teacher's interest in freedom of "teaching" and "learning" and the teacher's interest in Party membership. These two freedoms were more important than the individual interest at stake in the case, because of their importance to the continued welfare of the nation. In the words of Justice Harlan, the author of the majority opinion,

> Of course, broadly viewed, inquiries cannot be made into the teaching that is pursued in any of our educational institutions. When academic teaching-freedom and its corollary learning-freedom, so essential to the well-being of the Nation, are claimed, this Court will always be on the alert against intrusion by Congress into this constitutionally protected domain. But this does not mean that the Congress is precluded from interrogating a witness merely because he is a teacher. An educational institution is not a constitutional sanctuary from inquiry into matters that may otherwise be within the constitutional legislative domain merely for the reason that inquiry is made of someone within its walls.[40]

Justice Harlan explicitly recognized the nation's right of self-preservation when he analyzed the power of Congress to order these investigations. This right of self-preservation is a vein that has run—either explicitly or implicitly—through all of the issues that surround school speech, from *Gobitis* to *Tinker* to *Pico*. The *Barenblatt* majority opinion stated that Congress has "wide power" to legislate in the field of communist activity. This power rests on the right of self-preservation, "the ultimate value of any society." Since it was widely held that the tenets of the Communist Party include the overthrow of the government of the United States by force and violence, this justified Congress's interest in this area.

The Court distinguished this ruling from *Sweezy*, noting that the vice in that case had been questioning Sweezy, who was not known to be connected the Communist Party, about the content of his lectures. This the Court said, was very different from inquiring into the extent to which the Communist Party has infiltrated our universities and searching out persons committed to violent overthrow. Even the brief of the AAUP acknowledged that the right of self-preservation was an important one, but argued that when it collides with academic freedom rights, the government must set forth a "demonstrable justification" for intruding on those rights. The Court determined that this justification was present in this instance, and held that the inquiry was permissible.

Justice Black, joined by Justices Douglas and Brennan and Chief Justice Warren in dissent, argued that the rule Congress had promulgated that gave the House Committee its power was too vague to pass First Amendment scrutiny. (Justice Brennan also wrote a one-paragraph dissent; "the dissent" in this section refers to the Black dissent.) The dissenters would not have tolerated any balancing test at all. But even using one, the majority got it wrong, because it had taken too narrow a view of the interests that were to be balanced. The majority had ignored "the interest of the people as a whole in being able to join organizations, advocate causes and make political 'mistakes' without later being subjected to governmental penalties for having dared to think for themselves." Although the dissent did not mention academic freedom explicitly, it alluded to the special societal interest that universities carry. The ability to err politically keeps us strong as a nation, and it is "doubly crucial when it affects the universities, on which we must largely rely for the experimentation and development of new ideas essential to our country's welfare."

As for the right of self-preservation, the dissenters made the same argument we have seen in other cases. The dissenting justices believed the best way to preserve the Republic was through broad and deep rights of expression. Justice Black, though a dissenter here, would refine his view with regard to K–12 students ten years later. Recall that as far as Justice Black is concerned, these broad and deep rights do not extend to students protesting a war by wearing black armbands in school. In *Barenblatt* Justice Black warned:

the only constitutional way our Government can preserve itself is to leave its people the fullest possible freedom to praise, criticize or discuss, as they see fit, all governmental policies and to suggest, if they desire, that even its most fundamental postulates are bad and should be changed; "Therein lies the security of the Republic, the very foundation of constitutional government" [citing *De Jonge v. Oregon*, 299 U.S. 253 (1937)]. On that premise this land was created, and on that premise it has grown to greatness.

Justice Black asserted, "Our Constitution assumes that the common sense of the people and their attachment to our country will enable them, after free discussion, to withstand ideas that are wrong." Of course that assumes that the people have "common sense" or the education and cognitive skills to be able to sort the wheat from the chaff. Therein lies the conundrum, and it is a particularly difficult issue when dealing with students who are in the midst of gaining that knowledge and common sense and attachment to their country.

Justice Frankfurter, who had all but ordained teachers as priests in his *Wieman* concurrence, was less enthusiastic about freedom for teachers eight years later. This time, the Court was faced with an Arkansas statute that required every teacher, as a condition of employment in a state-supported school or college, to file an affidavit each year listing every organization to which he or she has belonged or regularly contributed within the preceding five years (*Shelton v. Tucker*, 364 U.S. 479 [1960]). Justice Frankfurter dissented from the majority opinion, which struck down the statute. Although the Court majority, in an opinion written by Justice Potter Stewart, acknowledged the state interest in determining the fitness and competence of the teachers it employed, it balanced that interest against the freedom rights of teachers that Frankfurter himself had celebrated in his *Wieman* concurrence. In fact, Justice Stewart buttressed his claim for these rights for teachers by quoting Justice Frankfurter's homage to the "free spirit of teachers."

For the Court majority, these rights overcame the state's interest in teacher fitness. To compel teachers to disclose their every associational tie would impair their right of free association, "a right closely allied to freedom of speech and a right which, like free speech, lies at the foundation of a free society." Indeed, in earlier proceedings in the case, a witness had testified that he intended to gain access to some of the information provided with a view to eliminating persons who supported certain organizations from the school system. Among such organizations he named the American Civil Liberties Union, the Urban League, the American Association of University Professors, and the Women's Emergency Committee to Open Our Schools. There was also some evidence that part of the motivation was to subvert the Supreme Court's rulings on school desegregation. The Court viewed the scope of the inquiry required by the Arkansas statute as unlimited, including church membership and support, political party membership and support, and "every conceivable kind of associational tie—social, professional, political, avocational, or religious." Many of these ties had no possible bearing on a teacher's occupational competence or fitness, and the statute thus swept too broadly.

But Justice Frankfurter was not convinced that teachers needed *this* much freedom. He maintained that the state had an interest in ascertaining whether the teacher was so overcommitted to organizations that it would affect the quality of time and effort he or she could put toward teaching. Nonetheless, Justice Stewart had thrown his own words at him in the majority opinion, and he needed to explain how his vote here was consistent with his past opinions. He maintained that his view in *Shelton* would actually enhance teacher liberty:

> If I dissent from the Court's disposition in these cases, it is not that I put a low value on academic freedom. See Wieman v. Updegraff, 344 U.S. 183, 194 (concurring opinion); Sweezy v. New Hampshire, 354

U.S. 234, 255 (concurring opinion). It is because that very freedom, in its most creative reaches, is dependent in no small part upon the careful and discriminating selection of teachers. This process of selection is an intricate affair, a matter of fine judgment, and if it is to be informed, it must be based upon a comprehensive range of information.

Because he saw nothing in the record that showed that the information would be used to terminate teachers because of membership in particular organizations, the Court should wait to see if that happened before striking down the statute.

Although the teachers won the case, the liberty it delineated was not unfettered. After *Shelton,* a state could ask teachers to reveal information, as long as the state could show that this information was tied to teacher fitness.

Ten years after it had upheld New York's Feinberg law in *Adler,* the Supreme Court struck it down on the basis of "vagueness and overbreadth," two doctrines the Court uses to analyze the language of statutes that infringe on speech. Justice William Brennan wrote for the majority in this instance, *Keyishian v. Board of Regents,* another 5–4 opinion.[41] He reasoned that because the statute affected academic freedom, the prohibited acts must be clear so that fear of the law does not corrupt a professor's selection of material and manner of teaching. The Court once again failed to define the right of academic freedom: "Ironically, this opinion, which voided a statute as unduly vague, is itself extraordinarily vague about the dimensions of the right of academic freedom."[42] But the Court's ardent tribute to academic freedom further validated the idea that academic freedom was something that courts and the Constitution must nurture:

Our Nation is deeply committed to safeguarding academic freedom, which is of transcendent value to all of us and not merely to the teachers concerned. That freedom is therefore a special concern of the First Amendment, which does not tolerate laws that cast a pall of orthodoxy over the classroom. The vigilant protection of constitutional freedoms is nowhere more vital than in the community of American schools. The classroom is peculiarly the "marketplace of ideas." The Nation's future depends upon leaders trained through wide exposure to that robust exchange of ideas which discovers truth "out of a multitude of tongues, [rather] than through any kind of authoritative selection."

This statement first focuses on the claim that academic freedom is important to society as a whole, not just to those claiming the liberty. Calling it a "transcendent" value imbues it with a burnished, perhaps even a sacred, luster. And academic freedom is not just an idea that has a First Amendment dimension; it is a *special* concern" of the First Amendment—implying that it, like political speech, has a higher place in First Amendment hierarchy. But the "careless" importation of Holmes's marketplace metaphor to the classroom was ill considered.[43] With regard to professorial research, the marketplace metaphor makes some sense: research will be examined and reviewed and critiqued by other scholars, finally gaining acceptance in some corner of the "marketplace" if it meets competence standards. But this is not necessarily so in the classroom. Although students must be exposed to a wide array of concepts and encouraged to discuss and defend their assertions, teaching does not always involve a free and unfettered exchange among equals.[44] As noted in Chapter 6, a biology teacher teaching the theory of evolution does not need the approval and blessing of the undergraduates in the class. Moreover, the marketplace analogy fails when it comes to the content of a particular course, as the professor may not have unlimited autonomy on that issue either.[45]

Justice Clark, with three other justices, would have allowed the state of New York to disqualify from teaching those who advocate the violent overthrow of the United States government or who are members of an organization that advocates such overthrow. For the dissenters, like so many of the majority and dissenting arguments I have reviewed throughout this study, the issue was again that of self-preservation—the ability to keep educators from teaching revolution to the nation's youth:

> The majority has by its broadside swept away one of our most precious rights, namely, the right of self-preservation. Our public educational system is the genius of our democracy. The minds of our youth are developed there and the character of that development will determine the future of our land. Indeed, our very existence depends upon it.[46]

When the hunt for communists in education died down, the Court's ardor about academic freedom died down with it. Yet despite the flawed premise of some of Justice Brennan's rhetoric, its theme was carried on in another context by Justice Lewis Powell in his famous lone opinion in *Regents of the University of California v. Bakke,* the first case about affirmative action in education.[47] Justice Powell agreed with four other justices that the particular affirmative action plan in place at the University of California at Davis violated the equal protection clause. Nonetheless, he maintained that admissions policies could treat race as one factor among others. He grounded his decision in one of the four essential freedoms of a university from Justice Frankfurter's concurrence in *Sweezy*: the university's freedom "to determine for itself on academic grounds . . . who may be admitted to study."

But the notion that the decision to obtain a diverse student population was academic rather than political had its roots in Justice Brennan's rhetoric in *Keyishian.* Exposing students to the "multitude of tongues," as he put it, necessary for robust debate depends on a classroom where students and professors with different life experiences come together in the community of learning. Justice Powell's *Bakke* opinion proposed that once a university could show that its policy was based on academic grounds, courts should defer to the university, even against the equal protection claim of a white applicant. Justice O'Connor reinvigorated this conception of institutional academic freedom in *Grutter v. Bollinger,* in which the Court revisited the affirmative action question. Citing *Sweezy, Shelton, Wieman,* and *Keyishian,* Justice O'Connor described those cases as "recognizing a constitutional dimension, grounded in the First Amendment, of educational autonomy."

This educational autonomy also played a part when a rise in student activism began to spawn lawsuits about grading policies. In 1977, the Supreme Court upheld a student's dismissal from the University of Missouri–Kansas City Medical School.[48] Although the case was couched in language about Fourteenth Amendment procedural due process rights rather than First Amendment speech rights, it is significant because of its deference to educational institutions and teachers who award grades. The decision to dismiss the student, the Court said, had rested on the "academic judgment" of school officials. Chief Justice Rehnquist, writing for the majority, connected this power of dismissal to a teacher's grading evaluation. "Like the decision of an individual professor as to the proper grade for a student in his course, the determination whether to dismiss a student for academic reasons requires an expert evaluation of cumulative information and is not readily adapted to the procedural tools of judicial or administrative decisionmaking." For a teacher, the grading evaluation is akin to speech, since it is his or her expression of professional judgment about the quality of a student's work.

A few years later another student came before the Court, claiming that his dismissal had been arbitrary and capricious, violating his Fourteenth Amendment "substantive due process rights" because he was not permitted to retake an examination he had failed. The court of appeals, reversing the district court opinion, ruled for the student. The Supreme Court reversed in a unanimous opinion. The Court simply stated that there was no room for judicial review of an academic decision unless "it was such a substantial departure from academic norms as to demonstrate that the faculty did not exercise professional judgment."[49] Again, although the decision was not explicitly based on teacher freedom of expression, it demonstrated the Court's willingness to defer to educators—at least educators who are college professors—when they make certain kinds of professional communications.

> It ain't what you don't know that gets you into trouble. It's what you know for sure that just ain't so.
>
> —Mark Twain

Given the approbation institutional and professorial academic freedom has been afforded, what are the rights of individual faculty members against administrators within the education institution? Remember that the AAUP Declaration of Principles addressed the *teacher's* freedom of inquiry and research, of teaching, and of extramural utterance. But Supreme Court opinions like *Bakke* and *Grutter* have championed a kind of institutional academic freedom that is rooted in institutional autonomy. Scholars have recognized that there is a friction between the ideas of institutional and of individual constitutional academic freedom.[50] The Supreme Court itself has observed that the part of academic freedom that supported the independent and uninhibited free exchange of ideas among faculty and students could sometimes be inconsistent with the part that supported autonomous decision making by the academy itself.[51] Resolving this complicated issue is, of course, beyond the scope of this chapter. But it has proved to be fertile ground for Supreme Court and lower court opinions.

The tension between institutional autonomy and teacher speech cloaked in academic freedom is revealed in a line of cases that arose around the same time students were pushing for more speech rights, in the late 1960s. As students sought more rights against the government as educator, public employees, including teachers, asked the courts to define their speech rights against the government as employer. The Supreme Court decided some cases regarding the free speech rights of individual faculty members in this context, and its analysis may have confused, rather than clarified, the issue. In *Pickering v. Board of Education,* a teacher sent a letter to the local newspaper criticizing the way the board had handled proposals to raise revenue. The board dismissed the teacher because it determined that the letter was detrimental to the efficient operation and administration of the district schools. The Illinois Supreme Court rejected the teacher's claim that his letter was protected by the First Amendment. The Supreme Court disagreed, explaining that teachers could not be compelled to relinquish the First Amendment rights they hold as citizens to comment on matters of public interest in connection with the schools where they work.[52] Unless a teacher knowingly or recklessly made false statements, "a teacher's right to speak on issues of public importance may not furnish the basis for his dismissal from public employment."[53]

Even so, Justice Thurgood Marshall, writing for six other justices, suggested that a teacher who made statements that impeded the proper performance of their daily duties in the classroom or interfered with the regular operation of the school would be less likely to be protected by the First Amendment. Note the parallel here between the standard set forth in *Tinker* regarding student speech rights: school officials cannot restrain student speech unless it substantially disrupts or materially interferes with the education process. The *Pickering* Court also warned that public statements that were so lacking in foundation as to call into question a teacher's fitness to perform classroom duties could be used as evidence of the teacher's general incompetence.

The State has different powers when it acts as an employer. It has an interest in the speech of its employees that differs from its interest in the speech of citizens in general. "The problem in any case is to *arrive at a balance* between the interests of the teacher, as a citizen, in commenting on matters of public concern and the interest of the State, as an employer, in promoting the efficiency of the public services it performs through its employees."[54] Thus what is known as the *Pickering* balancing test was born. After the decision, public employees, including teachers, would be protected from reprisals by the government only when they were speaking on matters of public concern.

In 1983 the Court revisited the *Pickering* test in *Connick v. Myers*.[55] That the speech was a matter of public concern, and not just a matter of personal interest, is the threshold requirement that each employee must meet. After that requirement is met, the employee's interest in free speech is balanced against the interest of the government employer in promoting the efficiency of the public service it provides. As part of its case the government may show that the speech slows down services, hurts morale, or affects discipline in the workplace.

At some point, a government employee's speech—when it takes place off the job and has content not related to the job—is not limited by the *Pickering/Connick* test.[56] But in 2006 the Supreme Court addressed the other end of the spectrum: speech that was part of the job performance itself. In *Garcetti v. Ceballos,* a district attorney supervising prosecutions wrote a memorandum that suggested that a police officer might have lied on an arrest warrant, and the attorney later testified for the criminal defendant under subpoena.[57] The attorney claimed that he had suffered reprisals from his employer because of his actions. In a 5–4 opinion, the Court determined that an employee in this circumstance has no First Amendment protection at all. "We hold that when public employees make statements pursuant to their official duties, the employees are not speaking as citizens for First Amendment purposes, and the Constitution does not insulate their communications from employer discipline."

The case was closely watched not only for what it would say about protections for whistleblowers but also because its holding might affect the speech rights of teachers and professors employed by public institutions. Justice Kennedy, writing for the majority, explicitly omitted educators from the ruling, at least for the time being: "There is some argument that expression related to academic scholarship or classroom instruction implicates additional constitutional interests that are not fully accounted for by this Court's customary employee-speech jurisprudence. We need not, and for that reason do not, decide whether the analysis we conduct today would apply in the same manner to a case involving speech related to scholarship or teaching." Thus the Court suggested that educators may have more First Amendment protection for on-the-job speech than other government employees. In his dissent Justice Souter expressed concern about how the case would affect academic freedom and wrote, "I have to hope that today's majority does not mean to imperil First Amendment protection of academic freedom in public colleges and universities, whose teachers necessarily speak and write 'pursuant to official duties.'" The upshot is that after *Garcetti,* the extent of any First Amendment protection—if it exists at all—is still a matter of speculation until the Court revisits the issue.

Leaving an issue open for another day is fine for the justices writing about a complicated opinion, but the lower courts have to continue to face the issue. The opinions emanating from these courts attempting to set the contours for protection of speech in the classroom have been confusing, to say the least. The opinions are especially murky when addressing the speech rights of K–12 teachers, who do not even have the weight of the AAUP guidelines behind them. One commentator has said that because academic freedom was conceived in the university context, "any role that it plays in the lower grades is derivative."[58] In addition, K–12 teachers are not generally researchers engaged in the search for truth. They operate in a different context, where they transmit knowledge while they are—as the Supreme Court has described it—inculcating the habits and manners of civility.[59]

Courts have used *Pickering, Hazelwood,* and even *Tinker* in their attempts to analyze K–12 teacher speech. Some courts using the *Pickering* test have determined that classroom speech is generally a matter of public concern. Other courts using the same *Pickering* test have determined that classroom speech is generally *not* a matter of public concern. Suffice it to say that lower court decisions "often yield contradictory results that strip the public concern prong of all predictability and leave both public employers and public employees uncertain of their rights."[60] Some courts do not use *Pickering* at all. Instead they have used *Hazelwood,* a case that was developed to delimit *student* speech rights. Under the *Hazelwood* test, school officials can restrain speech if their action is reasonably related to a legitimate pedagogical concern.[61]

Although the *Hazelwood* test at least recognizes the educational component of the analysis, it equates student speech with the teacher speech. It fails to take into account that the interest at stake in the teacher speech case is not that of a student who has not yet matured cognitively and who is in the process of obtaining knowledge while in the community of learning. It is one thing to curtail some student speech while the government is fulfilling its educative mission of instilling values in those students (though even that may raise hackles in some quarters). But the interests of teachers, while not boundless, are certainly *different* from those of their students. The courts that have conflated the two seem to be suggesting that the institutional interest in fulfilling its mission in the face of dissension or disruption makes the distinction between teacher and pupil irrelevant.

Given the different traditions of academic freedom and the different role that K–12 teachers play in the lives of their students, it is not surprising that their path to academic freedom has been even more tortuous than that of the college professor. The Supreme Court has been silent on the issue of K–12 teacher speech, except for the discussion of academic freedom in the cases about the teaching of evolution. To be sure, both *Epperson* and *Aguilllard* dealt with teaching in K–12 education, and Justice Brennan stated that academic freedom meant that teachers could "teach what they will," but this idea has never gained any traction, and there is no indication that the concept will secure any doctrinal clarity any time soon.

What of the teacher's right to receive speech? *Pico* addressed the rights of students to receive speech in the context of book banning at a school library. Recall that some justices in *Pico* asserted that since speakers have the right to expression, the recipient has a concomitant right to receive that expression. An interesting issue regarding the right of faculty to receive certain expression arose in *Urofsky v. Gilmore,* in which the Court of Appeals for the Fourth Circuit addressed a Virginia statute that prohibited any state employee from viewing "sexually explicit content" on computers owned or leased by the state.[62] Professors challenged the statute, arguing that it violated their constitutional right to academic freedom if they were to need this kind of material as part of their research.

In what one commentator has called "the worst case for academic freedom [in sixty years]," the court of appeals rejected the claim.[63] The court recognized that the statute violated the AAUP norms of academic freedom, but it stated that the Constitution protected only the academic freedom of the university, not of individuals. According to the court, the state has control over the professional speech of its employees, including professors, when the speech is part of the professor's duties. The court illustrated its point by explaining that the state has as much right to control the teaching, research, and scholarship of professors at state universities as to control the speech of other professionals in its employ— like the pleadings of state lawyers or the reports of state bureaucrats. *Garcetti*, in which the Supreme Court suggested that speech related to scholarship or teaching might be different from the speech of other government employees, had not yet been decided. But given the lack of any real guidance by the high court, it is by no means clear that *Urofsky* would have come out any differently even after *Garcetti*.

Understandably, the *Urofsky* opinion has been roundly denounced by scholars, but the Supreme Court denied certiorari in the case. If other courts agree with *Urofsky*, the divide between AAUP norms for individual academic freedom and that of the judiciary may become a wide chasm indeed.

There is certainly a wide chasm between the school speech of Mary Beth Tinker and that of Joseph Frederick, the plaintiff in the case that is the focus of the book's final chapter. Although *Morse v. Frederick* will undoubtedly not be the last word from the Supreme Court, it is the Court's most recent pronouncement at the time of the writing of this book. It is surely one of the oddest Supreme Court case on school speech to date. Chapter 8 examines this last word—for now—from the high court and then discusses the next frontier for school speech.

✦

A Long Way from Black Armbands

WHEN THE SUPREME COURT received the petition for certiorari in *Morse v. Frederick* in 2006, it had been twenty years since it had decided its last pure student speech case. To be sure, it had acted on other issues concerning speech in school, but cases like *Hazelwood School District v. Kuhlmeier* had the overlay of a school-sponsored newspaper; *Board of Education, Island Trees Union Free School District v. Pico* dealt with the right to receive speech; and *Lee v. Weismann* and *Santa Fe Independent School District v. Doe* addressed speech that was tangled up in the religion clauses.

There were certainly a number of school speech matters that had proved especially thorny for school officials and for the lower courts in the decades after the *Fraser* opinion. For example, where should teachers or judges draw the line between one student's First Amendment right of expression and another student's statutory right to be free from speech that he or she considers harassment? Put another way, how bad does speech have to be to meet the definition of harassment and what can a school administrator do to stop it when it occurs? What if the speaker asserts that the expression—something like "Homosexuality is shameful"—is part of their free exercise of religion? To what extent can school officials enforce a student dress code against a First Amendment speech claim? What can a teacher do when a student's creative writing contains violent themes?

One issue that has proved extremely difficult is that of student internet speech. The school landscape has changed since the time of *Tinker*, and "the Internet marks that landscape change as dramatically as the Front Range marks the end of the Great Plain."[1] Emails and websites about teachers and other students may have an effect on the learning environment that is the same as—perhaps even worse than—words in a face-to-face confrontation. Almost every school lawyer has received numerous questions about student internet speech, and the courts deciding lawsuits after schools have disciplined students for cyberspeech have struggled, without much success, to develop coherent rules of engagement. Issues surrounding school speech and the internet have been daunting, and they are not going away any time soon. With all of these issues bubbling and churning, it was time for the high court to weigh in.

So after showing little interest for decades, the Supreme Court granted certiorari in *Morse v. Frederick*. If the Court's renewed interest in school speech was a bit surprising after two decades of silence, its choice of this particular case as the vehicle in which to revive its school speech doctrine was astounding. Except in a very few instances, the Court gets to choose which cases it wishes to hear. Because of limited time and resources, the justices make a concerted effort to choose cases where the facts will help those trying to work through difficult issues that have a wide impact on the nation's institutions and its citizens. The bizarre facts of *Morse* made it an unlikely candidate for Supreme Court review.

The case is not about harassment or dress codes. It does not deal with violent or threatening speech, and it has nothing to do with the internet. Although the speech is undoubtedly by a student, he argued that he was not even connected to the school at the time of the speech. Unlike the Tinkers, who were trying to convey an idea, this student was in the odd position of having to argue that his speech had no meaning.

Despite these factual differences, there were some parallels with the *Tinker* case. In 2006, as in the time of *Tinker*, the United States was engaged in a war that had proved to be unpopular on the home front. The war's setting had moved from Vietnam to Iraq, but there were many in the press and in politics who often compared the two. But Joe Frederick was not protesting the war in Iraq, and he did not appear to be making any other political statement. In fact he claimed that he just wanted to see what his high school principal would do to him.

How did this bizarre case come about? On a winter day in 2002 the Olympic Torch Relay was scheduled to pass through the streets of Juneau, Alaska. This occurred during the school day, and it passed by the Juneau Douglas High School. The high school teachers were given the option of allowing their students to attend the relay as a class to view the torch. A number of the teachers elected to do so, and some of the students walked to the other side of the street to view the relay. The school pep band and cheerleaders added to the festivity. Joseph Frederick joined some other students and then, as the camera truck and the relay runner passed, he unfurled a fourteen-foot banner. It took several (at least nine) students to hold the banner, and it read in large letters, "BONG HiTS 4 JESUS."

Deborah Morse, the high school principal, was helping teachers and other staff supervise the student body, and she had spoken to students who had been throwing snowballs and bottles from the vicinity where Frederick was standing. When she saw the banner, she believed that the words "Bong Hits" connoted marijuana use and that the banner advocated using illegal drugs. This was not an especially fanciful conclusion. The word "bong" is a term that is generally understood to refer to a water-cooled pipe or pipe-like device for smoking marijuana. Similarly, the word "hit" means inhaling marijuana. The band Cypress Hill has recorded a song called "Hits from the Bong" that celebrates getting stoned. Because the school had a strong antidrug policy, Morse did not want students in the school to display a banner that appeared to be endorsing bong hits. She was also concerned that the banner would contribute to what was becoming an unruly situation. She told Frederick that the banner was inappropriate for a school activity. The other students dropped the banner, but Frederick argued that he had First Amendment rights and that Morse had no jurisdiction over him while he was across the street from school property. Morse confiscated the banner and told Frederick to come to her office. According to Morse's sworn affidavit, Frederick turned and walked in the opposite direction and did not go to her office. She had to track him down in a classroom.

Frederick claimed that he started quoting Thomas Jefferson regarding civil liberty while in Morse's office and that she doubled his suspension from five to ten days for doing so. Morse says that she never told Frederick that he would be suspended for five days, and that she does not remember the Jefferson quotation. She maintains that after hearing him out, she consulted the student handbook and his past disciplinary record. She decided on ten days' suspension on the basis of multiple infractions of the rules in the student handbook and Frederick's defiant attitude. Whatever the real story, scenes like this one, in which student and principal wrangle over discipline issues, are played out daily in many public schools.

Frederick appealed his suspension to the school board and testified at a hearing. He said he unfurled his banner as a humorous parody and that he first saw the phrase on a snowboard. He called attention to the website of a group called "Bong Hits For Jesus" that unfurls a banner at Mardi Gras in New Orleans to make fun of fundamentalist religious groups that protest the revelry. Frederick said he had tried to find a saying for the banner that was "pushy" (his term) because he wanted to see if Morse would try to suppress his speech outside of school grounds.

The school superintendent upheld the suspension in a nine-page memorandum. Frederick appealed that decision, and the school board upheld it. If Frederick had been at a private school, he would have had no federal constitutional claim to make in any court. But he was a student in a public high school. Frederick, who was 18 at the time, then decided to sue Morse and the school board for disciplining him. He requested that the defendants remove any reference to the discipline from his school records and that they amend his grades. He also asked for compensatory and punitive money damages and attorney's fees.

The district court decided that Morse did not have to pay money to her student since she was immune from money damages.[2] Government officials are immune from civil damages if their conduct does not violate a clearly established right; "clearly established" means that it must be clear to a reasonable official that the official's conduct was unlawful, either because there is published case law on point or because the official's actions were so far-fetched that the illegality is obvious. The court found no case law on point showing that Morse could not act as she did. On the contrary, the *Fraser* case had shown that it was objectively reasonable for Morse to believe that her action was proper. Frederick did not argue that Morse's actions were so far-fetched as to make the illegality apparent. Thus the district court ruled that Morse was immune from civil money damages.

Even if Morse could not be made to pay money to Frederick, he had also made claims asking for injunctive relief, so the court had to rule on the merits of the First Amendment claim. The trial court rejected Frederick's argument that his free speech rights had been violated. The court first determined that both the facts and common sense showed that the viewing of the torch relay was a school-sponsored activity. The court seems to be on firm footing here. Suppose there had been a disturbance among the student spectators, the teachers and principal had ignored it, and a student had been hurt. The parents of the hurt student would likely have a winning argument that the school staff had acted improperly by failing to supervise the students under their charge. If the event had been totally separate from the school, there would be no duty to intervene. It seems far-fetched to argue that this event, which occurred in front of the school, during school hours (when parents expect their children to be under school supervision) and after which the students immediately returned to their scheduled classes, was not connected to a school activity.

Since Frederick was at a school activity, the district court explained, the school had a greater degree of control over his expressive conduct. Unlike the students in *Tinker*, who had made a statement of personal opinion unrelated to the mission of the school, Frederick's statement directly contravened the school's policy regarding drug abuse prevention. Judge John Sedwick reviewed the Supreme Court opinion in *Fraser*, and stated that it had recognized that school officials could determine that certain speech does not teach students the boundaries of appropriate social behavior.

The school board in Juneau had a written policy that prohibited advocating illegal drug use. It was not unreasonable to read the message with the terms "bong hits" as advocating illegal drug use. Even Frederick admitted that the message could be read as referring to drug use. Principal Morse "had the authority, *if not the obligation*, to stop such messages at a school-sanctioned activity."[3]

Frederick's luck turned when he appealed his case to the Ninth Circuit Court of Appeals and found three judges who agreed not only that his First Amendment rights had been violated but that his high school principal had to pay him money damages because she had disciplined him.[4] The appeals court acknowledged that the case involved a school-authorized activity and that the statement on the banner expressed a positive statement about marijuana use, even if vague and nonsensical. But the appeals court maintained that the district court had focused on the wrong Supreme Court opinion.

Instead of *Fraser*, which dealt with speech that was offensive due to sexual innuendo, the district court should have used *Tinker* to resolve this case. Frederick's speech was "not 'plainly offensive' in the way sexual innuendo is." "Under *Tinker*, a school cannot discipline a student merely because a student advocates a position that is contrary to government policy." The Tinkers had protested war, and the federal government policy had been to advance the effort to win the war. If the Tinkers' speech undermining the war effort was protected, Frederick's speech undermining the school's policy against illegal drugs was also protected, according to the court of appeals.

Of course, this analysis could lead to some dubious consequences. Student speech that advocated cheating, indiscriminate unprotected sex, or drinking while driving could also be protected. But the court of appeals either did not see where its analysis could lead or chose not to address it. Indeed, the court was adamant that public schools could not suppress speech that undermines whatever mission it defines for itself. Once again we see how a court's mistrust of local school officials can drive its constitutional analysis.

After deciding that Joe Frederick's constitutional rights had been violated, the case was not over. Up to this point, no money was involved. The opinion simply meant that Frederick's disciplinary record would be expunged and that schools in the Ninth Circuit needed to follow the opinion's dictates in the future whenever they dealt with student speech that undermined their school's mission. But Frederick wanted more. He had asked that his former principal pay him money damages. The appeals court still needed to decide whether Morse had to pay Frederick; that is, whether the right was clearly established and whether it would have been clear to a reasonable school principal that her conduct was unlawful.

If the decision up to this point was somewhat surprising in the short shrift the court gave to the *Fraser* opinion, it was no less than astounding when it decided that student speech law was clearly established *and* that "the opacity in this particular corner of the law has been all but banished." If there is anything a reader of this book should take away from it, it is that this particular corner of the law is rife with complexity and controversy.

The court then analyzed whether Morse could have reasonably but mistakenly believed that her conduct did not violate Frederick's constitutional rights. Here the opinion reached a puzzling conclusion. Despite the fact that *a federal district court judge* had just ruled that there was no constitutional violation under these facts, the court of appeals ruled that a *school principal* could not have reasonably believed that her actions were acceptable.

The court of appeals based its opinion on an earlier Ninth Circuit case in which it had ruled that students were allowed to show disrespect for their teachers while involved in a labor dispute. In *Chandler v. McMinnville School District,* a school district hired replacement teachers to keep schools running during a teacher strike. Two students wore buttons that said "I'm not listening scab" and "Do scabs bleed?" When the students refused to remove the buttons, they were suspended, and they sued the school district. The school district moved to dismiss the complaint for failure to state a claim. As with the *Morse* case, the district court—finding the buttons "inherently disruptive"—ruled for the school district. The Ninth Circuit reversed. The court of appeals recognized that the term "scab" was used to refer to replacement workers during a strike and that it was usually meant as an insult or epithet. But *Tinker* requires that school officials must reasonably forecast substantial disruption of school activities. There was no showing at that stage of litigation that the buttons had caused this kind of disorder, so the district court had erred in dismissing the student's complaint.[5]

Based on the *McMinnville* case, the appeals court determined that Principal Morse should have known that her actions violated Frederick's rights. Thus she would have to pay money damages to Frederick.

> This case, therefore, wholly without constitutional reasons, in my judgment, subjects all the public schools in the country to the whims and caprices of their loudest-mouthed, but maybe not their brightest, students.
>
> —Justice Hugo Black

Joe Frederick may have been just like the students Justice Black had in mind in his *Tinker* dissent. Frederick's antics seem to have been motivated by the desire to get attention and cause trouble, and he showed a lack of respect toward his high school principal. The facts surrounding Frederick's dealings with Morse may seem humorous to some in the retelling. And perhaps as we read the dry record of the incident, her decision on discipline might seem a bit heavy-handed. But anyone who has worked in education lately realizes it is no easy task to teach and administer a public school. Teachers and principals have to make many decisions that affect their students every day. Every day, many educators see how the ravages of drug use in their young students erode their childhood and impair their future. Those who are attempting to maintain some form of discipline as they teach hundreds of students—many of whom are defiant and unruly—find little humor in the prospect of being ordered to pay money damages for disciplining a difficult student.

It may have been this aspect of the case that prompted the Supreme Court to hear it. During oral argument, some of the justices seemed to be particularly bothered by the damages Deborah Morse would have to pay Joe Frederick if the Ninth Circuit opinion stood.

Coming as it did after decades of silence and with its unusual facts, the case received a great deal of attention in the weeks preceding oral argument. Fifteen amicus briefs were filed. Chief Justice William Rehnquist had died the year before, so this was the first term in twenty-one years with a new chief justice. Another justice, Samuel Alito, was also new to the Court, replacing the Court's first woman Justice, Sandra O'Connor. Legal commentators were intensely interested in how the two new justices would affect the Court.

The Court heard oral argument on March 19, 2007. Former Solicitor General and Whitewater investigator Kenneth Starr, now the dean of Pepperdine Law School, took the podium to argue for the school. The theme of his argument was the serious problem of illegal drugs in schools and the glorification of the drug culture. He argued that when Morse saw a large banner about bong hits, she had to make a judgment on the spot. She made a reasonable judgment that this banner—either joking about or condoning drug use—was undermining the school's antidrug message. The Justice Department also sent a lawyer to argue along with Dean Starr, Deputy Solicitor General Edwin Kneedler. He wanted the Court to use the *Fraser*, standard. Under *Fraser* schools have the duty to inculcate civility and to prepare students for citizenship, and not violating the law is an important part of that.

Douglas Mertz, an attorney from Juneau, Alaska, argued the case for Joe Frederick. He started out by telling the Court, "This is a case about free speech. But Chief Justice Roberts immediately chimed in, "It's a case about money. Your client wants money from the principal personally for her actions in this case." The chief justice expressed his concern that principals and teachers around the country would fear that they might have to pay out of their own pockets whenever they took actions, pursuant to established school board policies, they thought were necessary to promote their school's educational mission. Justice Kennedy also remarked that Frederick was seeking damages in relation to "this sophomoric sign" from this principal "who has devoted her life to the school." Indeed, after the justices had wrestled with the First Amendment issue for an hour, it was hard for Mertz to argue that the issue was so clearly established that Morse was liable for money damages. As Justice Souter said, "We have been debating this in this courtroom for going on an hour, and it seems to me, however you come out, there is reasonable debate."

The merits of the First Amendment issue were debated with considerable energy. The crux of Mertz's argument was that as long as there was no physical disruption at school, the school had to tolerate student speech that undermined a school lesson, whether it be on drug use or anything else. Mertz was given a hypothetical: If a school initiated an antidrug program with movies, speakers, and police, is the school nonetheless required to allow a student to wear a button saying, "Smoke pot. It's fun"? Mertz answered that the school would have to tolerate a nondisruptive pin. Justice Kennedy asked if a student would be allowed to wear a pin that said "Rape is fun." When Mertz said this would be a problem because it would promote a violent act, he provoked some derisive comments from the Court. If it is only nonviolent crimes that a student cannot promote in school, then a sign saying "Extortion is profitable" would be okay, Justice Scalia noted. "This is a very, very, with all respect, ridiculous line," he remarked.

Justice Breyer summed up the difficulty of the issue, stating, "It's pretty hard to run a school where kids go around at public events publicly making a joke out of drugs. . . . He doesn't know the law, the principal. His job is to run the school. And so I guess what I'm worried about is a rule that would take [the student's] side; we'll see people testing limits all over the place in the high schools. But a rule [for the other side] may really limit people's rights on free speech. That's what I'm struggling with. Now, I want some help there, and I'm worried about the principal."

During Starr's rebuttal time, he reminded the Court that to allow a student to promote drugs in his school speech would "really be quite inconsistent with much of [the Court's] drug jurisprudence." He reminded the Court of the facts of *Tinker*, and declared, "We are light years away from that." When the red light at the podium blinked, Chief Justice Roberts stated, "The case is submitted."

The chief justice had the very next word on the case, as he wrote the majority opinion that was handed down on June 25, 2007. School speech must have been an important issue for the new chief; he could have assigned the opinion to any of the other justices in the majority, but he kept it to write himself. Chief Justice Roberts, joined by Justices Scalia, Kennedy, Thomas, and Alito, determined that "schools may take steps to safeguard those entrusted to their care from speech that can reasonably be regarded as encouraging illegal drug use." The Court held that the principal did not violate the First Amendment by confiscating the banner and suspending Frederick.[6]

None of the justices—not even those in dissent—seriously contended that Frederick was anywhere but at a school-sanctioned, school-supervised event. The key issue for the majority was whether a school principal could restrict student speech at a school event when that speech is reasonably viewed as promoting illegal drug use. Although the message on the banner was "cryptic," the majority determined that Morse's interpretation that it promoted illegal drug use was "plainly reasonable." It could be read as an imperative—"take bong hits"—or as celebrating bong hits.

The chief justice first reviewed *Tinker, Fraser,* and *Hazelwood* and then focused on cases about drug testing in school. When allowing drug testing at school in the face of a Fourth Amendment claim, the Court had recognized that deterring drug use by schoolchildren is an "important, perhaps compelling" state interest. Drug use can cause severe and permanent damage to the health and well-being of young people. Maturing nervous systems are more critically impaired by intoxicants than mature ones are, children become chemically dependent more easily than adults, and their rate of recovery is poor. Even students not taking drugs are affected, as it disrupts the educational process. Moreover, students are more likely to use drugs when the norms in school appear to tolerate such behavior.

The "special characteristics of the school environment," as discussed in every case beginning with *Tinker,* together with the governmental interest in stopping student drug abuse, allow schools "to restrict student expression that they reasonably regard as promoting illegal drug use." The danger from drug use is "serious and palpable." The Court refused to adopt a broader rule that all offensive speech could be proscribed, since much political and religious speech could be offensive to some. The problem with Frederick's banner was not that it was offensive, but that it promoted illegal drug use. Morse had to act on the spot when she saw Frederick's banner. Her failure to act would send a powerful message to her students. Put simply, "The First Amendment does not require schools to tolerate at school events student speech that contributes to the dangers of illegal drug use."

As we have seen so many times in the school speech cases, these issues can cause both fractured and fractious opinions. *Morse v. Frederick* was no exception, with five justices setting forth their views about "Bong Hits." Justice Alito wrote a concurring opinion, joined by Justice Kennedy. Justice Alito stated that he had joined the majority opinion with the understanding that it allowed schools to restrict only speech that a reasonable observer would interpret as advocating illegal drug use. He would not support an opinion that would allow restriction of speech that could plausibly be interpreted as commenting on any political or social issue.

Court watchers never really know how much amicus briefs influence the justices hearing a case, and *Morse v. Frederick* is no exception in that regard. But Joe Frederick had attracted some strange bedfellows in his support. Along with groups that are generally viewed as being on the liberal side of the political spectrum (like the Student Press Law Center and the Lambda Legal Defense and Education Fund), groups that are generally viewed as more conservative also supported him (like the Christian Legal Society and the Liberty Legal Institute). These groups feared that a broad ruling that schools could restrain speech that did not fit in with the school's mission would allow "politically correct" school districts and administrators to silence speech supporting certain religious or political issues. This argument may have resonated with Justices Alito and Kennedy.

Justice Alito recognized that the speech rules in school were different from the general rules about free speech. But he was unwilling to treat public school officials as if they were in loco parentis. This unequivocal rejection of in loco parentis is in tension with some other school cases the Court had decided before Justice Alito joined the bench. In two drug-testing cases, the Court defined the authority of the school as custodial and tutelary.[7] This meant that school officials are allowed to act as a reasonable custodian would while supervising students. Although not precisely the in loco parentis power, this custodial power could be read as being broad and deep. Justice Kennedy signed on with the majority in both drug-testing cases, and it may be that he had a change of heart in the intervening years. It is not clear whether Justice Alito—adamant that school officials do not have the delegated power of a parent—would sign on to an opinion that described school authority as that of a custodian.

Since he was unwilling to countenance any change in the general rules about speech or parental delegation, Justice Alito needed another theory. He pointed out that one special characteristic of the school setting is the unusual threat to the physical safety of the students. Justice Alito observed that parents cannot control the school setting, and students might not be able to avoid threatening persons or situations in the same way they could outside school. Because of this special feature of the school environment, "schools must have greater authority to intervene before speech leads to violence." This theory, if read more broadly, could have an impact beyond this particular case in instances where schools are faced with student threats and other violent speech.

Although speech that advocates illegal drug use may not be as obvious a threat as speech advocating violence, Justice Alito pointed out that illegal drug use "presents a grave and in many ways unique threat to the physical safety of students." Thus public schools may ban speech that advocates illegal drug use. But Justice Alito warned that this was at "the outer reaches of what the First Amendment permits."

Justice Breyer concurred in part and dissented in part. He would not have reached the merits of the constitutional question. He would have merely decided the qualified immunity issue and determined that the student could not collect money damages from his high school principal on these facts.

Justice Breyer certainly had no sympathy for Joe Frederick: "What is a principal to do when a student unfurls a 14-foot banner (carrying an irrelevant or inappropriate message) during a school-related event in an effort to capture the attention of television cameras? Nothing? In my view, a principal or a teacher might reasonably view Frederick's conduct, in this setting, as simply beyond the pale. And a school official, knowing that adolescents often test the outer boundaries of acceptable behavior, may believe it is important (for the offending student and his classmates) to establish when a student has gone too far."

But Justice Breyer was concerned that the Court's opinion could authorize other viewpoint-based restrictions beyond the context of illegal drugs. He believed that the Court did not need to decide the difficult First Amendment issue. Rather, the Court should merely state that Morse need not pay Joe Frederick money damages because she did not clearly violate the law when she confronted him. Even the dissenting justices all agreed about this. Other appellate courts have observed that the *Tinker, Fraser,* and *Hazelwood* tests are complex and often difficult to apply and that none of them clearly governs this case. Deciding that Morse simply did not have to pay damages could leave the First Amendment issue for another day.

Although Justice Breyer's solution of dodging the question may have been one way to get the Court off the hook, the problem with this suggestion is that Frederick's complaint asked for more than just money damages. He also asked for declaratory relief (a declaration that Morse violated his First Amendment rights) and for two injunctions (one prohibiting Morse from violating his rights or those of other similarly situated students and another requiring the school to remove references to the incident from his school record). Justice Breyer tried to get around this hurdle by suggesting that Frederick was suspended on "non-speech-related grounds" because he failed to report to the principal's office and because of his "defiant [and] disruptive behavior" and "belligerent attitude" when he finally did report. This explanation is not especially persuasive, as the parties did not argue this and none of the courts below discussed it. Although Frederick's antagonistic attitude might have been sufficient grounds for punishment in Justice Breyer's view, the evidence in the record indicated that his problems with Morse were rooted in that fourteen-foot banner.

Justice Thomas also wrote a separate concurrence, and he would have gone farther than the majority. Indeed, Justice Thomas was ready and willing to overrule *Tinker* in its entirety: "The standard set forth in Tinker v. Des Moines Independent School District is without basis in the Constitution." Justice Thomas argued that the First Amendment, as originally understood, does not protect speech in public schools. Although the Court has narrowed some of the broad strokes painted by the *Tinker* majority, not since Justice Black's famous dissent had any justice called for its demise.

The *Morse* opinion is a perfect vehicle to explore the differing views of some of the justices on the role of the courts in constitutional interpretation. The battle between Justices Frankfurter and Jackson in the mid-1900s was a part of this debate about the role of the judiciary. The issue is alive and well in 2007. Justice Thomas's view of the role of courts is that judges should attempt to interpret the original understanding of the constitutional text. To an originalist like Justice Thomas, this keeps judges within certain boundaries and does not allow the judge—who is not elected by the people—to import his or her own views and biases into constitutional decision making. If society has changed so that this original interpretation is obsolete, then the Constitution has provided a way for the people, not judges, to amend it. Judges like Justice Breyer have a different view. They believe a judge's role is to interpret and reinterpret the meaning of the Constitution continually in light of changes in societal norms. Under this view, the meaning of the Constitution changes; the Constitution is a "living document." But these changes are not made through the democratic process. They are based on the norms of a majority of the Court at any given time. Some justices—at times Justice Souter is in this camp—rely heavily on previous cases from the Court. Even if some of these cases may have been based on incorrect doctrinal analysis at the outset, they have become so intertwined with the understanding of what the Constitution means that it would be too disturbing and confusing to overrule them.[8]

The Thomas opinion explores the history of public schools, pointing out that when public schools began to emerge during the 1800s, no one doubted their ability to educate and discipline students just as private schools did. The doctrine of in loco parentis allowed schools to discipline students and to regulate their speech. The *Tinker* opinion conflicted with the traditional understanding of the judiciary's role in regard to the public school and the doctrine of in loco parentis that had governed the schoolhouse from the time of Blackstone. *Tinker* had "effected a sea change in students' speech rights, extending them well beyond traditional bounds."

Justice Thomas insisted that the cases the *Tinker* Court cited in favor of its "bold proposition" about the schoolhouse gate do not support it. He is correct that the *Tinker* Court made little attempt to ground the opinion in the history of education or in the original understanding of the First Amendment. One case *Tinker* cited involved a challenge by a private school; another involved a challenge by parents who wished to send their children to private schools.

Neither provides support for the idea that students have free speech rights in school. Justice Thomas pointed out the Court has since cut back on *Tinker*, creating exception after exception, including the new one that the Court set forth in *Morse*. The new rule seems to be that "students have a right to speak in school—except when they don't." Although the idea of treating children as if it were still the nineteenth century would find little support today, he argued that there is no constitutional imperative to allow all student speech.

Not only did Justice Thomas insist that *Tinker* was wrong as a matter of constitutional interpretation; he also maintained that it had harmed the country's public schools. "In the name of the First Amendment, *Tinker* has undermined the traditional authority of teachers to maintain order in the public schools." The case at hand was a perfect example. "To elevate [Frederick's] impertinence to the status of constitutional protection would be farcical, and would indeed be 'to surrender control of the American public school system to the public school students'" (quoting Justice Black's *Tinker* dissent).

Justice Thomas did not convince any other justice to join him in calling for the end of *Tinker*. But as we have seen in other cases, these separate opinions, even dissents, sometimes have a way of becoming a part of later opinions in surprising ways. Only time will tell if this opinion by Justice Thomas will have an influence on the next chapter of the school speech story.

Justice Stevens, joined by Justices Souter and Ginsberg, wrote a rather curious dissent. He first found fault with the school for punishing Frederick for expressing a view with which it disagreed. For support for this viewpoint on the discrimination theory, Justice Stevens unearthed Justice Harlan's *Tinker* dissent in which he would have allowed the school to restrict student speech unless the decision was based on something "other than legitimate school concerns." An example Justice Harlan gave for a concern that was illegitimate was a desire to prohibit the expression of an unpopular point of view while permitting the expression of the dominant opinion. Of course, illegal drug use is not so much "unpopular" with school officials as it is considered harmful and dangerous to the students in their charge. And unlike troop withdrawal, smoking marijuana is illegal. Moreover, there is nothing in the case that suggests that Morse allowed a fourteen-foot antidrug banner while taking down Frederick's bong hits message.

Later in his dissent, even Justice Stevens acknowledged that the custodial and tutelary supervision by school officials might make it "appropriate to tolerate some targeted viewpoint discrimination in this unique setting." He also admitted that the general speech rules about restricting speech that advocates illegal conduct—incitement to imminent lawless action—possibly "ought to be relaxed at school." His main bone of contention with the majority, therefore, seemed to be that the "Bong Hits" message, in his view, did not *advocate* illegal drug use, since it would not actually persuade even the dumbest student to take illegal drugs.

Under this analysis, Frederick's speech apparently could be restrained only if his banner said something like "*Take* Bong Hits for Jesus" or "*Enjoy* Bong Hits for Jesus," *and* only if it could persuade other students to change their behavior. But without the necessary verb and persuasive operation, a speech making light of drug use or celebrating drugs would be permissible. A principal dealing with the issue presumably would need to parse out the phrase to determine the level of advocacy that was requested. Justice Stevens did not discuss why a school might wish to avoid an environment in which irreverent satire and celebration of bong hits—or "doobies," or "crystal," or "horse," or "XtC," or "rocks," or "snow," or "crank," or "toot," or "love doves," or "smack"—is considered acceptable for students.

Perhaps uncomfortable with where this line of reasoning might lead, Justice Stevens changed course near the end of his dissent. He turned the opinion into a referendum on the importance of protest and discussed the importance of "unfettered debate, even among high school students, about the wisdom of the war on drugs or of legalizing marijuana for medicinal use." This issue is certainly important, and it would be good for the Court to address it in a case where it was raised by the parties. But even if the justices could agree that the hallways of the public schools are a proper forum for heated debate and protest about social issues, this issue was simply irrelevant to the case before the Court. Joe Frederick never hinted that his banner was intended to be part of a political protest. He repeatedly said that he raised it to get the attention of television cameras and to see what Principal Morse would do about it. Should the next student with a "Bong Hits" banner intend it for political protest, the lower courts will have to address that issue separately.

Near the end of the majority opinion, Chief Justice Roberts noted that even the dissent had admitted that it might be appropriate to tolerate some viewpoint discrimination in the unique school setting and that other rules could be relaxed as well. He pointed out that the difference between the dissent and the majority was a narrow one: whether the banner constituted promotion of illegal drug use. The majority believed it did, and "the dissent's contrary view on that relatively narrow question hardly justifies sounding the First Amendment bugle."

Despite Chief Justice Roberts's attempt to calm the waters, the opinion caused quite a stir. A *New York Times* editorial said that the Court had mangled "sound precedent and the First Amendment."[9] A *Los Angeles Times* editorial said that the Court had "drained the life" out of one of the court's landmark pronouncements that children "do not shed their constitutional rights to freedom of speech or expression at the schoolhouse gate."[10] The *Worcester* (MA) *Telegram* insisted that the principal had no jurisdiction over Frederick, since he was not on school grounds, and declared that historians would find the opinion a "low point" for the Roberts Court.[11]

Underlying much of the commentary decrying the *Morse* opinion is the idea that students in public schools are treated as second-class citizens because they are not afforded the same constitutional rights as adults. But the law in other contexts has consistently recognized that minors are different. It protects minors in some areas because of their vulnerability, and in other areas it refrains from affording them the full rights of citizens because of their lack of maturity. It is not only small children who have different capabilities from those of adults. Recent scientific evidence has emphasized the difference between adolescents and adults. Some segments of the legal system have traditionally recognized these differences. Minors cannot drive, drink alcohol, or buy tobacco products. Their constitutional rights to abortion are more limited than those of adults. They are treated differently from adults in tort law and in contract law. Their freedom of movement may be restricted by local curfew laws. They may not even vote—certainly one of the most important right afforded to any citizen—because they are viewed as not having the maturity to understand how to exercise the franchise.

In *Roper v. Simmons,* briefs submitted to the Supreme Court argued that minors' lack of maturity and responsibility, together with their vulnerability and susceptibility, made them different enough from adults so that they should not be executed for crimes for which adults might receive the death penalty. In holding that it was unconstitutional to execute persons who committed a capital crime while under the age of eighteen, the Supreme Court emphasized that adolescents were different from adults and more prone to immature and irresponsible behavior. The Court acknowledged that drawing categorical age rules at eighteen "is subject to the objection always raised against categorical rules, [but] that is the point where society draws the line for many purposes between childhood and adulthood."[12]

If adolescents have such different social and biological developmental differences in these contexts such that they are not deemed capable of responsibility, do they somehow change when it comes to exercising their right of expression in school? Some of the cases that arise in the public school systems indicate that they do not. Allowing teachers and school officials to constrain some expression of children and adolescents while they are trying to educate them in the public school system is not so different from what the law has recognized long ago about the young.

> Hey kid, rock and roll,
> Rock on.
> And where do we go from here?
> Which is the way that's clear?
>   —Def Leppard, "Rock On"

We are in the middle of a fascinating story, and there is no way to tell how it will come out. The *Morse* school speech case entered the fray at what may be a significant time for the Court. Its legacy is yet to be determined. Despite rulings where Chief Justice Roberts delivered the judgment of the Court, he could not unite the five conservatives in his reasoning in *Morse,* or in some of the other controversial cases that came down at the end of the term. Unity on the Court at this point came from the four more liberal justices, who often joined together in a single dissent rather than writing separate opinions.

Perhaps the justices have found a new interest in school speech issues, and they will decide to hear more cases in the near future. Although the pundits claim that the Court's June 2007 rulings have a decidedly conservative edge, both Justices Alito and Kennedy distanced themselves from Chief Justice Roberts's majority opinion in *Morse,* carving out a safe haven for "political speech." It will be up to the lower courts to determine to what extent speech is "political" and to what extent it will be protected. Perhaps the next Joe Frederick need only write "Vote for Bong Hits" on his banner to receive First Amendment protection.

But "Bong Hits" banners are not the only issues on the new frontier for school speech. Suppose Joe Frederick had composed his message on a laptop at his home, and a friend had opened it in school where many other students could see it. Chief Justice

Roberts hinted at a scenario like this in *Morse* when he said, "There is some uncertainty at the outer boundaries as to when schools should apply school-speech precedents, see Porter v. Ascension Parish School Bd., 393 F.3d 608, 615 n. 22 (CA5 2004), but not on these facts" (meaning the facts in *Morse*). In *Porter,* a student had claimed that his First Amendment rights had been violated when he was removed from school and placed in an alternative school because he had made a sketch depicting a violent siege on the school. The student had completed the drawing at home and had stored it in his closet for two years; it had been taken to school by his brother. The court of appeals found that the speech was not on-campus speech or directed at campus and was protected. (The principal nonetheless was protected by qualified immunity.) The part of *Porter* to which the Chief Justice specifically referred describes the difficulty courts have had dealing with this issue:

> We are aware of the difficulties posed by state regulation of student speech that takes place off-campus and is later brought on-campus either by the communicating student or others to whom the message was communicated. Refusing to differentiate between student speech taking place on-campus and speech taking place off-campus, a number of courts have applied the test in *Tinker* when analyzing off-campus speech brought onto the school campus. *See Boucher v. Sch. Bd. of Sch. Dist. of Greenfield,* 134 F.3d 821, 827–28 (7th Cir.1998) (student disciplined for an article printed in an underground newspaper that was distributed on school campus); *Sullivan v. Houston Indep. Sch. Dist.,* 475 F.2d 1071, 1075–77 (5th Cir.1973) (student punished for authoring article printed in underground newspaper distributed off-campus, but near school grounds); *LaVine,* 257 F.3d at 989 (analyzing student poem composed off-campus and brought onto campus by the composing student under *Tinker*); *Killion v. Franklin Reg'l Sch. Dist.,* 136 F.Supp. 2d 446, 455 (W.D.Pa.2001) (student disciplined for composing degrading top-ten list distributed via e-mail to school friends, who then brought it onto

campus; author had been disciplined before for bringing top-ten lists onto campus); *Emmett v. Kent Sch. Dist. No. 415,* 92 F.Supp. 2d 1088, 1090 (W.D.Wash.2000) (applying *Tinker* to mock obituary website constructed off-campus); *Beussink v. Woodland R-IV Sch. Dist.,* 30 F.Supp. 2d 1175, 1180 (E.D.Mo.1998) (student disciplined for article posted on personal internet site); *Bystrom v. Fridley High Sch.,* 686 F.Supp. 1387, 1392 (D.Minn.1987) (student disciplined for writing article that appeared in an underground newspaper distributed on school campus). [And compare] *Thomas v. Bd. of Educ., Granville Cent. Sch. Dist.,* 607 F.2d 1043, 1050–52 (2d. Cir.1979) (refusing to apply *Tinker* to student newspaper published and distributed off-campus); *Klein v. Smith,* 635 F.Supp. 1440, 1441–42 (D.Me.1986) (enjoining suspension of student who made a vulgar gesture to a teacher while off-campus); *see also Killion,* 136 F.Supp. 2d at 454 ("Although there is limited case law on the issue, courts considering speech that occurs off school grounds have concluded [relying on Supreme Court decisions] that school official's authority over off-campus expression is much more limited than expression on school grounds."); Clay Calvert, *Off-Campus Speech, On-Campus Punishment: Censorship of the Emerging Internet Underground,* 7 B.U.J. Sci. & Tech. L. 243, 279 (2001) (noting that *Tinker* is ill-suited to deal with off-campus student expression that is unintentionally brought on-campus by others).

By referring explicitly to this note, Chief Justice Roberts seems to be acknowledging that there is a controversy brewing in the lower courts regarding off-campus speech that makes its way onto school grounds. *Morse* will surely be a case lower courts will use as they grapple with this issue. Recall how far the *Tinker* opinion has strayed from its moorings. Soon after it was decided, it was used in arguments to support all kinds of student speech, from hair length to school plays. The Supreme Court may soon need to accept another school speech case to decide about the "long arm" of *Tinker* and off-campus speech.

A related issue that has proved vexing for education institutions and lower courts is student speech that is dark, violent, or threatening. This kind of speech—on or off campus—may be verbal, or it may appear in student journals or other creative writing. Teachers at all levels of education are put in the position of judging whether their students' work is creative expression or disturbed ranting. Since the rash of school shootings, including the one at Columbine, questions about the appropriate reaction have become common in schools and in the courts, as school officials attempt to respond to violent speech before it turns into violent action. The mass murders at Virginia Tech in April 2007 prompted calls for some kind of action when student writings are filled with violence after reports surfaced about the writings of the killer, Cho Seung-Hui.

At the university level, federal privacy and antidiscrimination laws affect how the institution may deal with a student whose writings and behavior might indicate mental illness. In most situations, the university cannot tell parents about the behavior or release information in education or medical records without the student's consent. Most state laws do not permit university officials to bring students to hospitals unless there is imminent risk to the student or others.

Universities are put in a difficult position. If they fail to act, they may be liable if they do not prevent a murder or suicide. When a student at Massachusetts Institute of Technology wrote suicide notes and used university counseling services before committing suicide by setting herself on fire, the state court allowed her parents—who had not been told—to sue the school for $27.7 million. (The case settled for an undisclosed amount.) But universities may also be liable if they take action when a student exhibits troubling behavior. City University of New York paid money damages to a student who sued after being barred from her dormitory after hospitalization for a suicide attempt, and George Washington University reached a confidential settlement for suspending a student who had sought hospitalization for depression.[13]

Teachers and principals in middle and high schools have no easier task. Many schools have policies that involve parents, school counselors, and other health providers (even police) when a student's behavior appears to pose a risk of harm to the student or others. But schools also have disciplinary procedures for students who threaten teachers or others. Schools may revert to the *Tinker* rule and assess whether the speech or writing would cause a substantial disruption or material interference with school activities, or they may use a legal doctrine that assesses whether speech is a "true threat," which is not protected.

Students who sue school officials after they are disciplined for threatening speech typically claim that the speech was a joke or the writing was merely fiction, and they did not intend to do harm. For instance, ninth-grader Rachel Boim wrote about her sixth period class: "Yes, my math teacher. I lothe [*sic*] him with every bone in my body." The story continued, "I stand up and pull the gun from my pocket. BANG the force blows him back and everyone in the class sits there in shock." Rachel claimed her work was fiction and that she was punished for exercising her First Amendment rights. The school principal was concerned about the violence in the writing, particularly since Rachel had math during sixth period with a male teacher.[14] When she was disciplined with a school suspension, she sued the school and the principal.

Teacher and principals have a difficult call to make in these cases. Mental health professionals cannot always assess with certainty when and if an *adult* will act out violently, even if they have been treating a patient for some time. Teenagers are even more difficult to figure out. Research studies report that from ages eleven to fourteen, young teens lose connections between cells in the part of the brain that enables them to think clearly and make good decisions.[15]

"Teenagers often make poor decisions because their brains haven't attained an adult level of organization." Indeed, a coalition of psychiatric and legal organizations used the science of neural development in a brief before the Supreme Court arguing against the death penalty for juveniles.[16] In other contexts outside the school—at an airport, for instance—people understand that any speech about violence, even made in jest, will be taken seriously. If violence in school is more commonplace than airplane hijackings, it is not surprising that school officials sometimes are willing to err on the side of student safety rather than on the side of free expression. The courts, perhaps even the Supreme Court, will have the last word on when and if school officials can act in these kinds of circumstances. As they determine what rules schools must follow, judges will be well aware of the social context spawned by both Columbine and Virginia Tech, just as judges who served in years past were well aware of senate hearings and war protests.

Are there other forms of speech that would be excepted from the *Tinker* rule? May a public school prohibit students from wearing tee shirts with messages that condemn homosexuality? Prohibiting anti-gay messages because of the content of the message runs the risk of trampling some tenets of First Amendment rights, because it is viewpoint discrimination, as well as a restraint on "political" speech. In some instances, religious speech may also come into play. For example, a student group in one high school in California had a "Day of Silence" to promote tolerance, particularly of homosexual students. One student, Tye Harper, who disagreed with the theme of the event, wore tee shirts on two separate days. On the day of the event, he wore a shirt that said "I will not accept what God has condemned" on the front and "Homosexuality is shameful. Romans 1:27" on the back. The next day he wore a shirt that said "Be ashamed. Our school embraced what God has condemned" on the front, with the same message on the back as the previous day. When he refused to remove the shirt or turn it inside out, he was punished.

The Ninth Circuit Court of Appeals (the same court that had allowed Joe Frederick's banner and student tee shirts saying "Scabs Bleed") refused to allow Tye Harper to wear the tee shirt.[17] The opinion backed away considerably from *Tinker*, which had cautioned that suppressing student speech required more than "a mere desire to avoid the discomfort and unpleasantness" that arises when hearing an unpopular opinion. It also backed away from court holdings that addressed another part of *Tinker*. Recall that *Tinker* said that schools could suppress speech that caused substantial disruption or material interference *or* speech that "impinge[s] on the rights of others." But courts addressing that last part of *Tinker* had said that the speech had to be of such a serious magnitude that it would amount to a civil tort. The Ninth Circuit changed course, stating that the tee shirt was a psychological attack that infringed on the rights of gay and lesbian students, and that schools could ban it.

The court limited its holding only to remarks directed at a student's minority status, such as race, religion, or sexual orientation. Tee shirts that said "Young Republicans Suck" or "Young Democrats Suck" could not be banned. These shirts might not be civil, but the court decided that they would not be sufficiently damaging to the individual or to the educational process. (The court did not mention if schools might be able to ban words like "suck" from student speech at school because of vulgarity.)

Perhaps Justice Thomas was right in his *Morse* concurrence when he stated that the current speech rules mean only that "students have a right to speak in schools except when they don't." Determining when they do and when they don't will continue to be a developing story as courts and schools struggle to come to terms with how the First Amendment fits in the school setting. The vague legal lines that began with *Tinker* have not become clearer over the decades. There will be no dearth of opportunity to add new chapters. Despite the ban on prayer, students will continue to push against the boundaries for declaration and distribution of religious speech in school. Issues regarding what material students have a right to receive will continue to arise as Congress passes legislation trying to protect children from harmful material on the internet. Teachers will remonstrate that their speech is part of academic freedom. The Pledge of Allegiance furor will erupt again. There will be more tee shirts, more banners, more websites.

The school speech story is one that plumbs the soul of the nation. It reveals our past in ways that we may not have perceived when viewing it through another lens. It colors our future in ways that we cannot yet comprehend. It uncovers fissures both at our highest levels of government and at the most local level, about the role of courts and the mission of schools.

This book began the tale of school speech with a quotation from Abraham Lincoln about self-preservation. He asked how a government could "walk the line," that is, allow enough liberty for its citizens to be free, but not so much that its citizens would ultimately destroy it. How do we determine how much liberty is necessary in our public schools for students to gain an abiding respect for our fundamental freedoms without destroying the order that is necessary for them to obtain a serious education? The school speech story presents no concrete solution, and there are troubling costs when the line is drawn too far to one side or the other. It is a frustrating exercise at times, but I suspect that Mr. Lincoln was well aware that there is no easy answer. Perhaps the most significant mainstay of our system is that we continue to ask the question.

Notes

1. Outside the Schoolhouse Gate

1. Thomas Jefferson to James Madison. December 20, 1787, Paris. The papers of Thomas Jefferson, Ed. by Julian P. Boyd et al. (Princeton, N.J.: Princeton University Press, 1950) 12:440.
2. West Virginia v. Barnette, 319 U.S. 624 (1943).
3. Spence v. Washington, 418 U.S. 405 (1974).
4. Police Dept of Chicago v. Mosley, 408 U.S. 92 (1972).
5. Grayned v. City of Rockford, 408 U.S. 104 (1972).
6. United States v. O'Brien, 391 U.S. 367 (1968).
7. Abrams v. U.S., 250 U.S. 616 (1918).

2. The Vietnam War and "Hazardous Freedom"

1. Tinker v. Des Moines Independent Community School District, 258 F. Supp. 971 (1966).
2. Tinker v. Des Moines Independent Community School District, 383 F.2d 988 (8th Cir.1967).
3. Tinker v. Des Moines Independent Community School District, 393 U.S. 503 (1969).
4. Paul Goodman, "The New Reformation," *New York Times,* September 14, 1969, 32, 33.
5. 363 F.2d 744 (5th Cir. 1966).

6. Abe Fortas, *Concerning Dissent and Disobedience* (New York: Signet Books, 1968).

7. Id. at 22.

8. See discussion in Chapter 4.

9. Fred P. Graham, "Freedom of Speech, but Not License," *New York Times,* March 2, 1969, E11 (predicting—wrongly—that the new freedom would not mean that students could successfully challenge school rules about "hippie hair styles").

10. Paul G. Haskell, "Student Expression in the Public Schools: Tinker Distinguished," 59 *Geo. L. Rev.* 37, 37 (1970–1971).

11. Herbert G. Lawson, "Some Students Find They Can Win Demands by Suing Their School," *Wall Street Journal,* November 25, 1969, 1.

12. Id.

13. Id.

14. Id.

15. Wisconsin v. Yoder, 406 U.S. 205 (1972).

16. Linda Lyons, "Teens Stay True to Parents' Political Perspectives," Gallup Poll News Service, January 4, 2005.

17. Heart of Atlanta Motel v. United States, 379 U.S. 241 (1964); Loving v. Virginia, 388 U.S. 1 (1967).

18. 363 F.2d 744 (5th Cir. 1966).

19. Blackwell v. Issaquena County Board of Education, 363 F.2d 749 (5th Cir. 1966).

20. Fortas, *Concerning Dissent and Civil Disobedience,* 60, 61.

21. Id. at 61.

22. See Hugh W. Divine, "A Note on Tinker," 7 *Wake Forest L. Rev* 539, 543 (1971).

23. Diane Felmlee et al., "Peer Influence on Classroom Attention," 48 *Soc. Psychol. Q.* 215, 223 (1985).

24. Tinker v. Des Moines Indep. Community School Dist., 393 U.S. 503, 518 (1969) (Black, J., dissenting).

25. Goss v. Lopez, 419 U.S. 565 (1975).

26. United States Constitution, amendment XIV.

27. United States Constitution, amendment IV.

28. New Jersey v. T.L.O., 469 U.S. 325 (1985).

29. Ingraham v. Wright, 430 U.S. 651 (1977).
30. Richard Arum, *Judging School Discipline* (Cambridge, Mass.: Harvard University Press, 2003).
31. Id. 24–25.
32. Rendell-Baker v. Kohn, 457 U.S. 830 (1982).
33. W. Stuart Stuller, "High School Academic Freedom: The Evolution of a Fish out of Water," 77 *Neb. L. Rev.* 301 (1998).
34. Id. Healy v. James, 408 U.S. 169 (1972).
35. Papish v. Board of Curators of the University of Missouri, 410 U.S. 667 (1973).

3. The Second Wave and the Constraint of Civility

1. Bethel School Dist. v. Fraser, 478 U.S. 675 (1986).
2. Jonathan Yardley, "We Have Met the Future and It Is Us," *Washington Post,* June 11, 1995, 3. Unsigned review of *1939, The Lost World of the Fair,* by David Gallanter, *Book World,* WBK 3 (1995).
3. The Civil Rights Attorney's Fee Act of 1976, 42 U.S.C. § 1988.
4. Mark Brown, "A Primer on the Law of Attorney's Fees under Section 1988," 37 *Urb. Law.* 663 (2005).
5. Id.
6. FCC v. Pacifica Foundation, 438 U.S. 325 (1985).
7. 438 U.S. 726 (1978).
8. See Haskell, "Student Expression in the Public Schools: Tinker Distinguished," 59 *Geo. L. J.* 37, 57–58 (1970).
9. Linda Greenhouse, *Becoming Justice Blackmun* (New York: Holt, 2005).
10. Papish v. Board of Curators of the University of Missouri, 410 U.S. 667, 672 (1973) (Burger, C. J., dissenting).
11. According to the National Center for Education Statistics (http://nces.gov), about 48,574,000 students were enrolled in the public schools in 2006.
12. 319 U.S. 624 (1943) and 347 U.S. 483 (1954).
13. 441 U.S. 68 (1979).
14. Bethel School Dist. v. Fraser, 1985 WL 667979 (Brief of the United

States as Amicus Curiae Supporting Petitioners); citing Charles and Mary Beard, *The Beards' New Basic History of the United States* (Doubleday, 1968).

15. D. W. Brogan, "The Quarrel of Charles Austin Beard and the American Constitution," 18 *Economic History Rev.* 199 (1965).

16. Pope McCorkle, "The Historian as Intellectual: Charles Beard and the Constitution Reconsidered," 28 *Legal History* 314 (1984).

17. Richard Hofstadter, *The Progressive Historians: Turner, Beard, Parrington* 344 (New York: Alfred A. Knopf, 1968).

18. Ambach v. Norwick, 441 U.S. 68 (1979), 76–77.

19. Cohen v. California, 403 U.S. 15 (1971). Texas v. Johnson, 491 U.S. 397 (1989).

20. Ginsberg v. New York, 390 U.S. 629 (1968); Board of Education v. Pico, 457 U.S. 853 (1982); FCC v. Pacifica Foundation, 438 U.S. 7726 (1978).

21. See New Jersey v. T.L.O., 469 U.S. 325 (1985). The doctrine of in loco parentis is "in tension with contemporary reality and with the teachings of this Court." "[S]chool officials act as representatives of the State, not merely as surrogates for the parents, and they cannot claim the parents' immunity from the strictures of the Fourth Amendment."

22. The seven words were *shit, piss, fuck, cunt, cocksucker, motherfucker,* and *tits.* 438 U.S. 726 (1978) Appendix to Opinon of the Court.

23. The statute allowed the FCC to forbid the use of "any obscene, indecent or profane language by means of radio communications." The FCC did not impose a formal sanction but wrote an order for the radio station's license file. If subsequent complaints were received, the FCC would review the file to determine whether to impose further sanctions.

24. After an appeal by producer David O. Selznick, the film industry's self-regulatory body, the Production Code Administration, gave permission with a Code seal for the Rhett Butler character to say "damn" but fined the film $5,000 for violating the Code's provision against profanity. Contrary to popular belief (and apparently that of

Justice Stevens) the nation had been shocked by the word *damn* in a film even before *Gone with the Wind* was released in 1939; the word had been spoken by two characters in *Pygmalion* (1938) and in *Alice Adams* (1935). *"Gone with the Wind": Original Motion Picture Soundtrack,* deluxe ed. liner notes. Rhino/Weu (original CD release date October 15, 1996)

25. Matthew Fraser, email message to the author, January 23, 2007.
26. He is also executive director of Education Unlimited, a company that runs academic summer programs for kids and teens in California and on the East Coast. Fraser thinks his case "largely gutted the Tinker v. Des Moines decision by lowering the standard for what constitutes disruption to such a low level as to effectively make the concept meaningless in practice." Id.
27. Matthew Fraser, email message to University of Georgia law student Guy Milhalter, August 22, 2006, on file with author.
28. Minersville District v. Gobitis, 310 U.S. 586, 598 (1939).
29. Tussman, *Government and the Mind* 54 (New York: Oxford University Press, 1977).
30. 42 U.S.C. §2000d.
31. Bryant v. Independent School Dist., 334 F.3d 928 (2003). Courts dealing with Title VI racial harassment in school have turned to the standards set forth by the U.S. Supreme Court for sexual harassment since there is no Title VI case directly on point from the Supreme Court.
32. 20 U.S.C. §1681(a).
33. Cannon v. University of Chicago, 441 U.S. 677, 694–698 (1979).
34. Gebser v. Lago Vista Independent School Dist., 524 U.S. 274 (1998).
35. Davis v. Monroe County Board of Education, 526 U.S. 629 (1999).
36. Montgomery v. Independent School Dist., 109 F. Supp. 2d 1081 (D. Minn. 2000).
37. Jon B. Gould, *Speak No Evil: The Triumph of Hate Speech Regulation* (Chicago: University of Chicago Press, 2005).
38. Id. at 5.
39. Id. at 5.

40. Id. at 25.

41. These facts come from Judge Avern Cohn's description in Doe v. University of Michigan, 721 F. Supp. 852 (E.D. Mich. 1989).

42. UWM Post v. University of Wisconsin, 774 F. Supp. 1163 (E.D Wis. 1991); Dambrot v. Central Michigan, 55 F.3d 1177 (6th Cir. 1995); University and Corry v. Stanford University, no. 740309 Cal. Super. Ct. (filed February 27, 1995).

43. 505 U.S. 377 (1992).

44. 315 U.S. 568 (1942).

45. Robert A. Sedler, "Speech Codes Are Still Dead," review of *Speak No Evil,* by Jon B. Gould, *Academe,* (May–June, 2006), www .aaup.org/AAUP/pubres/academe. Can also be found at http://find articles.com/p/articles/miqu3860/is200605/ain1718445.

46. Gould, *Speak No Evil.*

47. Id. at 5–6.

48. Id. at 6.

49. Sedler, "Speech Codes Are Still Dead."

50. Gould, *Speak No Evil,* at 6.

51. Bair v. Shippensburg University, 280 F. Supp. 2d 357 (M.D. Pa. 2003).

52. For more on this issue see Gould, *Speak No Evil,* chap. 4.

53. A report in 1992 stated that over 60 percent of American colleges and universities had such policies, and another 11 percent were considering enacting them." Vince Herron, "Increasing the Speech: Diversity, Campus Speech Codes, and the Pursuit of Truth," 67 *So. Cal. L. Rev.* 407, 439 n. 32 (1994) (citing Stephen F. Rohde, "Campus Speech Codes: Politically Correct, Constitutionally Wrong," *Los Angeles Lawyer,* December 1991, 23.

54. Saxe v. State College Area School Dist., 240 F.3d 200 (3d Cir. 2001).

55. Sypniewski v. Warren Hills Regional Bd. of Educ., 307 F. 3d 243 (3d Cir. 2002).

56. Gould, *Speak No Evil,* at 140.

57. Id. at 6. This would also be true for racial harassment.

58. Gould speaks only of sexual harassment, but his theory has some force with regard to racial harassment also.

59. Gould, *Speak No Evil,* at 142.

60. Id. at 144, 146.

61. Id. at 141.

62. Timothy Shiell, *Campus Hate Speech on Trial* (Lawrence University Press of Kansas, 1998).

63. "Bullying Widespread in U.S. School, Survey Finds," news release, National Institute of Child Health and Human Development, National Institutes of Health, April 24, 2001, wwnichd.nih.gov/news/releases/bullying.cfm.

64. Sheri Bauman & Cindy Hurley, "Teachers' Attitudes and Beliefs about Bullying: Two Exploratory Studies," 4 *J. School Violence* 49, 50 (2005).

65. U.S. Dept. of Education, National Center for Education Statistics, "Indicators of School Crime and Safety: 2006," in *Indicator 11: Bullying at School* (2007), http://nces.ed.gov/programs/crimeindicators/ind_11.asp.

66. Marianne D. Hurst, "When It Comes to Bullying, There Are No Boundaries," *Education Week,* February 9, 2005 (quoting Andrew Mellor, manager of the Anti-Bullying Network at the University of Edinburgh, an organization funded by the Scotland government to provide schools and students with information and support).

67. John Gravois, "Mob Rule," *Chronicle of Higher Education,* April 14, 2006.

68. Kathleen Hart, "Sticks and Stones and Shotguns at School: The Ineffectiveness of Consitutional Anti-bullying Legislation as Response to School Violence," 39 *Ga. L. Rev.* 1110–1111 (2005) (describing tapes by the shooters and interviews with their classmates).

69. *The Final Report and Findings of the Safe School Initiative: Implications for the Prevention of School Attacks in the United States,* www.secretservice.gov/ntac/ssi_final_report.pdf; S. A. Reid, "Teen Tired of Bullying May Now Face Five Years in Jail," *Atlanta Constitution,* May 5, 2004.

70. "Does School Bullying Lead to Crime?" September 4, 2003, http://stacks.msnbc.com/news/961312.asp.

71. John Dayton & Anne Dupre, "From the Common Bully to the Cyber Bully: Finding Effective Law and Policy Remedies" (draft manuscript on file with author). One commentator reported in 2004 that sixteen states had passed such legislation. Kathleen Hart, "Sticks and Stones and Shotguns at School: The Ineffectiveness of Constitutional Anti-bullying Legislation as a Response to School Violence," 38 *Ga. L. Rev.* 1109 (2005). Hart divides the legislation into five categories based on how the statute defined bullying: (1) Tort-based definition (wilful attempt to inflict injury) (Georgia: *O.C.G.A.* §20-2-751.4(a)(1)); (2) *Tinker*-based definition (insults that cause substantial disruption with the orderly operation of the school) (New Jersey: *N.J. Stat. Ann.* §18A: 37-14(b)); hostile environment definition (so severe, persistent, or pervasive that it creates an intimidating, threatening, or abusive educational environment) (Louisiana: *La. Rev. Stat. Ann.* §17:416.13 (B)(2)(b)); fighting words–based definition (likely to intimidate or provoke disorderly response) (New Hampshire: *N.H. Rev Stat.* §193-F:3(II)(a)); and intent to ridicule–based definition (intent to ridicule, humiliate, or intimidate while on school grounds) (Connecticut: *Conn. Gen. Stat. Ann.* §10-222d).

72. Sam Howe Verhovek, "Washington: Bullying Measure Opposed," *New York Times,* May 4, 2001, at A 18.

73. *Mich. Comp. Laws* §380.131a(2); Smith v. Mt. Pleasant Public Schools, 285 F. Supp. 2d 987 (E.D. Mich. 2003) (quoting the policy).

74. Julie Blair, "New Breed of Bullies Torment Their Peers on the Internet," *Education Week,* February 5, 2003, 6.

75. Paul M. Secunda, "Title IX and School Bullying," 12 *Duke J. of Gender Law and Policy* 1 (2005).

76. J.S. v. Bethlehem Area Sch. Dist., 807 A.2d 837 (Pa. 2002).

77. Emmett v. Kent Sch. Dist., 92 F. Supp. 2d 1088 (W.D. Wash. 2000).

78. Tom Wolfe, *I Am Charlotte Simmons* (New York: Farrar, Straus, Giroux, 2004).

4. Student Press Rights and Responsibilities

1. Hazelwood School Dist. v. Kuhlmeier, 484 U.S. 260 (1986). I have written in depth about this case elsewhere. See Anne Proffitt Dupre, "The Story of *Hazelwood v. Kuhlmeier:* Student Press and the School Censor," in Dupre, *Education Law Stories* (New York: Foundation Press, 2007). This chapter is based in part on research from that project.

2. The facts are taken from the district court opinion, Kuhlmeier v. Hazelwood School District, 607 F. Supp. 1450, 1452 (E.D. Mo. 1985). Quotation is from Bruce Hafen, "Hazelwood School District and the Role of First Amendment Institutions," 1988 *Duke L.J.* 685.

3. Frasca v. Andrews, 463 F. Supp. 1043 (E.D.N.Y. 1979).

4. Kuhlmeier v. Hazelwood School Dist., 795 F.2d 1368 (1986).

5. Blackwell v. Issaquena County Board of Education, 363 F.2d 749, 754 (5th Cir. 1966).

6. Note, "Administrative Regulation of the High School Press," 83 *Mich. L. Rev.* 625, 641 (1984). ("Limiting school action under the invasion-of-rights justification to torts or potential torts means that a school can refer to previously defined legal standards to decide if it may constitutionally restrain student expression.")

7. Christopher Meazell, media attorney, personal communication, March 23, 2007.

8. Hazelwood School District v. Kuhlmeier, 484 U.S. 260 (1988).

9. Anne Proffitt Dupre, "Should Students Have Constitutional Rights? Keeping Order in the Public Schools," 65 *Geo. Wash. L. Rev.* 49 (1996) (pointing out that the *Hazelwood* majority opinion revived the standard set by Justice Harlan in his *Tinker* dissent).

10. Joan Biskupic, "Ex-Supreme Court Justice Byron White Dies," *USA Today,* April 15, 2002. In 1998 Hutchinson published a biography of White, entitled *The Man Who Once Was Whizzer White.*

11. Al Kamen, "Power to Censor Student Publications Widened; Basic Educational Mission Takes Precedence," *Washington Post,* January 14, 1988, A1.

12. Stuart Taylor Jr., "Court 5B3 Widens Power of School to Act as Censor," *New York Times,* January 14, 1988, A1.

13. David A. Savage, "Justices OK Censorship by Schools: Say Educators Can Control Content of Pupil Publications," *Los Angeles Times,* January 14, 1988, 1.

14. Judy Mann, "Principal as Publisher," *Washington Post,* January 15, 1988, C3.

15. Rosemary C. Salamone, "Free Speech and School Governance in the Wake of *Hazelwood*," 26 *Ga. L. Rev.* 253 (1992). *Hazelwood* was also one of nine cases chosen to be highlighted in Dupre, *Education Law Stories.*

16. 482 U.S. 78 (1987).

17. www.firstamendmentcenter.org/speech/studentexpression/topic.

18. Poling v. Murphy, 872 F.2d 757, 762 (6th Cir. 1989).

19. Crosby v. Holsinger, 853 F.2d 801 (4th Cir. 1988).

20. Miles v. Denver Public Schools, 944 F.2d 773 (10th Cir. 1991).

21. Lacks v. Ferguson School Dist., 147 F.3d 718 (8th Cir. 1998).

22. Desilets v. Clearview Regional Board of Education, 266 N.J. Super. 531 (Superior N.J. App. Div. 1993).

23. Pennsylvania and Washington have administrative codes that offer some protection for student journalists.

24. Pangle v. Bend-Lapine School Dist, 169 Ore. App. 376 (Ore. App. 2000).

25. https://ecf.cacd.uscourts.gov/cgi-bin.

26. Adams v. Los Angeles Unified School Dist. no. BC235667. "California Teacher Wins Harassment Suit Stemming from Underground Paper," *Student Press Law Center Report,* March 15, 2002. The school district was granted a new trial in 2004 because of post-judgment changes in the harassment law, which had retroactive effect (language that would allow the jury to consider the extent of the employer's control), but as of January 2007, the case was still pending; 2004WL1834405.

27. Kincaid v. Gibson, 236 F.3d 342 (6th Cir. 2001) (en banc).

28. There is no apostrophe in the university name.

29. Hosty v. Carter, 325 F.3d 945 (7th Cir. 2003).

30. Hosty v. Carter, 412 F.3d 731 (7th Cir. 2005)(en banc).
31. See Emily Gold Waldman, "Returning to Hazelwood's Core: A New Approach to Restrictions on School-Sponsored Speech," 60 *Florida Law Review* 63 (January 2008).
32. "Court Lets Student's Libel, Privacy Claims Move Forward; School District Appeals Decision," *Student Press Law Center Report,* January 23, 2006.
33. "Cartoon about the Holocaust Truly Appalling," *Miami Herald,* May 3, 2004, 1B.

5. Banning Books from School

1. Pico v. Bd. of Ed., 638 F.2d 404, 419 (2d Cir. 1980).
2. The brief of amicus curiae American Library Association, the New York Library Association and the Freedom to Read Association, Board of Education v. Pico, in support of Respondents (the students), at 4, gives some of the history of book banning, citing A. Haight & C. Grannis, *Banned Books, 387 B.C. to 1978 A.D.*
3. Amicus Brief for Long Island Library Association Coalition, Board of Education v. Pico, in support of Respondents, at 12, refers to an address by Salisbury in Connecticut in 1978. I was unable to locate the text of that address, but Salisbury delivered a similar lecture in 1983 that is available from the Library of Congress. See Harrison Salisbury, "The Book Enchained," lecture sponsored by the Center for the Book in the Library of Congress and the Authors League of America, presented at the Library of Congress, September 28, 1983.
4. President's Council, Dist. 25 v. Community School Board, 457 F.2d 289, 292 (2nd Cir. 1972).
5. Pico v. Board of Education, 474 F. Supp. 387 (E.D.N.Y. 1979).
6. See Todd v. Rochester Community Schools, 200 N.W. 2d 90 (Mich. App. 1972), for judicial appraisals of *Slaughterhouse Five.* See also Judge Mansfield's dissent in the *Pico* case at the Court of Appeals level, 683 F.2d 404 (2nd Cir. 1981).
7. 425 U.S. 748 (1976).

8. 408 U.S. 753, 762-63 (1972).

9. In narrower terms, the Court addressed whether the statute that gave the attorney general the right to exclude Mandel was unconstitutional.

10. Minarcini v. Strongsville City School Dist, 541 F.2d 577 (6th Cir. 1976).

11. Zykan v. Warsaw County Community School Corp., 631 F.2d 1300 (7th Cir. 1980).

12. 457 F.2d 289 (2nd Cir. 1972).

13. 393 U.S. 97 (1968).

14. Epperson v. Arkansas, 393 U.S. 97, 104 (1968).

15. Pico v. Board of Education, 474 F. Supp. 387, 396 (E.D. N.Y. 1979).

16. 638 F.2d 404, 416 (2nd Cir. 1980).

17. 638 F.2d 404, 419 (Newman, J., concurring).

18. 638 F.2d 404, 420 (Mansfield, J., dissenting).

19. Brief of Petitioners.

20. Keyishian v. Board of Regents, 385 U.S. 589, 603 (1967).

21. Respondent's Brief at 15.

22. 638 F.2d 404, 419.

23. See., e.g., Student Press Law Center v. Alexander, 778 F. Supp. 1227 (D.D.C. 1991) ("The Supreme Court has noted in a variety of contexts that the First Amendment 'protects the right to receive information and ideas'" (quoting *Pico*)); Schuloff v. Fields, 950 F. Supp. 66 E.D.N.Y. 1997 ("The First Amendment protects 'the right to receive information and ideas'" (citing *Pico*)); U.S. v. Miami University, 91 F. Supp. 1132 (S.D. Ohio 2000) ("It is well settled that the right to receive information 'is an inherent corollary of the rights of free speech and press that are explicitly guaranteed by the Constitution. . . .'" (quoting *Pico*)); Ruiz v. Hull, 957 P.2d 984 (Ariz. 1998) ("In Board of Education v. Pico, 457 U.S. 853, 867, the Court recognized that 'the right to receive ideas is a necessary predicate to the recipient's meaningful exercise of his own rights of speech, press and political freedom.'"); Rossignol v. Voorharr, 316 F.3d 516, 522 (4th Cir. 2003) ("The First Amendment protects both a speaker's right to communicate information and ideas to a broad au-

dience and the intended recipients' right to receive the information and those ideas" (citing *Pico*)): Counts v. Cedarville School Dist., 295 F. Supp. 2d 996, 999 (W.D. Ark. 2003) ("the right to read a book is an aspect of the right to receive information and ideas," an "inherent corollary of the rights of free speech and press that are explicitly guaranteed by the Constitution" (citing *Pico*)); Student Members of SAME v. Rumsfield, 321 F. Supp. 2d 388, 394 (D. Conn 2004) ("the Supreme Court has called the right to receive 'an inherent corollary of the rights of free speech and press that are explicitly guaranteed by the Constitution'" (citing *Pico*)).

24. Justice Blackmun not only refused to join all of Justice Brennan's opinion; he also hinted that he had voted against hearing the case at all. He pointed out the absence of a factual record from the trial court, observing that this underscored the views of those who believed that the case should not have been taken in the first place. Nonetheless, "the case is here and must be decided."

25. Nat Hentoff, "Censorship Did Not End at Island Trees: A Look Ahead," in *New Directions for Young Adult Services* 85 (Ellen Li-Bretto ed.; (New York: Bowker, 1983).

26. Id.

27. Id.

28. Respondent's Brief.

29. Ambach v. Norwick, 441 U.S. 68 (1979) n. 9.

30. Respondent Brief at 16.

31. Id.

32. Id.

33. Mt. Healthy City School Dist. Bd. of Educ v. Doyle, 429 U.S. 274 (1977).

34. 385 U.S. 589, 603 (1967).

35. (Washington, D.C.: Government Printing Office, 1974).

36. For number of school districts in the United States see *Digest of Education Statistics: 2005*, http://nces.ed.gov.programs.digest.d05 .tables/ dt05_084.

37. T. Emerson, "Developments in the Law-Academic Freedom," 91 *Harv. L. Rev* 1045 (1968).

38. San Antonio Sch. Dist. v. Rodriguez, 411 U.S. 1, 50 (1972)(separate opinion).

39. 539 U.S. 134 (2003).

40. Mailloux v. Kiley, 323 F. Supp. 1387 (1971).

41. James v. Bd. of Educ., 461 F2d. 566, 574 (2d Cir. 1972).

42. See Parducci v. Rutland, 316 F. Supp. 352, 358 (M.D. Ala. 1970).

43. Mailloux v. Kiley, 323 F. Supp. 1387 D. Mass. 1970, aff'd 448 F.2d 1242 (1st Cir 1971).

44. Petitioner's Brief.

45. Petitioner's brief quoting Epperson v. Arkansas, 393 U.S. 97, 106 (1968).

46. "Look Out, Harry Potter! Book Banning Heats Up," interview with Mark West, professor of North Carolina at the University, www .education-world.com/admin.

47. Challenges are most often made by parents who attempt to remove books from school curricula or libraries. www.ala.org/ala/oif/banned booksweek/challengedbanned/challengedbanned.htm.

6. Religious Speech: On a Wing and a Prayer

1. Lee v. Weisman, 505 U.S. 577 (1992) (citations omitted).

2. Id.

3. Id. The U.S. Supreme Court has not used a separate free exercise standard for religious exercise and speech in public schools. Kristi L. Bowman, *Public School Students' Religious Speech and Viewpoint Discrimination.* 110 West Va. L. Rev. 187, 196–197 (2007).

4. 319 U.S. 624 (1943).

5. 310 U.S. 586 (1940).

6. Leoles v. Landers, 184 Ga. 580 (Ga. 1937).

7. Hamilton v. Regents of University of California, 293 U.S. 245 (1934).

8. Hering v. State Bd. of Educ., 117 N.J.L. 455 (N.J. 1937).

9. Gabrielli v. Knickerbocker, 82 P. 2d 391 (Cal. 1939).

10. Gobitis v. Minersville School Dist., 24 F. Supp. 271 (E.D. Ap. 1938).

11. 21 F. Supp. 584–85.

12. 24 F. Supp. 274.

13. 108 F.2d 683, 684 (3d Cir. 1939).

14. Id. at n. 3. Erich Frost, "Watchtower," April 15, 1961, p. 244. (Pronouncement of Adolf Hitler, April 4, 1935).

15. West Virginia State Bd. of Educ. v. Barnette, 319 U.S. 624 (1943), (Frankfurter, J., dissenting).

16. Jones v. Opelika, 316 U.S. 584 (1942).

17. 521 U.S. 203 (1997).

18. West Virginia State Bd. of Educ. v. Barnette at 637.

19. H.P. Rep. no. 83-1693 at 1–2, reprinted in *USCCAN* 2339, 2340 (1954).

20. Texas v. Johnson, 491 U.S. 397 (1989).

21. Newdow v. U.S. Congress, 328 F.3d 466 (9th Cir. 2002).

22. Myers v. Loudoun County Public Schools, 418 F.3d 395 (4th Cir. 2005).

23. Lynch v. Donnelly, 465 U.S. 716 (Brennan, J., dissenting).

24. See Abington Township Sch. Dist. v. Schempp, 374 U.S. 203 (1963) (Brennan, J., concurring), for a list of courts.

25. 379 U.S. 421 (1962).

26. Justice Stewart was quoting Zorach v. Clausen, 343 U.S. 306 (1952).

27. James E. Clayton, "Wave of Protests Follows Ruling on Prayer in School," *Washington Post,* June 27, 1962, A1.

28. Alexander Burnham, "Court's Decision Stirs Conflicts," *New York Times,* June 27, 1962, 1.

29. "President Urges Court Be Backed on Prayer Issue," *New York Times,* June 28, 1962, 1.

30. "Mail Pours into Court on the Prayer Decision," *New York Times,* June 29, 1962, 11.

31. Anthony Lewis, "Court Again under Fire," *New York Times,* July 1, 1962, 14.

32. Id.

33. School District of Abington Township v. Schempp, 374 U.S. 203 (1963).

34. Ann Seamon, *The Most Hated Woman in America: The Life and*

Gruesome Death of Madalyn Murray O'Hair (London: Continuum Books, 2005).

35. Quotation from Lawrence Wright, *Saints and Sinners: Walker Railey, Jimmy Swaggart, Madalyn Murray O'Hair, Anton LaVey, Will Campbell, Matthew Fox* (New York: Vintage Books, 1995) (quoted in Bryan F. LeBeau, "Becoming the Most Hated Woman in America: Madalyn Murray O'Hair," 26 *J. Amer. Culture* 153 (2003); Jane Howard, "The Most Hated Woman in America," *Life,* June 19, 1964; Bryan F. LeBeau, *The Atheist* (New York University Press, 2003).

36. Jaffree v. James, 544 727 (S.D. Ala. 1982).

37. Everson v. Board of Education addressed a town's reimbursement to parents of money they spent on buses transporting their childern to Catholic schools. 330 U.S. 1 (1947).

38. William Crosskey, "Charles Fairman, 'Legislative History' and the Constitutional Limitations on State Authority," 22 *Chicago L. Rev.* 1 (1954).

39. 49 *Colum. L. Rev.* 735, 736 (1949).

40. 705 F.2d 1526, 1532 quoting *Engel* at 429B30.

41. Jaffree v. Wallace, 705 F.2d 1526 1532 (11th Cir. 1983) (emphasis in original).

42. 472 U.S. 38 (1984).

43. 310 U.S. 296, 303 (1940).

44. Reynolds v. United States, 98 U.S. 145, 164 (1879).

45. Illinois ex rel. McCollum v. Bd. of Educ., 333 U.S. 203 (1948) (Jackson, J., concurring).

46. 728 F. Supp. 68 (1990).

47. 909 F.2d 1090 (1990).

48. I was employed as an attorney at Shaw Pittman from 1989 to 1994.

49. "The Twenty-five Most Influential Evangelicals in America," *Time,* February 7, 2005.

50. Lee v. Weisman, 505 U.S. 577, 622 (1992) (Souter, J., concurring).

51. ACLU, Rhode Island, www.riaclu.org/friendly/churchstatecspf .html.

52. 492 U.S. 573 (1989) (Kennedy, J., concurring in the judgment in part and dissenting in part).

53. The discussion of the oral argument comes from the transcript and from my own firsthand observations. The transcript can be found at Lee v. Weisman, 505 U.S. 577 (oral transcript at 1991 WL 636285 and 1991 U.S. Trans Lexis 145).

54. Lee v. Weisman, 505 U.S. 577 (1991).

55. Id. 592.

56. Id. 593.

57. Id. 595.

58. 463 U.S. 783 (1983).

59. Lee v. Weisman, 505 U.S. 577, 632 (1991).

60. Jones v. Clear Creek Independent School District, 977 F.2d 963, 968–72 (5th Cir. 1992).

61. Doe v. Santa Fe Independent School Dist., 933 F. Supp. 647 (1996).

62. Doe v. Santa Fe Independent School Dist., 168 F.3d 806 (5th Cir. 1999).

63. Id. 823.

64. Santa Fe Independent School Dist. v. Doe, 530 U.S. 290 (2000).

65. 168 F.3d at 809 (discussing the district court ruling).

66. Id. at 810.

67. *Morning Edition*, National Public Radio, March 29, 2000.

68. 933 F. Supp 650.

69. David Firestone, "Action at School Games Seeks to Skirt Court's Church State Ruling," *New York Times*, August 26, 2000.

70. Adler v. Duval County, 250 F.3d 1330 (11th Cir. 2001) (8–4 en banc).

71. Lassonde v. Pleasanton Unified School Dist., 320 F.3d 979, 984 (9th Cir. 2003).

72. Warnock v. Archer, 443 F.3d 954 (8th Cir. 2006).

73. 152 Tenn. 424 (1925).

74. State v. Epperson, 242 Ark. 922 (Ark. 1967).

75. Epperson v. Arkansas, 393 U.S. 97 (1968).

76. Aguillard v. Treen, 634 F. Supp. 426 (E.D. La. 1985); 765 F.2d 1251 (CA5 1985).

77. Edwards v. Aguillard, 482 U.S. 578 (1987).

7. Teacher Speech and the "Priests of Our Democracy"

1. Tinker v. Des Moines Independent Community School Dist., 393 U.S. 503, 506 (1969)(emphasis added).

2. Michael Olivas, "Reflections on Professorial Academic Freedom: Second Thoughts on the Third 'Essential Freedom,'" 45 *Stan. L. Rev.* 1835 (1973).

3. McAuliffe v. Mayor of New Bedford, 29 N.E. 517 (Mass. 1892).

4. See David M. Rabban, "The First Amendment in Its Forgotten Years," 90 *Yale L.J.* 514, 520 (1981) (with one exception, free speech claimants lost pre–World War I Supreme Court cases).

5. Academic Freedom and Tenure: A Handbook of The American Association of University Professors, Ed. Louis Joughin (Madison: University of Wisconsin, 1967), p. 158.

6. Id.

7. Walter P. Metzger, "Profession and Constitution: Two Definitions of Academic Freedom in America," 66 *Tex. L. Rev.* 1265, 1275 (1988).

8. Id.

9. Id. at 1275.

10. Id. at 1275.

11. Id. at 1265, 1275.

12. Id. at 1265, 1275 (citing AAUP Report on the Committee of Inquiries on Conditions at the University of Utah, July 1915).

13. Id. at 1276 (citing L. Metzger, Professors in Trouble: A Quantitative Analysis of Academic Freedom and Tenure Cases (1978)).

14. Id. at 1266.

15. See id. at 1246.

16. Id. at 1246.

17. Id. at 1286.

18. Adler v. Board of Education, 342 U.S. 485 (1952).

19. Id. at 492.

20. Douglas, J., dissenting, at 508.
21. Id. at 510–11 (emphasis added).
22. Metzger, "Profession and Constitution," at 1289.
23. 344 U.S. 183 (1952).
24. Frankfurter, J., concurring, at 221.
25. 354 U.S. 234 (1957).
26. Sweezy v. State of New Hampshire, 354 U.S. 234 (1957).
27. J. Peter Byrne, "Academic Freedom, a 'Special Concern of the First Amendment,'" 99 *Yale L. J.* 251, 289 (1989).
28. See id., citing cases.
29. Accord, id. at 291, 251, 289.
30. Frankfurter, J., concurring, at 266.
31. See Roper v. Simmons, 543 U.S. 551 (2005).
32. *The Open Universities in South Africa,* published on behalf of the Conference of Representatives of the University of Cape Town and the University of the Witwatersrand, Johannesburg, held in Cape Town on 9, 10, and 11 January 1957 (Johannesburg: Witwatersrand University Press, 1957).
33. Richard Hiers, "Institutional Academic Freedom vs. Faculty Academic Freedom in Public Colleges and Universities: A Dubious Dichotomy," 29 *J. College and University Law,* 35, 59 (2002).
34. Id.
35. Byrne, "Academic Freedom," at 292.
36. Id.
37. David M. Rabban, "Can Academic Freedom Survive Postmodernism?" 86 *Calif. L. Rev.* 1377 (1998) (reviewing *The Future of Academic Freedom,* ed. Louis Menand).
38. Byrne, "Academic Freedom," at 291.
39. 360 U.S. 109 (1959).
40. Id. at 112.
41. 385 U.S. 589 (1967).
42. Byrne, "Academic Freedom," at 295.
43. Id. at 297.
44. Accord, id. at 297.
45. Accord, id.

46. 385 U.S. 589, 628 (Clark, J., dissenting).
47. 438 U.S. 265, 312 (1978).
48. Board of Curators of the University of Missouri v. Horowitz, 435 U.S. 78 (1978) (despite lack of formal hearing no procedural due process violation where student was fully apprised of faculty dissatisfaction with her work).
49. Regents of the University of Michigan v. Ewing, 474 U.S. 214, 227 (1985).
50. Richard Hiers traces the development of these two freedoms in "Institutional Academic Freedom vs. Faculty Academic Freedom," at 35.
51. Regents of the University of Michigan v. Ewing, 474 U.S. 214 (1985).
52. 391 U.S. 563 (1968).
53. Id. at 574.
54. Id. at 568 (emphasis added).
55. 461 U.S. 138 (1983).
56. City of San Diego Police Dept. v. Roe, 543 U.S. 77 (2004) (per curiam).
57. 126 S. Ct. 1951.
58. Byrne, "Academic Freedom," at n. 137.
59. Bethel School Dist. v. Fraser, 478 U.S. 675 (1986).
60. Karin B. Hoppmann, Note, "Concern with Public Concern: Toward a Better Definition of the Pickering/Connick Threshold Test," 50 Vand. L. Rev. 993, 1008 (1997).
61. See J. Peter Byrne, "The Threat to Constitutional Academic Freedom," 31 J.C. & U.L. 79 (2004), nn. 203–10, and cases cited therein.
62. Urofsky v. Gilmore, 216 F.3d 401 (4th Cir. 2000).
63. See Byrne, "Threat," at 79.

8. A Long Way from Black Armbands

1. Beidler v. North Thurston School Dist., no. 99-2-00236-6 (Thurston Cty. Super. Ct., July 18, 2000), quoted in "Student Suspended for Website Wins Free Speech Lawsuit Against District,"

Student Press Law Reporter vol. XXI, no. 3, p. 35 (fall 2000) (case upholding student expression, citing *Tinker*).

2. Frederick v. Morse, 2003 WL 25274689 D. Alaska, May 27, 2003 (no. J02-008 CV JWS), order issued May 29, 2003.

3. Emphasis added.

4. 439 F.3d 1114 (2006).

5. 978 F.2d 524 (9th Cir. 1992).

6. Morse v. Frederick, 127 S.Ct.2618 (2007).

7. Vernonia School Dist. 47J v. Acton, 515 U.S. 646 (1995); Board of Educ. of Independent School Dist. No. 92 of Pottawatomie County v. Earls, 536 U.S. 822 (2002).

8. Charles Krauthammer, "From Thomas, Original Views," *Washington Post,* June 10, 2005, A23.

9. "Three Bad Rulings," *New York Times,* June 26, 2007, A20.

10. "Student Speech: No," *Los Angeles Times,* June 26, 2007, A22.

11. "Dubious Ruling," *Worcester* (MA) *Telegram,* June 29, 2007.

12. 125 S. Ct. 1183. See also Kevin W. Saunders, "Do Children Have the Same First Amendment Rights as Adults?" 79 *Chicago-Kent L. Rev.* 257 (2004) (discussing maturity).

13. Tamar Lewin, "Laws Limit Colleges' Options When a Student Is Mentally Ill," *New York Times,* April 19, 2007, A1.

14. Boim v. Fulton County, no. 06-14732 (2007).

15. Robert Boyd, "Teenagers Can't Think Straight, Scientists Say," *Orlando Sentinel,* December 21, 2006.

16. Bruce Bower, "Teen Brains on Trial," *Science News,* May 8, 2004, 299.

17. Harper v. Poway Unified School Dist., 445 F.3d 1166, 1171 (9th Cir. 2006).

Case Index

Adams v. Los Angeles Unified
   School District, 268n26
Adler v. Board of Education, 209,
   210, 214, 219
Adler v. Duval County, 275n70
Agnostini v. Felton, 151
Aguillard v. Treen, 199, 201,
   202
Ambach v. Norwick, 50, 52, 53, 127

Bair v. Shippensburg University,
   264n51
Barenblatt v. United States,
   214–216
Bethel School District v. Fraser, 39,
   43
Blackwell v. Issaquena County Board
   of Education, 28, 29, 83
Board of Curators of the University
   of Missouri v. Horowitz,
   278n48
Board of Education, Island Trees
   Union Free School District v.
   Pico, 53, 54, 107, 109, 110–117,
   119, 121, 122, 124–132, 134, 136,
   215, 228, 230

Board of Education of Independent
   School District No. 92 of Potta-
   watomie County v. Earls, 279n7
Boim v. Fulton County, 279n14
Bowers v. Hardwick, 91
Brown v. Board of Education, 15, 28,
   50, 152
Bryant v. Independent School Dis-
   trict, 66
Burnside v. Byars, 28

Cantwell v. Connecticut, 177
Chandler v. McMinnville School
   District, 237
Chaplinsky v. New Hampshire, 54,
   62
Cohen v. California, 262
Connick v. Myers, 225
County of Allegheny v. ACLU, 186
Crosby v. Holsinger, 268n19

Desilets v. Clearview Regional Board
   of Education, 95, 268n22
Doe v. University of Michigan, 264
Donnelly v. Lynch, 186, 273n23

Edwards v. Aguillard, 276n77
Engel v. Vitale, 164, 166, 171, 172,
    175, 176, 274n40
Epperson v. Arkansas, 115, 198–200,
    228, 270n14

FCC v. Pacifica Foundation, 43, 44,
    53–55, 61, 261n6
Frasca v. Andrews, 80, 267n3

Gabrielli v. Knickerbocker, 272n9
Garcetti v. Ceballos, 225, 226,
    229
Ginsberg v. New York, 53–55,
    262n20
Gitlow v. New York, 178
Goss v. Lopez, 31, 32, 34, 35, 40,
    260n25
Grutter v. Bollinger, 222, 223

Harper v. Poway Unified School Dis-
    trict, 279n17
Hazelwood School District v.
    Kuhlmeier, 45, 74, 76, 81, 83, 87,
    88–104, 106, 130, 227, 230, 241,
    244, 267n1
Healy v. James, 36–38
Hering v. State Board of Education,
    272n8
Hosty v. Carter, 101, 102, 104, 268,
    269n30

Jaffree v. James, 274n36
Jaffree v. Wallace, 169, 170, 177
Jones v. Clear Creek Independent
    School District, 190, 275n60
Jones v. City of Opelika, 149, 273n16

Keyishian v. Board of Regents, 120,
    130, 214, 219, 221, 222, 270n20
Kincaid v. Gibson, 99, 103, 106,
    268n27
Kleindienst v. Mandel, 111, 113, 122

Lacks v. Ferguson School District,
    268n21
Lee v. Weisman, 163, 169, 180, 230,
    272n1, 274n50, 275n59
Lemon v. Kurtzmann, 168, 193
Leoles v. Landers, 272n6

Mailloux v. Kiley, 272n40
Marsh v. Chambers, 188
McAuliffe v. Mayor of New Bedford,
    205, 208, 276n3
Miles v. Denver Public Schools,
    268
Minarcini v. Strongsville City School
    District, 112, 116, 270n10
Minersville School District v.
    Gobitis, 141, 143, 146–157, 160,
    210, 215, 263n28
Morse v. Frederick, 229–239, 241,
    242, 244, 245, 247–249, 251–253,
    257
Murray v. Curlett, 166
Myers v. Loudoun County Schools,
    273n22

Newdow v. United States Congress,
    158, 161, 162, 176, 273n21
New Jersey v. T.L.O., 32, 260, 262n28

Pangle v. Bend-Lapine School Dis-
    trict, 268n24

Papish v. the University of Missouri, 37, 39, 48, 261n35
Parducci v. Rutland, 272n42
Pickering v. Board of Education, 224, 225, 227, 278n60
Poling v. Murphy, 268n18
Porter v. Ascension Parish School Board, 252
President's Council v. Community School Board, 114–117, 119, 269n4

Qualls v. Cunningham, 66

R.A.V. v. City of St. Paul, 62
Regents of the University of California v. Bakke, 221–223
Regents of the University of Michigan v. Ewing, 278n49
Rendell-Baker v. Kohn, 35, 261
Reynolds v. United States, 179, 274n44
Roe v. Wade, 91
Roper v. Simmons, 250, 277n31

Santa Fe Independent School District v. Doe, 182, 230
Saxe v. State College Area School District, 264n54
Schneider v. State, 178
School District of Abington Township v. Schempp, 166–172, 273n24
Scopes v. State, 197, 198, 201
Shelton v. Tucker, 217–219, 222
Sweezy v. State of New Hampshire, 210, 214, 215, 218, 221, 222, 277n26

Texas v. Johnson, 262, 273n20
Thomas v. Board of Education, 39, 253
Tinker v. Des Moines Independent School District, 10, 13–16, 18, 20–43, 46–49, 52–57, 72, 74, 79–81, 83, 87–90, 92, 93, 96–98, 122, 123, 140, 155, 164, 198, 199, 204, 215, 224, 227, 231, 232, 235–238, 240–242, 244–247, 252–257
Turner v. Safly, 93

United States v. O'Brien, 7, 259n6
Urofsky v. Gilmore, 228, 229, 278n62

Vernonia School District 47J v. Acton, 279n7
Virginia Board of Pharmacy v. Virginia Citizens Consumers Council, 110–113, 116, 122

Wallace v. Jaffree, 169, 177, 274n41
Warnock v. Archer, 275n72
West Virginia v. Barnette, 49, 141, 144, 145, 150–157, 159, 161, 178, 259, 273n15
Wieman v. Updegraff, 210, 217, 218, 222
Wisconsin v. Yoder, 26, 260n15

Zykan v. Warsaw County Community School Corporation, 113, 114, 119, 270n11

Subject Index

Academic Bill of Rights, 116
Academic freedom, principle of, 9,
 108, 116, 199–229
Affirmative action, 130, 133, 221,222
American Association of University
 Professors (AAUP), 9, 206,
 207–214, 218
American Bar Association Commit-
 tee on the Bill of Rights, 157
American Civil Liberties Union, 152,
 156, 157, 163, 186, 218
Amicus briefs, 51, 132, 160, 238, 242
Anti-*Hazelwood* legislation: in gen-
 eral, 96–99, 104; Arkansas Student
 Publications Act, 96; the College
 Campus Press Act (Illinois), 104
Archer, Jerome, 109
Arum, Richard, 33, 34
As-applied challenges (to laws), 7

Beard, Charles Austin, 50–54
Beard, Mary Ritter, 50–54
Best Short Stories by Negro Writers
 (Hughes), 108
Bill of Rights: in general, 4, 5, 35,
 139, 154, 163, 172–174, 178, 197,

203, 210; made applicable to
 states, 139
Black Boy (Wright), 108–109
Black, Hugo (justice), 5, 22, 48, 49,
 54, 89, 123, 149, 152, 153, 155,
 164, 165, 173, 199, 209, 216, 217,
 238, 245
Blackmun, Harry (justice), 63, 110,
 111, 113, 122–123, 177, 184, 185,
 187, 188, 271n24
Blackstone Commentaries, 9, 189,
 246
Blaine Amendment, 174
Blanding, Sandra, 186, 187
Brennan, William (justice), 55, 90,
 106, 109, 120–123, 125, 126, 128,
 162, 168–170, 177, 200, 203, 216,
 219, 221, 228, 271n24
Bullying, 68–71
Burger, Warren (justice), 48, 50, 51,
 53, 123
Byrne, Peter (professor), 211

Campus Hate Speech on Trial
 (Shiell), 67, 68
Cardozo, Benjamin (justice), 4

Carvin, Michael, 182
Catch-22 (Heller), 112
Cat's Cradle (Vonnegut), 112
Childress, Alice, 108
Cianci, Vincent "Buddy", 183
Civil Rights Act of 1964, Title VI of,
    11, 58, 67
Civil Rights Attorney's Fees Act of
    1976, 41, 55, 56, 73
Civil Rights Movement, 3, 26, 29,
    141
"Clear and Present Danger" prin-
    ciple, 6, 96, 98, 146, 150, 151
Cleaver, Eldridge, 109, 129, 130
Coercion test, Justice Kennedy's,
    184–187, 189, 192–194
Cold War, 19, 158
Colleges. *See* Higher education
Columbine shootings, 3, 13, 69, 86,
    254, 256
Commercial speech, 6, 110
Communism, 158, 165, 169, 172.
    See also *Barenblatt v. United
    States; Sweezy v. New Hampshire*
Conduct as speech, 5, 58, 60, 65, 69,
    156
Constitutional interpretation, 176,
    178, 186, 194, 245–247
Content-based restrictions, 5, 7, 38,
    45, 55, 63, 83, 84, 90, 95, 112,
    116–120, 256
Cooper, Charles J., 181–187
Cyber-bullying, 70, 71

Darwin, Charles, 197–198, 202
Daschle, Tom, 159
Declaration of Principles, 206, 208,
    223
Deference to educators (by courts),
    47, 79, 82, 88, 95, 222

Dewey, John, 50
Discrimination, 19, 58–60, 64, 65,
    123, 152, 156, 163, 247–249,
    256
Dissents, 3, 22, 23, 25, 26, 46–49,
    54–56, 85, 88–93, 98, 103, 110,
    119, 123, 124, 148–150, 152, 156,
    157, 164, 165, 169, 176, 179, 180,
    188, 192–194, 199, 200, 209,
    216–218, 221, 226, 238, 241
Diversity, 2, 63, 82, 129–131, 141,
    147, 154, 180
Douglas, William O. (justice), 5,
    25–27, 48, 149, 152, 155, 175, 209,
    216
Down These Mean Streets (Thomas),
    108, 115
Drug testing in schools, 33, 241, 243

Easterbrook, Frank (judge),
    102–104, 189
Education amendments of 1972,
    Title IX of, 58
Eighth Amendment, 33
En banc review, 14, 99, 100, 102,
    119
Endorsement test, Justice
    O'Connor's, 179, 186, 191–193,
    201
Establishment clause, 138, 140,
    159, 161, 162, 164, 165, 168, 169,
    172–177, 179, 181, 184–189,
    191–193, 199, 200
Evolution, 116, 126, 133, 197–202,
    220, 228

Facial challenges (to laws), 7, 193
Fairman, Charles (professor), 173,
    174, 178

Feinberg Law, the (New York), 208,
209, 214, 219
"Fighting words," 6, 8, 54, 62,
63
First Amendment: in General, 3, 5,
6, 9, 22, 35–37, 39, 44, 46, 53–55,
62, 63, 65, 76, 81, 85, 86, 88,
90, 92, 94–96, 98, 100–105,
110–113, 115–118, 120–126,
128, 130, 132, 138, 140, 146, 147,
154–156, 160, 161, 163, 171–174,
176–178, 190, 198, 199, 204–206,
208, 209, 212–216, 220, 222, 224,
226, 230, 231, 233–235, 239–242,
244–247, 249, 251, 252, 255–257;
establishment clause, 138, 140,
159, 161, 162, 164, 165, 168,
169, 171–177, 179, 181, 184–189,
192, 193, 196 199, 200, 202; free
exercise clause, 138–140, 146,
147, 156, 161, 172, 176, 177,
190, 198, 199; free Speech
clause, 5–7, 9, 35, 62, 63, 76, 90,
111-113
Fixer, The (Malamud), 108,
126
Flag of the United States, Its History
and Symbolism, The (Moss),
145
Fortas, Abe (justice), 15–22, 198,
199
Fourteenth Amendment: in general,
5, 31, 139, 143, 161, 163, 171,
173, 174, 176-179, 210, 222; Due
Process Clause, 5, 31, 32, 87, 139,
143, 150, 163, 177, 178, 210, 211,
222; incorporation, 139, 163, 171,
173, 174
Fourth Amendment, 32, 33, 91, 241
Frankfurter, Felix (justice),
146–149, 152, 153, 156, 157,
160, 210, 212, 213, 217, 218,
221, 245

Gluckman, Ivan, 92
Go Ask Alice (Anon.), 108, 113
Goodman, Paul, 259n4
Gould, Jon (professor), 59, 63, 64,
66, 67
Government and the Mind (Tuss-
man), 57

Hand, Brevard (judge), 172–175,
177
Hand, Learned (judge), 12
Hate speech, 62–64, 66, 68, 71
Harry Potter series (Rowling),
136
Hentoff, Nat, 126, 136
Hero Ain't Nothing But a Sandwich,
A (Childress), 108, 129
Higher education, 37, 59, 65, 99,
102, 103, 111, 120, 130, 203, 205,
208
Hofstadter, Richard, 51
Holmes, Oliver Wendell (justice), 5,
8, 152, 156, 205, 208, 220
Horowitz, David, 203, 207
Hughes, Langston, 108

Incorporation, of the Bill of Rights,
139, 161, 163, 171–174
In loco parentis doctrine, 9, 10, 32,
40, 53, 243, 246
Intelligent design, 201, 202
Intermediate scrutiny, 7
Internet, 3, 70, 132, 148, 231, 253,
258
Iraq War, 232

Jackson, Robert (justice), 49, 141, 144, 148, 150–156, 178, 179, 245

Jefferson, Thomas, 1, 145, 173, 179, 233

Judging School Discipline (Arum), 33

LaFarge, Oliver, 109

Laughing Boy (LaFarge), 109

Lehrfreiheit, 206

Lemon test, 168, 171, 176, 178, 181, 184, 186, 187, 189, 191–193, 199, 200

Lernfreiheit, 206, 207

Lincoln, Abraham, 1, 2, 160, 258

Lovejoy, Arther O. (professor), 207

Malamud, Bernard, 108, 126

Maris, Albert Branson, 143–146, 148

"Marketplace of ideas" metaphor, 7–9, 103, 113, 120, 220

McCarthy era, 155, 208–214

Mertz, Douglas, 239, 240

Metzger, Walter (professor), 207, 208

Morris, Desmond, 108

Moss, James (colonel), 144, 145

Murray, Madalyn, 166

Naked Ape, The (Morris), 108, 128

Obscenity, 6, 71, 132

Off-campus speech, 70, 252–254

O'Hair, Madalyn Murray, 166, 167

Open forum, 79. *See also* Public forum

Over-breadth doctrine, 8, 61, 117, 219

Pitts, Leonard, 105

Pledge of Allegiance, 140–143, 146, 149, 156–164, 258

Political speech, 6, 220, 221, 242, 251, 256

Powell, Lewis (justice), 37, 48, 50, 90, 124, 131, 175, 177, 200, 221, 222

Powell, Thomas Reed (professor), 157

Prior restraint, 6

Private schools, 5, 35, 36, 41, 56, 87, 88, 208, 234, 246

Public forum, 79–81, 88, 89, 100, 103, 104

Qualified immunity, 244, 252

Rational-basis scrutiny, 7

Reader for Writers, A (Archer), 109, 129

"Red Monday," 211

Rehnquist, William (justice), 48, 124, 125, 132, 160, 179–181, 183, 184, 187, 188, 193, 194, 197, 200, 222, 238

Right to receive speech, 44, 228, 230, 258

Roberts, John G. (justice), 156, 177, 178, 183, 197, 239–241, 249, 251–253

Rowling, J. K., 136

Salisbury, Harrison, 108

Schempp, Edward, 166–169

School prayer, 139, 162–167,
169–171, 176–180, 182, 185–197,
202
School-sponsored speech, 45, 79–81,
86, 89, 90, 92–96, 98, 192, 230,
234
Sekulow, Jay, 182
Sexual harassment, 58, 59, 66, 67,
196
Shiell, Timothy, 67–68
Slaughterhouse Five (Vonnegut), 108
Soul on Ice (Cleaver), 109
Speak No Evil (Gould), 63
Standing doctrine, 113, 116,
160–162
Starr, Kenneth, 239, 240, 183, 186
State as educator, 9, 57, 86, 202
State as employer, 9, 124, 205,
224–227
State as sovereign, 9, 124, 125
Steinbeck, John *(Of Mice and Men)*,
136
Stewart, Potter (justice), 6, 48, 71,
165, 169, 199, 217, 218
Strict scrutiny, 6, 7, 92
Student Press Law Center, 104, 242
Stuller, W. Stuart, 36
Summary judgment, 117, 119, 191,
197

Teacher speech, 9, 14, 24, 50, 258
Thomas, Clarence (justice), 160, 161,
176, 184, 187, 188, 194, 241, 245,
246–247, 257
Thomas, Piri, 108, 115
Threatening speech, 68, 69, 71, 96,
243, 244, 254, 255
Time, place, and manner restrictions,
7, 100, 118

Tussman, Joseph (professor), 57, 202
Twain, Mark *(Adventures of Huckleberry Finn),* 136

Universities. *See* Higher education
Unprotected speech, 8, 62, 66, 101,
127

Vagueness doctrine, 7, 8, 61, 62,
66, 70, 72, 134, 199, 216,
219
Vietnam War, 3, 11–15, 18–20, 23,
30, 36, 47, 60, 208, 232
Violent speech. *See* Threatening
speech
Virginia Tech shootings, 86, 254,
256
Vonnegut, Kurt, 108, 112, 134
Vouchers, 36
Vulgarity, 71, 73, 124, 257

Welcome to the Monkey House
(Vonnegut), 134
White, Byron, 65, 88–91, 110, 123,
188, 200
Wolfe, Tom, 72
Workplace mobbing, 68
World War II, 3, 141, 158, 166
Wright, Richard, 108–109
Wright, Susan Webber (judge), 46,
47, 196, 197

Yardley, Jonathan, 40

Zirkel, Perry (professor), 24